Narrative, Identity and Ethics in Postcolonial Kenya

Bloomsbury Studies in Religion, Gender, and Sexuality

Series Editors: Dawn Llewellyn, Sonya Sharma and Sîan Hawthorne

This interdisciplinary series explores the intersections of religions, genders and sexualities. It promotes the dynamic connections between gender and sexuality across a diverse range of religious and spiritual lives, cultures, histories and geographical locations, as well as contemporary discourses around secularism and non-religion. The series publishes cutting-edge research that considers religious experiences, communities, institutions and discourses in global and transnational contexts, and examines the fluid and intersecting features of identity and social positioning.

Using theoretical and methodological approaches from inter/transdisciplinary perspectives, *Bloomsbury Studies in Religion, Gender, and Sexuality* addresses the neglect of religious studies perspectives in gender, queer and feminist studies. It offers a space where gender can critically engage with religion, and for exploring questions of intersectionality, particularly with respect to critical race, disability and postcolonial and decolonial theories.

Becoming Queer and Religious in Malaysia and Singapore, Sharon A. Bong
Beyond Religion in India and Pakistan, Navtej K. Purewal and Virinder S. Kalra

Narrative, Identity and Ethics in Postcolonial Kenya

The Young Women's Christian Association

Eleanor Tiplady Higgs

BLOOMSBURY ACADEMIC
LONDON • NEW YORK • OXFORD • NEW DELHI • SYDNEY

BLOOMSBURY ACADEMIC
Bloomsbury Publishing Plc
50 Bedford Square, London, WC1B 3DP, UK
1385 Broadway, New York, NY 10018, USA
29 Earlsfort Terrace, Dublin 2, Ireland

BLOOMSBURY, BLOOMSBURY ACADEMIC and the Diana logo are trademarks of
Bloomsbury Publishing Plc

First published in Great Britain 2021
This paperback edition published 2023

Copyright © Eleanor Tiplady Higgs, 2021

Eleanor Tiplady Higgs has asserted her right under the Copyright, Designs and
Patents Act, 1988, to be identified as Author of this work.

For legal purposes the Acknowledgements on p. vi constitute an extension
of this copyright page.

Cover design: Toby Way
Cover image: The Museum of Fine Arts, Houston, Museum purchase funded by the
Caroline Wiess Law Accessions Endowment Fund, 2016.81 ©2015 Wangechi Mutu

All rights reserved. No part of this publication may be reproduced or transmitted
in any form or by any means, electronic or mechanical, including photocopying,
recording, or any information storage or retrieval system, without prior permission
in writing from the publishers.

Bloomsbury Publishing Plc does not have any control over, or responsibility for, any
third-party websites referred to or in this book. All internet addresses given in this
book were correct at the time of going to press. The author and publisher regret any
inconvenience caused if addresses have changed or sites have ceased to exist, but can
accept no responsibility for any such changes.

A catalogue record for this book is available from the British Library.

Library of Congress Control Number: 2021935675

ISBN: HB: 978-1-3501-2980-1
PB: 978-1-3502-4795-6
ePDF: 978-1-3501-2981-8
eBook: 978-1-3501-2982-5

Series: Bloomsbury Studies in Religion, Gender, and Sexuality

Typeset by Newgen KnowledgeWorks Pvt. Ltd., Chennai, India

To find out more about our authors and books visit www.bloomsbury.com
and sign up for our newsletters

Contents

Acknowledgements	vi
List of abbreviations	vii
Map of Kenya with locations of YWCA branches	ix
Part 1	1
Introduction	3
1 Identity and ethics in narrative	20
Part 2	45
2 Imperial maternalism, 1855–1965	47
3 From welfare to development, 1965–2000	73
4 African, Christian, feminist? 2000–12	99
Part 3	125
5 Controversial faith issues	127
6 'We are Christians'	151
7 Everyday Christian ethics	175
Postscript	200
Notes	203
References	209
Index	231

Acknowledgements

I wrote the majority of this book during the coronavirus pandemic of 2020, on lockdown in Birmingham, UK, during the last months of my postdoctoral research fellowship at the University of Cape Town. It was a strange time to be writing a book, but I was grateful for the distraction. First and foremost, I would like to extend my gratitude to everyone who was a part of Kenya YWCA in 2012. *Asanteni sana* for facilitating my research with generosity, openness and good humour. The research for this book was undertaken as part of my doctoral studies at SOAS, University of London. My research was supervised by Sîan Hawthorne, whom I thank for her guidance, attentive critique and ongoing support. I am also grateful to Adriaan Van Klinken and Awino Okech, who examined my thesis. Their supportive criticism has made this work far stronger than it would otherwise have been. I acknowledge the grants I received from the Sir Richard Stapley Educational Trust, the Sidney Perry Foundation, the Gilchrist Educational Trust and the Roger and Sarah Bancroft Clark Charitable Trust which enabled the research upon which this book is based, as I pursued my doctorate with no institutional funding. Without the additional funds generously offered by Nanna and Elaine, I would not have completed the PhD. Thanks also to Peta, who not only helped me heal my back with Pilates but also provided my non-academic side gig, which has become my main source of income. These are the material realities of attempting to forge an academic career doing critical feminist work in the humanities in these neoliberal times. Finally, to my family, there are no words to adequately thank you for your care and support, not only during the process of writing this book but in all things.

Abbreviations

AAWORD	Association of African Women for Research and Development
AIC	African Independent Church/African Instituted Church
AIDS	Acquired Immune Deficiency Syndrome
BHESP	Bar Hostess Empowerment and Support Programme
CEDAW	Convention on the Elimination of All Forms of Discrimination against Women
CEDPA	Centre for Development and Population Activities
Circle	Circle of Concerned African Women Theologians
FBO	Faith-Based organization
FGM	Female Genital Mutilation
FIDA-K	Federation of Women Lawyers, Kenya
GNP+	Global Network of People Living with HIV
HIV	Human Immunodeficiency Virus
ICPD	International Conference on Population and Development
IMF	International Monetary Fund
IPPF	International Planned Parenthood Foundation
KCLF	Kenya Christian Leaders Forum
KESWA	Kenya Sex Workers Alliance
KHRC	Kenyan Human Rights Commission
LBTQI	Lesbian, Bisexual, Trans, Queer, Intersex
LGBTQ	Lesbian, Gay, Bisexual, Trans, Queer
LKWV	League of Kenyan Women Voters
NCCK	National Council of Churches of Kenya
NCWK	National Council of Women of Kenya
NEPHAK	National Empowerment Network for Persons Living with HIV and AIDS in Kenya
NGO	Non-governmental Organization
PLWHA	People Living with HIV and AIDS
RHRA	Reproductive Health and Rights Alliance
SDA	Seventh Day Adventist (church)
SRHR	Sexual and Reproductive Health and Rights
UKAID	An operating name of DfID since 2009

UN	United Nations
UNAIDS	Joint United Nations Programme on HIV and AIDS
UNICEF	United Nations International Children's Fund
UNIFEM	United Nations Fund for Women
USAID	United States Agency for International Development
WB	World Bank
YMCA	Young Men's Christian Association
YWCA	Young Women's Christian Association

Map of Kenya with locations of YWCA branches

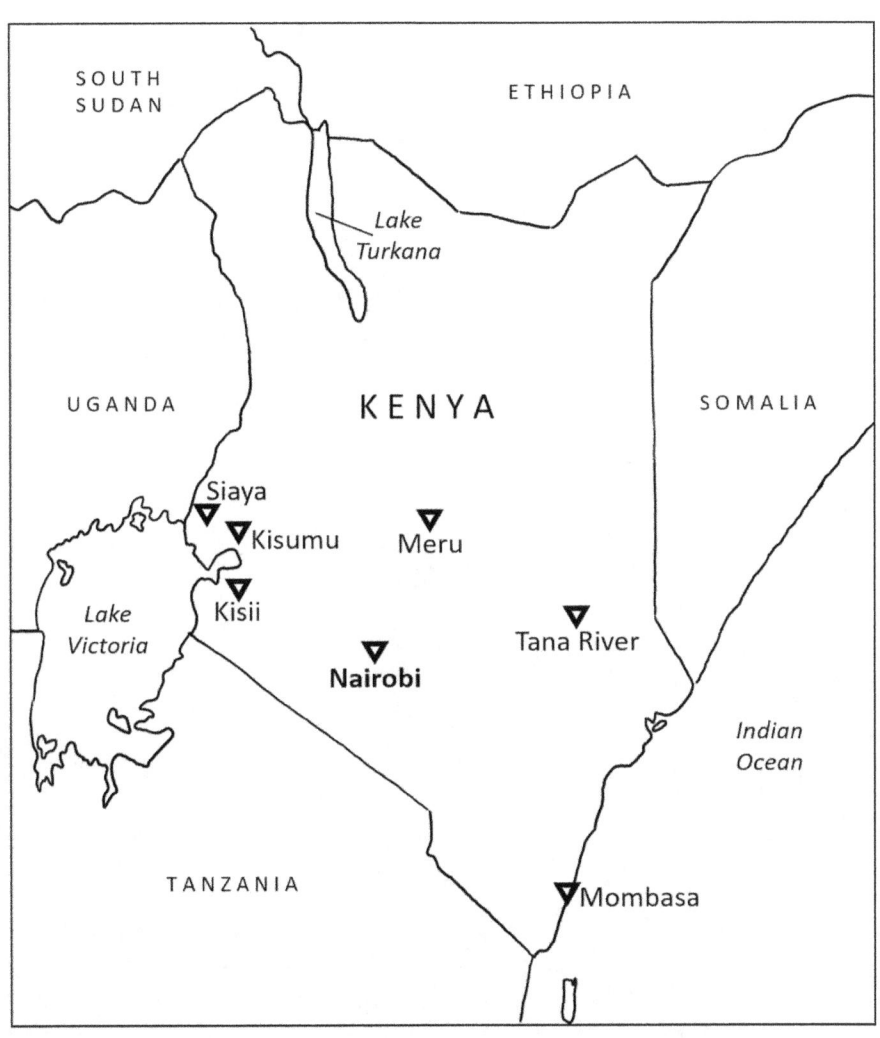

Part 1

Introduction

'So, what is your aspiration? Are you going to serve in the church?' Winnie asked me.¹ We were sitting together at a small circular table in a canteen at the Nairobi headquarters of the Young Women's Christian Association of Kenya (to which I refer as simply 'the YWCA' or 'the Association'). Evidently, Winnie had assumed that I was a Christian. We had been talking for more than an hour, and I felt a little surge of anxiety run through me. Had I misrepresented myself? Keen to correct this, I told an abbreviated autobiography, mentioning my mostly non-religious upbringing in the UK and explaining that my interest in theology was mainly academic, and political – growing from a curiosity about the contradiction between official, mainstream church teachings and practices and the radical edges of Christian thought in liberation, Black and postcolonial feminist theologies. Winnie had presumed not only that I was a Christian but also that I had a specifically Christian project, vocation or ambition. She thereby expressed one of the central contentions of this book: that 'being (a) Christian' is understood to entail certain kinds of ethical conduct, and vice versa: that observing certain conduct leads many to infer a Christian identity.

Throughout conversations about this research, both with research participants and new acquaintances, I was asked countless times: 'What church do you go to, back home?' This question was most often small talk, but it was always an attempt to get a hold on who I was and what I was doing in Kenya; sometimes it was an attempt to make a connection, to see if we both belonged to the same denomination, or if we shared an identity. I was always slightly sad to disappoint with my stock answer: 'I don't go to church.' It occasionally crossed my mind to lie and tell people I was Anglican, to facilitate a connection by telling them what I thought they wanted to hear. I did not employ this tactic, but experiencing the temptation to do so was instructive: it helped me to understand the affective dimension of sharing a religious identity, and the social rewards of claiming one, in a place where the assumption of Christianity is as strong as it is in Kenya. The staff, leaders and volunteers I interacted with at the YWCA often highlighted their Christian faith in conversation, and explicitly claimed it as an identity for a wide range of reasons, including pragmatic and spiritual reasons. Almost all expressed pleasure in being part of the YWCA as a Christian organization: pride, a sense of belonging, affirmation, satisfaction. It is significant that the YWCA brings people together and names itself for positions or identities that are (or are likely to be) unchosen: being a woman, a Christian and/or young. My research participants' words made it clear that desire and choice underlie their decisions to foreground these identities in their construction of moral identities, not least because the YWCA is a membership organization that relies on voluntarism.

The YWCA in Nairobi

I did not deliberately set out to study identity and narrative. I went to Nairobi to ask the YWCA questions about how, and what, it knew about Christian ethics in relation to, and as a result of, making programmatic interventions for the benefit of women and girls. I took certain assumptions with me into the field; based on broader tensions between feminism and Christianity, I was curious to find out what it meant for the YWCA to be a Christian women's organization in the twenty-first century. I did not have much idea what that might be exactly, but I did assume there was something there to be studied. This turned out to be the case, as I found the organization concerned to 'emphasize' its Christian identity in response to its perception of potential controversy about some aspects of its sexual and reproductive health and rights (SRHR) interventions. The YWCA's past as a colonial institution also continued to inform its structure and its operations that, since the 1970s, have seen it positioned on the periphery of what I will call the 'development industry' (following Cornwall and Jolly 2009). My own arrival in Nairobi mirrored that of the women who established the YWCA a century earlier, in 1912.

On 10 January 2012, I said a very tearful goodbye to my partner and boarded a plane from Heathrow to Nairobi; only the fourth time I had boarded a plane, and my first time travelling outside Europe. When I landed, I crossed the city by taxi to stay with Marie, a white German woman who worked for the United Nations (UN), in the apartment she shared with her Black Kenyan partner Elijah. Marie's place was on the third floor of a building in a small compound, a few minutes' walk from Valley Arcade, in a middle-class residential area. Like the

YWCA's earliest beneficiaries, I journeyed to eastern Africa as a young, single, white woman, and upon my arrival I plugged into a loose network of white European 'ex-pats', living lives totally unlike the lives of the majority of Black Kenyans. Like my forebears, I arrived with my own project in mind and had the financial means (however precariously) to pursue it. However, unlike the white settlers who established the YWCA, upon my arrival I found a city built upon more than a century of colonial material and ideological infrastructure upholding capitalism and persistent white supremacy which in 1912 had only just begun to be built.

Within hours of landing in Nairobi, I was on-board a *matatu* (a minibus, part of an informal network of public transport) with Marie, on my way to a party for one of her UN colleagues in another part of the city. I spent a lot of time in January and February travelling by *matatu* or by bus. My destinations were usually middle-class spaces or institutions – most often, the YWCA headquarters, but inevitably also malls, bookshops, university campuses, cafés and friends' places. I therefore spent many hours sitting in Nairobi's infamous traffic jams, gazing out of bus windows at the buildings, street sellers, trees and road signs; it afforded me great opportunities to observe the life of the city. On a hot and sunny January morning, I made my way to the YWCA headquarters for the first time. I travelled by *matatu* from Valley Arcade to Serena, and walked the last leg of the journey up Nyerere Road, with the park on one side and hotels and office buildings on the other. The YWCA stands on the corner of Mamlaka Road and Nyerere Road, overlooking Central Park. The plot on which the YWCA was built was acquired in 1913, on what was then called Kirk Road, on the leafy green edge of the nascent city's centre. In 2012 its immediate neighbours included the Zambian Embassy and St Andrew's Presbyterian Church. In the next few streets are located the University of Nairobi, and many other hostels for students, the Serena Hotel, some other embassies, State House and many churches. The area between Mamlaka Road, the University of Nairobi and Central Park is sometimes called 'church island' due to the proximity of All Saints' Anglican Cathedral, Nairobi Central Seventh Day Adventist Church, St Paul's Catholic Church, Mamlaka Hill Chapel and the Lutheran Church.

The YWCA compound is arranged on a gentle hillside, which informs the positions and shapes of the buildings. From the road, I could see the white façade of the 1950s-built hostel, Beecher Hall, behind trees and a fence. Walking up Mamlaka Road, I found the entrance to the YWCA on the right – a reddish wood gate with a guard's station. A sign displayed the YWCA's blue triangular symbol and simply advertised 'Hostel, Conference Halls, Cafeteria, Parking,

Salon'. The original YWCA building, opened in 1917, was now in front of me; it was known simply as 'The Hostel' until 1933, when it was named Windsor House (Harley 1995: 38). Windsor House is impressively solid, with exposed grey stone walls on the inside as well as outside, criss-crossed by dark wooden beams in a mock-Tudor style. Its more modern neighbours are rendered in white plaster since weathered and faded to a spectrum of pale yellows and greys. It has only two storeys, so it is dwarfed by the larger, more modern blocks built in the 1960s and 1970s, four or five storeys tall, which sit behind it towards Nyerere Road. The jumble of buildings and extensions that comprise the headquarters testifies to the long history of the organization on this plot and its near-continuous programme of expansion. In the past, it was the demand for accommodation for single women that motivated the expansion of the YWCA's hostels, but in recent years the addition of new buildings has been part of wider efforts towards financial self-sustainability. Inside, Windsor House opens into a large hall and a cafeteria, through which you can exit on the other side into a narrow passage formed by the space between it and an extension. There, you find a window which, when open, serves as a kiosk for the convenience of residents. Stopping for directions to the headquarters offices, I found myself navigating the passage, heading down through a terraced garden of low shrubs between the buildings, and along a path to the car park on the other side of the compound. The headquarters offices are in a building that was constructed especially to house them in 1960. I went up the external concrete staircase to a balcony on the first floor; a climbing plant with bright flowers wound itself around the railings of the balcony, making it seem less like offices and more like a holiday villa. This impression was reinforced by the large windows taking in the view of the park across the road. In fact, when it was built it included accommodation for two members of staff, their flats now converted into offices.

I found Wandia in her office on the first floor, next to a small conference room with walls painted in lilac and a bold graffiti-style mural. On the top floor were offices occupied by the National General Secretary and the National Chairperson. Wandia welcomed me warmly into the slightly cramped room, full of her files and piles of pamphlets publicizing the YWCA's projects. The sun beamed in through single-pane windows in flaking metal frames. Having already communicated briefly with Wandia by email, we got to know one another quickly. She was married, with children, and living in a nearby residential area while working full-time for the YWCA and pursuing postgraduate studies. This basic socio-economic and personal profile was shared by many of my research participants. Wandia gave me a few leaflets detailing YWCA projects, and we casually discussed my research. We chatted in a way that was new to me at that time, as I pared down my research agenda to brief statements of themes and areas of interest: ethics, the women's movement, theology. This would soon become a familiar, even rehearsed, way of talking about myself, as I repeated and refined my account of my research in each conversation with a new research participant.

Most significantly for my research, it was at this first meeting that Wandia asked me, 'Have you read Vera's book?' She pulled out of her desk drawer Vera Harley's *Rickshaws to Jets: A History and Anecdotes of the Kenya YWCA 1912–1965* (hereafter, *Rickshaws to Jets*). Yes, I told her. She was pleased to hear that I was familiar with *Rickshaws to Jets*, perhaps because it meant she did not need to tell me the YWCA's history herself. Wandia told me not only that I should read *Rickshaws to Jets* but also that she and her colleagues had done so, and that they continued to refer to it. I was amazed that I had serendipitously managed to find a copy of this book that was so important to the YWCA that Wandia kept a copy in her desk drawer. I began immediately to think about the implications of this: on one hand, I could read Harley's account of the YWCA as Wandia seemed to, as truthful. It also presented the opportunity to analyse the way the YWCA was understood, and represented, by a staff member from another period of the organization's history. What did it mean that the only published history of Kenya YWCA, to which the organization itself referred for information about its past, was written by a white British woman? I did not realize the full significance of *Rickshaws to Jets* until later in my research: as a key piece of the construction and circulation of a distinct organizational identity that emphasized Christianity, and evidence for how that had changed over time.

Throughout February I conducted interviews and had informal conversations with staff and others at the YWCA headquarters. I was invited as an observer to several meetings including a 'strategic planning' meeting and a Female Genital Mutilation (FGM) Programme meeting, at both of which I was able to observe the internal operations of the YWCA as an organization.[2] At these meetings, I saw at first-hand how explicitly Christian practices were integrated into the YWCA's conduct. I listened to the ways in which people within the organization used tropes, themes and vocabularies established in Christian, international development, and feminist narratives and the interactions between them. In 2012, its centenary year, the YWCA claimed a total of 23,449 members, making it the fourth largest YWCA in the world. It had reached tens of thousands of beneficiaries through its welfare and development projects, youth groups, microcredit schemes and women's groups. Nationally, it was led by approximately 175 volunteers and representatives, and administered by approximately 100 members of staff, a small number of whom worked at the YWCA's headquarters in Nairobi. Through its seven branches in Nairobi, Mombasa, Kisumu, Kisii, Siaya, Meru and Tana River, the YWCA operated youth clubs, known as 'Y Teens', and offered wide-ranging projects and programmes to its members and beneficiaries. The YWCA's hostels, for which the YWCA movement is perhaps best known, provided accommodation for travellers and longer-term tenants, typically students. The YWCA is constituted by four groups: staff, fee-paying members, representatives and programme beneficiaries (Figure 1). There are overlaps between these groups: many staff have been members, all representatives and volunteers must first be members and many beneficiaries are also members or become members through their involvement in a programme. However, the distinct interests of each group were occasionally reflected in a degree of tension emerging between staff and representatives on decision-making bodies – the committees that set the direction and aims of projects and govern the organization.

As my interviews progressed, I became more and more aware of recurring themes that were spoken of in relation to the Association's sexual health programmes. It became clear that my research participants, at least in their capacities within the YWCA, were concerned about the ethical implications

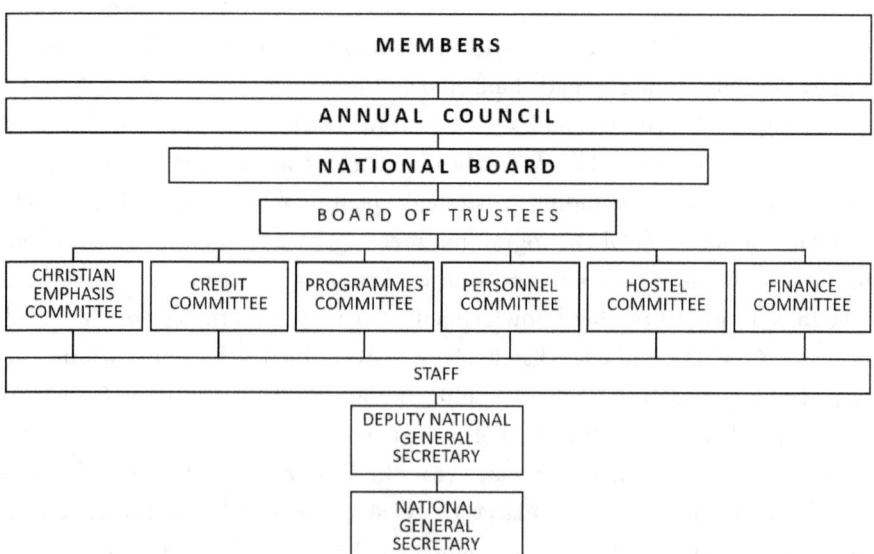

Figure 1 An organization chart describing the internal structure of the YWCA.

of these 'controversial faith issues'. Discovering the concept of controversial faith issues and the ways they allowed the YWCA to talk about its SRHR programmes was critical to my developing understanding of the organization's identity narratives. All the while, I was very conscious of how easy it would be to accidentally ask a leading question. 'I'm interested in why the YWCA does what it does', I would say. I wanted to hear an answer to 'why' in relation to what seemed to be broad areas of tension, even outright opposition, between ecumenical Christianity, the women's movement and development industry deployments of feminism – and postcolonial/anti-colonial rejections of all three. After I found out about controversial faith issues, I learned to ask, 'Why does the YWCA work on SRHR?'

In mid-February I moved to the YWCA, after staying for about a month at Marie's place. My room in Parkview Suites had a small balcony looking out over Central Park towards the city centre, which meant I had a vantage point from which I could observe the city from afar. In an effort to move away from reliance on external donors to fund projects, the YWCA constructed Parkview Suites to attract business travellers and tourists. The income generated by the hostels, now mainly occupied by students at the nearby University of Nairobi, was not enough to support the organization's ambitions. Situated on the northern side of the headquarters compound, Parkview Suites offers serviced one-room apartments at a much higher rate than the more basic hostel rooms. The building faces away from the rest of the YWCA compound, and has its own entrance on Nyerere Road, reflecting a degree of separation between the business travellers anticipated to stay in Parkview Suites and the students in the hostels who are explicitly approached as potential YWCA members. A laminated notice was tacked to the wooden room divider between the living area and the bedroom, advising guests of information about housekeeping and various rules. It also said that the rooms were only available to couples if they were married and could show a marriage certificate upon check-in to prove it. This was the only suggestion visible to the average guest that Parkview Suites was owned and operated by a Christian organization. Living on the same compound as the headquarters offices allowed me to observe the YWCA's day-to-day life, as well as being close to my research participants. However, I was there for only a couple of weeks before my research with the YWCA was put on hold when I sustained an injury to my back at the end of February, and was hospitalized. I returned to the UK for a period of four months, which I spent recovering at my parents' house and working in a sweet shop to raise funds to continue my research. In July I flew back to Nairobi and moved into another room at Parkview Suites.

Methods and fieldwork

This study is an interdisciplinary examination of ethics, identity and narrative through the prism of the YWCA in light of its colonial history, written by a white British feminist scholar. It would be remiss of me to consider the significance of identity for ethics while ignoring the effects of my identity as the researcher and author responsible for this project. Most significantly, I am an 'outsider' in respect of all the identities that are significant in this project. My interest in the YWCA is not a result of having a Christian identity or faith myself – I am, at most, 'culturally Christian' – nor was it generated by previous contact with the YWCA. YWCA members are connected to one another primarily by their involvement in the organization, but those I interviewed also regularly invoked their shared Kenyan and Christian identities, and their status as mothers, as relevant frames for their collective ethical positions. I was not able to include myself in these shared identities, and this inevitably had a range of effects for my research.

Throughout the design and execution of this research project I have been sensitive to the dynamics of power and representation inherent in the research process, particularly in terms of the political effects of the production of knowledge about 'African women'. Initially, I posed this question as an issue of how I could minimize the perpetuation of the ever-present asymmetrical power relations of feminism (Grewal and Kaplan 2000: 2). In my interpersonal relationships with my research participants I framed my research as a process of gathering expert knowledge about the YWCA, intentionally positioning myself as a student and my research participants as authoritative sources based on their professional knowledge and personal experience. In approaching my research participants as a young, single student I was able to activate the YWCA's hierarchies, both in terms of its structure and its ethos of Christian maternalism. This starting point was inspired by the work of feminist theologian Musa Dube, who describes that she and her research assistants 'always clearly stated [to research participants]: "We have come to learn from you"' (Dube 2000: 186). This approach dovetailed with a relatively hierarchical organization of relationships within the YWCA. The women I interviewed were all in professional leadership and managerial positions, they were all older than me, they were all married and they were all either mothers or grandmothers. The fact that I was young, unmarried and childless helped to construct our relationships along more than one axis of social power, not only between the more powerful researcher and 'the researched'. My research participants often responded to my junior status, as I asked curious questions and received guided tours. Participating in my research involved performing aspects of their positions as leaders and experts. Of course, these interpersonal relations did not mitigate any of the wider structural dynamics that privileged me relative to most of the women about whom I write in this book. Moreover, there is no way of getting around the fact that I imposed my idea to research ethics with the YWCA, rather than responding to an interest or a need that the Association itself identified in advance. However, my research agenda was broad to begin with and I consciously adapted it to respond to the themes and ideas my research participants introduced in conversation.

This book results from about four-and-a-half months of fieldwork in Nairobi, conducted in 2012, and seven years of wider research conducted for my PhD at SOAS University of London. If the reader doubts that eighteen weeks could be sufficient time to generate data for a comprehensive study of the YWCA, I admit that I share those doubts. My fieldwork was intended to be longer, but my back injury, the time it took me to recover and the financial impact it had all required me to change my plans. It is difficult to account for the myriad effects this interruption had on my study; at least, it meant that I took much longer to complete the project. It hampered my ability to establish myself as a reliable presence at the YWCA, as I left suddenly and returned with little warning. However, the short time I spent 'in the field' reflects the kind of project this became. I am very clear that my work is not an ethnography; I do not take 'Kenya', 'Kenyan women' or 'Kenyan Christians' as my object of study. I intentionally make smaller observations about the YWCA in Kenya; where I connect these observations to wider theoretical claims, I do so in the service of thinking better about women's everyday Christian ethics in respect of gender and sexuality.

As a feminist interdisciplinary scholar trained in ethics, the study of religions and gender studies, I applied a mixture of methods to observe and understand the YWCA's practices and the relationship of identity narratives to its activities. My research methods have been informed by feminist and postcolonial interventions in social and cultural anthropology – informed conversations, recorded interviews and consensual participant observation – but I am not an anthropologist. I combined these methods with archival research in the YWCA's own records, the collection and analysis of YWCA publications, such as its Annual Council Reports, and ephemera. These provided rich insights into the life of the YWCA in the late twentieth and early twenty-first century, and a snapshot of the ways in which the YWCA presents itself to internal and external audiences. I focused primarily on identifying, accessing and interpreting texts, including texts generated by transcribing recorded interviews. Alongside observation and casual conversation with YWCA staff and volunteers, I completed twenty formal interviews, eleven of which were in-depth and recorded digitally. The headquarters is where I spent most of my time, but I also went to visit the YWCA's Nairobi branch in Eastlands. To recruit research participants for interviews, I applied a method known as 'snowball' or 'chain' sampling, in which a participant is asked to identify and refer the researcher to other participants. This method was a pragmatic response to the fact that prior to arriving at the YWCA I was appointed a contact, Wandia, who became my key informant. In the course of conducting my fieldwork, my sampling method became less like a chain and more like a web, as Wandia became a 'gatekeeper' through whom I met most, but not all, of my research participants. Due to her intimate knowledge of the research context, and her professional network, Wandia was able to identify and contact persons of interest far more easily than I could have done without her help. However, 'snowball' sampling and similar techniques reliant on 'gatekeepers' tend to reflect the existing power relations in the research context, and preserve rather than challenge them. In my case, Wandia's perception, anticipation or awareness of my research interests may have influenced her to connect me more often with senior-level managerial staff and leaders. The women I formally interviewed were all highly educated, middle-class professionals and fluent in English in addition to other languages. Their experiences and evaluations of the YWCA were made possible by their shared access to a certain degree of power and influence within it; only someone who has served on a national committee or attended project planning meetings, for instance, can report about how the YWCA operates at the national level. The socio-economic class of my research participants and their position in the YWCA's hierarchy set them apart from most YWCA members, illustrative of the ways in which its structure tends to preserve a hierarchy of age and class.

Reflecting on the positions of relative class privilege occupied by the YWCA women I spoke with suggests dwelling on the issue of power in narrative. This book contains many stories, including my own, those told to me about the YWCA as well as wider stories or metanarratives about colonization, sexuality and Christianity. I am by necessity selective and creative with the many stories and complex truths of my research and its results. While I write about the uses of institutional stories and memories, the whole project is filtered through and facilitated by my own memories, now recalled in narrative form. Institutional memories are recalled as stories, in which the one remembering often often takes centre stage. These remembered stories are fallible, partial and continuously reinterpreted in light of new experiences. I remember some dimensions of my field research well, others less so, and I am unaware of many things that I have forgotten. The reasons behind what I remember are not always clear to me, although some of the gaps may be the result of the medication I was prescribed to deal with the back injury. The things that stand out above my other memories are inevitably the exceptional experiences – whether enjoyable, surprising or disappointing – while, as may be expected, more mundane experiences have faded. The memories of my research to which I have paid most conscious attention are aided by digital audio recordings of my interviews and conversations, and transcripts I made of those recordings in the course of analysing the story-data they collected. While these form the explicit centre of my research and writing efforts, they sit against a background of what I learned through my day-to-day experiences and encounters. Noting my memory's fallibility is not intended to suggest that what follows is untrue, or unusually subjective. Rather, because I have been thinking about and reading narratives, I am very conscious of the way that a good story can be as convincing as a good argument, if not more so.

Summary and outline

I argue in this book that identity and ethics are fundamentally, not trivially, connected to the narratives we hear and tell. Who we are, what we do and what we make of the outcomes of our conduct are deeply rooted in the narratives we hear and pay attention to – both those we seek out and those that address themselves to us. With institutional or organizational narratives, this is also the case in terms of how people, discussions, occasions and sequences of events are remembered, recorded, chosen and reread in the present, and what effects these readings have. The organization acts as author and audience as it tells its own stories to itself. This circularity between production and reception does not change the necessity of interpreting the narrative, in an effort to answer the question of the relationship between what 'we' say and what 'we' do (Miller 2005: 12–13). Stated another way, the central question that I attempt to answer with my research participants is: the YWCA's identity narratives say that it is a Christian organization, but does its conduct support that claim? In the first chapter, I outline the theoretical resources that I have used to think this through.

In the second part, I offer a postcolonial history of the YWCA from 1912 to 2012 to outline the changes and continuities in its interventions for social change over the course of the century. Originating in Victorian England during a period of industrialization and Protestant revival, the YWCA organized middle-class women for the moral and physical protection of young working women in Britain's growing cities. The YWCA is one of the oldest women's organizations in eastern Africa. It was established in 1912 by a small group of white British women who had come to the region as dependents of colonizer and missionary men. The hostels it set up provided a 'home away from home' for young white women, mainly British, who were arriving in the region to work. It further offered older, upper-class colonizer women positions of authority through which to fulfil their feminine social responsibilities, a form of white colonial gender power to which I refer as 'imperial maternalism'. Thereby, the YWCA played a small but significant role in supporting white European missionary activity and British colonization of the region. Throughout the twentieth century, the YWCA grew and changed. Its activities became increasingly formalized in recent decades, and it is now a non-governmental organization (NGO) working nationally in the field of women's rights and gender equality. However, the YWCA is still a membership organization, not a charity or a development agency, and it actively retains the Christian identity in its name.

The twentieth century also saw the YWCA develop a worldwide network of Associations, served and coordinated by the World YWCA, an umbrella organization founded in 1894. The World YWCA, to which each national YWCA must be affiliated, requires that YWCAs implement a highly formal internal structure and quasi-democratic processes of representation and decision-making. Like the YWCA movement around the world, Kenya YWCA is led by women, almost exclusively staffed by women and operates primarily to benefit girls and young women, but often operates more broadly with youth and older women. Both in the colonial era and in the very different context of Kenya in the early twenty-first century, the YWCA's narrative and programmatic activities offered an opportunity for Christian women to reinforce their sense of being Christian and behaving accordingly. While there is no single, obvious or coherent 'Christianity' to which such an identity refers – rather, there are many Christianities – many Christians and Christian institutions, including the YWCA, speak and act as though there is.

Christianity has been a crucial factor in justifying misogyny and patriarchy, as well as motivating women's resistance to them. This is true in the narrow sense of explicit Christian doctrine and tradition, as church institutions have put power in the hands of elite men and developed moral theologies associating sex and women's bodies with impurity and sin. It is also true in the broader sense that Christianity has informed everyday life in much of Europe, from the influence of the Ten Commandments on law and ethics to the influence of Bible stories in popular culture. Despite the ubiquity of Christianity, it is typically marginal to accounts of the development of Western feminisms[3] except as a source of sexism. As I have already suggested, my interest in this book is in how Christianity has facilitated women's resistance to men's dominance. I do not give a comprehensive overview of the ways Christian theology and culturally Christian assumptions have informed the ethical positions taken by white Western women's movements, nor the norms implicit in moral philosophy, social theory, anthropology and so on. Instead, I offer a small contribution towards rethinking the relationships between Christianity and development industry work on gender and sexuality through the history of the YWCA in Kenya. In particular, I highlight the ways whiteness and coloniality were deeply embedded in, and constitutive of, the narration and negotiation of Christian ethics of sex, sexuality, reproduction and mothering, and how these overlaps continued into the twenty-first century. The YWCA represents an opportunity to examine Christian women's collective action for social change, and the ethics that accompanies this conduct, outside the control of the churches and away from the patriarchal leadership of male clergy.

The history of the YWCA is divided across three chapters, in which I also present the context of colonization and the development industry in which the YWCA has worked, with a focus on Christianity's place within these. The course of its history demonstrates the YWCA's transformation from a white colonial women's organization into a 'multiracial' Christian Association, and then into an agent of development, while maintaining its structure and identity as a membership organization and part of the World YWCA movement. In Chapter 2, I sketch the YWCA's imperial maternalism as an expression of structural and theological commitments common to the YWCA movement, British colonizers and missionaries. Chapter 3 draws these themes into the second part of the twentieth century and examines their legacies in the international development industry, with an emphasis on the YWCA's increasing NGO-ization and its focus on SRHR. Finally, in Chapter 4 I outline the YWCA's interventions in FGM, HIV and youth SRHR in the twenty-first century, examining the ways these embed ethical assumptions established by the ascription of an identity. The effects of Christian institutions' moralizing include shoring up the borders of group belonging – that is, who is and is not considered to be 'a Christian' – by allowing the exclusion of others in order to define the nation, the family or the church. Doing this kind of 'boundary work' inherently implicates ethics, since establishing an identity implies an associated range of commitments and interests. Answers to the question of 'who I am' are fundamental to knowing who and what I care about; in other words our personal sense of identity 'provides the frame' within which we make evaluative judgements about what is good, bad, right, wrong and what we stand for or against (Taylor 2006: 27). Herein, I identify four major identity categories that frame and provide context for the YWCA's ethical stance; these are 'Christianity', 'African-ness', 'feminism' and 'development'.

In the final section of the book, I offer an account of how these narratives and discourses have contoured the YWCA's identity and ethics. In Chapter 5, I discuss 'controversial faith issues', presenting my research participants' words to sketch the positions it takes on condoms, abortion and non-normative sexualities. I introduce the YWCA's concept of 'controversial faith issues' and explain why condoms, abortion and non-normative sexualities might be categorized as 'controversial'. This is so for a wide range of reasons to do with hegemonic 'conservative' interpretations of Christian ethics, African responses to Christianity's position relative to British colonization of eastern Africa and ongoing dynamics of coloniality in Christian institutions and discourses, international development and feminist/women's movements. The YWCA responds to controversial faith issues with a range of planned interventions for social change around SRHR, and it explains the reasons for these interventions by giving a narrative, historical account of its Christian identity. This is possible because narrative practices and moral tales are central to everyday ethical conduct, and there are particular stories and modes of storytelling that are peculiar to Christians and to institutions that provide resolutions to ethical questions.

The mostly unarticulated sense of a somehow obvious set of Christian values which 'require no explanation' has been observed in other Anglophone African contexts, particularly in Christian resistance to lesbian, gay, bisexual and transgender (LGBTQ) rights and the associated assumption of Christian heteronormativity (e.g. Van Klinken 2014: 265). Recent debates in Kenya, particularly those concerning abortion, seem to suggest that Christian sexual morality only receives explicit attention from clergy and other leaders at moments of tension or challenge. Feminist critiques of patriarchal religious institutions have pointed out how sweeping declarations about sexual ethics target the pleasure, capacities, health and autonomy of women's and LGBTQ people's bodies. Such institutions typically refute and ridicule feminist challenges to these norms and practices as threatening to morality itself, often using the weighted language of 'family values' to reiterate the hetero-patriarchal and repronormative definition of the family. Christian women's organizations like the YWCA are therefore faced with a choice whether to contest the legitimacy of these sexual morality projects – and if they decide to do so, whether to stand publicly in opposition to them or be more subtle. The YWCA has tended to take the latter approach and remain non-confrontational.

In Chapter 6, I discuss how the tensions arising from controversial faith issues are addressed through a narrative emphasis of the YWCA's Christian identity. I focus on the implications of the narrative constitution of identity as a key venue for the articulation of ethical or moral positions, explaining why everyday understandings of what constitutes Christian ethics remain largely tacit. These include appeals to origins, the construction of unity and establishing connections between the personal moral identities of the members of the organization and the organization's identity. The YWCA engages all three of these strategies. Many organizations function in this way – by inducing their leaders and members to learn significant organizational stories such as the origin of the organization or the biography of a significant individual and to retell them as if they were their own stories (Linde 2009). In my research I heard two major YWCA narratives of Christian values and identity: 'controversial faith issues' and 'Christian emphasis'. These are embedded to varying degrees of formality in the structure of the organization. The first of these Christian identity narratives is a complex operation whereby 'controversial faith issues' are identified by asserting the existence of a controversy surrounding a topic in sexual ethics which is in some way implicated in the YWCA's activities. This creates opportunities to reiterate the ways in which its programmatic interventions conform to or deviate from the accepted/expected Christian responses to these 'issues'. The second, 'Christian emphasis', is a self-conscious narration of a set of practices aimed at recentring worship, prayer and pastoral care in the Association's structure and regular schedule of activities. The incorporation of the Christian faith of its members into the organization is a central element in Christian emphasis, which has its roots in the historical ecumenism of the World YWCA and the sociopolitical significance of ecumenism in contemporary Kenya.

In an institutional setting, narrative accounts of identity implicate memory and history. Identity narratives typically account for conduct, and therefore they offer resources for 'everyday' articulations of ethics; at the YWCA, both identity and ethics are narrated in relation to the organization's Christian history and context. The YWCA considered that its interventions around youth sexuality and sexual health required narrative resolution to avoid controversy, and it achieved this by further emphasizing its Christian identity. The YWCA engages in a set of narrative practices that tell internal and external audiences 'who we are', or what the YWCA is and what it does, in order to emphasize its Christian identity. Narratives of Christian emphasis construct Christianity as something that has been lost or forgotten, creating the conditions in which it can be presented as if newly rediscovered. The structure of this narrative has parallels with redemption or 'born-again' narratives, which require a period of trouble in order to give weight to the transformation caused by a turn, or return, to God. The YWCA told these narratives in response to my conversational prompts and questions about ethics and the YWCA's programmes and, on that basis, I began to explore the connections between Christian identity and everyday Christian ethics.

In Chapter 7, the final chapter and conclusion, I outline 'everyday Christian ethics' as a way of approaching organizational Christian ethics informed by the results of my work with the YWCA. Since its institutional identity narratives were central to its everyday ethics, I argue that stories through which the YWCA tells 'who we are' are of considerable significance for what it does, in terms of its programmatic interventions for social change, and for how it explains this conduct. This is crystallized in the YWCA's vision statement, a common strategy through which organizations represent themselves to their audiences and members. The YWCA's vision is typically included prominently alongside the related 'mission' statement on signs, leaflets and its website, and in 2012 it was 'a society where girls and women live fulfilled lives'. The value of 'fulfilled lives' is a mainstream expression within Christian theology and ethics that can also be seen in the YWCA's and Young Men's Christian Association's (YMCA) assertions of purpose at the World level, and widespread in articulations of African theology and Christian ethics. It connects the YWCA's programmatic interventions to improve women's material circumstances to a central concern of Christian theology, summarized in a multivalent ethics of 'life'.

Everyday Christian ethics is derived from combining insights from the fields of ordinary ethics, ordinary theological ethics and postcolonial African women's theologies. That ethics is 'everyday' means that it is fundamentally part of ordinary life, and not only found in academic abstraction or exercises of clerical authority. That everyday ethics is narrative means that ethical ideas are expressed in the form of stories or biographies, and that the content of quotidian storytelling practices is a window into the values and norms of a family, community, society or organization. A feminist theory of everyday Christian ethics recognizes that Christian women are not passive recipients of patriarchal, heterosexist, pro-natal religious morals: they promote or contest these using ideas, arguments and stories from within and without a wide Christian corpus, tradition, doctrine and theology in combination with wider public narrative resources. Therefore, I argue, when Christian women's conduct appears to differ from hegemonic Christian values, this is not necessarily evidence of a misunderstanding or of resistance to hegemony. It is evidence of the ways in which everyday Christian ethics are responsive to, and embedded in, the circumstances in which they are articulated.

1

Identity and ethics in narrative

> *So, one time, I was with a friend of mine … they were going for a YWCA meeting. I was not yet a member … I said, 'Which organisation is this?' … 'Young Women's Christian Association' – You know, when I heard that I said, 'This is the group that I should be with' … So I went [to the meeting] without invitation … and I was encouraged, just because it's a Christian organisation, and I felt, if it's a Christian organisation then they live true to their promises of the organisation, not like these other women['s groups] … So that's how I became a member.* (Nyaboke, interview, 2012)

I met Nyaboke, one of the YWCA's national leaders, at the organization's Nairobi headquarters. I waited for her in a small lobby, as two administrative staff worked at a reception desk. The layout of the building reflects the assumptions of the time in which it was constructed; its veranda faces the green space of Central Park, giving sweeping views of the city. The two offices occupied by national YWCA leaders have windows facing that direction. At the back of the building is a narrow service entrance, a small passageway with service doors into both offices, leading to a kitchenette and small cupboard-like filing rooms housing storage and a photocopier. These were still used by catering and administrative staff, while the offices and reception area served as the public-facing headquarters. During my meeting with Nyaboke, tea and lunch were served to us through these doors, suggesting that the infrastructure of the organization continued to reinforce hierarchies of power in class, seniority and professional status. Describing her introduction to the YWCA, Nyaboke recalled a chance invitation to attend a YWCA meeting with a friend, and joined because she felt that the YWCA reflected her Christian convictions. Nyaboke then rose through the ranks over a span of fifteen years, beginning as an ordinary member, then serving on the executive committee of her branch, becoming Branch Chairperson and finally holding a position in the national leadership team. In many ways, Nyaboke's story is a paradigmatic leader's journey through the YWCA, demonstrating commitment to the organization and her Christian faith. When I asked about Nyaboke's motivation for taking on increasing responsibility over time, she cited her training as a teacher and interest in working with young people, and her status and experience as a mother. As a mother of daughters and a survivor of FGM (or as Nyaboke put it, 'I was cut') she was particularly keen to address the practice in her community. Convinced of its 'disadvantages', Nyaboke refused to have it done to her own children. The YWCA offered her an institutional framework through which to talk to her community, using the YWCA's resources and her own experience, her success as an 'entrepreneur' and her position as a married mother of five children, as proof that customary understandings of the effects of refusing to perform circumcision on girl children are not accurate (Nyaboke, interview, 2012).

What Nyaboke had come to understand as good, and what she stood for, were rooted in her understanding of herself, including her personal sense of Christian identity which informed her decision to join the YWCA. This mutual influence between personal conduct, identity and group membership is the foundation of my approach to the YWCA's narrative constitution of a Christian organizational identity; 'understanding who I am is crucial to understanding how I should live; and understanding how I live is crucial to understanding who I am' (Atkins 2008: 1). In my view, the 'understanding' to which philosopher Kim Atkins refers here is sustained and recreated in 'ontological narratives' – stories that explain conduct by reference to identity. The YWCA itself, and its members, can speak as African, Kenyan, Christian, as mothers or as gender and development workers – and from vantage points constituted by the overlaps between these positions informed by their identities. Identity, in the sense in which I discuss it in this book, is constituted collaboratively through narrative, creating the impression of coherence, establishing continuity over time and making meaning out of raw experience (Atkins 2008; Cavarero 2000; MacKenzie and Poltera 2010; Somers 1994). In this chapter I offer a theoretical account of how personal and group identities are constituted in narrative, and connect this to the concepts of moral identity and moral narrative to suggest how the YWCA contends with moral positions and values established in dominant narratives of development and Christianity, sometimes affirming them and at other times deviating from them.

1.1 Narrative and identity

In the study of religion and gender, narrative approaches have been applied to diverse research projects. As a method and methodological perspective, narrative offers religious studies scholars a point of access to subjective religious experience (Johannsen, Kirsch and Kreinath 2020). As objects of study, religious texts and their interpretations can be approached as narratives and analysed using narrative theories. Often, narrative has been used to explain and analyse the construction of individual religious identities, primarily in stories of conversion and entering a religious community (Jindra et al. 2012: 2–4; Linde 2009: 171–7). Paying attention to narratives claimed as 'Christian' highlights the uses and effects of recurrent plots, characters and themes in different contexts and for different audiences – in sermons, theological texts, political campaigns, charity work and so on. Such narratives can be used in the construction of Christian group boundaries because they connect the group's identity to a cause, a way of life and/or a set of values. A shared social identity, like 'Christian', is defined in these stories through commitments that give meaning to belonging in the group, which means exclusion from the group can be premised on the failure or refusal to share or demonstrate those commitments. For instance, biblical narratives that describe sexual 'deviance' (such as the story of Sodom and Gomorrah) or accounts of invasion or conquest have been, and continue to be, used for this kind of boundary work and in turn to justify mission and colonization (Kwok 2005: 140–2).

The identity under study in this book is a collective social identity, but on a smaller scale than other types of collective social identity that are often studied narratively, like nation or gender. I am concerned with the 'self'-representations the YWCA makes to its various stakeholders in a postcolonial Kenyan social context, and to account for the effects of systemic unequal power relations on, and within, its identity narratives. Power is relevant to narrative analysis because the dialogic or reciprocal nature of narrating an identity often occurs between distinctly unequal interlocutors, and the narrative resources from which speakers draw in the telling of their identities are constrained by the operations of power. We do not hear some stories, while others become ubiquitous; *whose* stories are quietened or silenced is not random or arbitrary. It is the result of specific operations of power, which I describe in detail throughout this book. Some stories are more audible than others because they have been invested with authority, while others have a limited number of recognizable and acceptable interpretations: in other words, 'texts are always linked to the material circumstances of the history that produces and receives them' (Warhol 2012: 9).

The material history in which the YWCA is located is one in which, for instance, Christian narratives have been used to justify misogyny.

The interactions of language use and unequal power relations, and the effects of these on the material conditions of life, are often analysed using a conceptual vocabulary of 'discourse' informed by the work of Michel Foucault. Distinguishing between narrative and discourse is a complex task because they are often synonymous in everyday use, referring broadly to ways of speaking or patterns of expression. In my view, narrative is distinct from and subordinate to discourse, so I switch perspective occasionally from 'story to discourse and back again' (Culler 2000: 108). Narratives are components or units of discourse, so 'any minimal linguistic act' can be approached as narrative because an audience can infer a narrative from any text or speech if they read or hear it in the appropriate context – in its intertextual position within a wider matrix of other narratives (McQuillan 2000: 10–12; Tonkin 1992: 2–3; Wertsch 2008). Stories refer to one another, as 'new' stories borrow plots and characters from previous stories, or build on established themes and metaphors, and so on. The organizational narratives under discussion in this book have a chronological structure, sequencing past events in time and space, as well as having expressive and evaluative characteristics. I discuss large-scale narratives that circulate as underlying explanations for the way things are, as well as highly specific smaller-scale stories, and those in-between that knit together the global and the local. An example of the former is the narrative of 'progress' that anchors pervasive, racist ideas of human development, and ranks cultural and social formations in terms of the degree to which they have 'advanced' towards an assumed white-Western zenith; I discuss this in Chapter 3. Institutional histories, like the history of the YWCA movement, are examples of the latter as they typically combine biographical stories of key figures, and the story of the institution itself, with wider national or international developments.

While narratives of identity reflect the influences of surrounding cultures and histories, they also represent interventions into those cultures and histories, producing and renewing their connections with(in) them (Somers 1994: 621–6). Thus, approaching narratives with attention to power highlights the ways speakers cooperate with, or contest, oppressive structures and contexts. One of the ways storytellers reflect the power that circulates in narratives is by accepting or resisting the ways they create belonging or exclusion. For example, when Christian women have sought ordination or access to positions of ecclesial leadership, they have narrated women's experiences of exclusion therefrom as well as retelling biblical narratives of female leaders, using stories already recognized as authoritative by their churches to challenge exclusionary logics. Feminist theorists in a range of disciplines have turned to narrative – examining widespread practices of storytelling, the linguistic and structural forms of the narratives told and the effects of these on our theories, politics and theologies, and thus on people's lives. My theoretical framework for this book is based on insights from feminist social theory, moral and political philosophy and gender studies, connecting the dots between the narrative constitution of identity, the uses of narrative in institutions and the narrative form and content of everyday ethics.

The particular value of a narrative frame of analysis in this study of the YWCA is that it will allow me to understand the Association's identity and activities as constructed and contingent upon context, and therefore not arbitrary; the shifts within the organization's narratives of its identity and history need not be explained away. Neither are they the natural result of changes in a self-evident and coherent Christianity. Rather, these shifts reveal important relationships and interactions between, within and around the YWCA in its postcolonial Kenyan context. This will become clear in my analysis of the YWCA's deliberate reframing of its identity as Christian in the 1950s. Narrative offers a way of understanding how social action is connected to identity without relying on essentialist notions of identity that attribute conduct to immutable bodily and psychological differences. 'Women', for example, no longer appear as a self-evident social group, but as a narrative construction deeply contingent upon the (re)iteration of sexist and heteronormative public narratives: 'That social identities are constituted through narrativity, social action is guided by narrativity, and social processes and interactions – both institutional and interpersonal – are narratively mediated provides a way of understanding the recursive presence of particular identities that are, nonetheless, not universal' (Somers 1994: 621). In this frame, the historical and contemporary similarities and convergences between girls' and women's experiences are explained with reference to the narratively constituted positions in and of social groupings, not a shared essential 'nature' as women (Somers 1994: 610–12). To extend the above example, the reason that African women could become YWCA members in the 1950s was not because the British-Anglophone gender category 'women' applied to them in any straightforward 'natural' sense. Rather, extending YWCA membership beyond white settlers was conceivable only after 'Africans' were considered sufficiently Christianized, and recognizable as 'women' in the sense relevant to the YWCA. The induction of African YWCA members, who initially remained a separate constituency to 'European' members, required the organization narratively to emphasize a different dimension of its identity as Christian. As will be made clear throughout this book, when I refer to identities such as 'African', 'women' or 'Christian', it is always as mutually co-constitutive, changeable positions in complex networks of power relations. These identities have been narratively constructed and reconstructed out of the 'textual resources' of the postcolonial Kenyan historical, cultural and material circumstances that gave them meaning (Wertsch 2008: 122).

1.2 Organizational identity

The autobiographical collection and deployment of stories to explain and construct a sense of who and what one is – an identity – reflects the multiple constraining and enabling influences of generic social institutions, such as family, education, church and empire, and specific collective identities in a person's life (Miller 2005: 138). From their first moments, people and organizations both rely on the storytelling abilities of those involved in nurturing them to shape their lives. Institutions and organizations themselves require people to inhabit their structures and tell their stories in order to exist as such (Linde 2009). Organizational identity narratives are a form of knowledge production and transmission, in which information about an organization is archived, retrieved, evaluated and put to use, and through which the organization's purpose, character and boundaries are managed and modified. The YWCA's origins, history and development are memorialized in narratives that establish its origins, its Christian basis and its continuity over time. The identities of individuals, social groups and organizations, and the relationships between them, are constructed through the interaction of 'ontological' and 'public' narratives. Drawing on the work of Margaret Somers (1994), I apply a definition of ontological narratives as those which describe and contour the existence of a person, family, community or institution, by establishing a relationship between its existence, its 'being' (hence, *ontological*) and its practices or conduct – its 'doing' (Somers 1994: 617–20). Personal and collective identities are established and sustained through a continual process of giving accounts of conduct in ontological narratives, which are usually told in the first person ('I'/'we'), and less often in the third person ('they'/'it'), and sometimes in the second person ('you'). Strictly speaking, as an organization the YWCA ought to be referred to with the pronoun 'it', as I do throughout this book. However, my research participants' use of the first-person plural 'we' to refer to the YWCA was absolutely consistent across all my conversations with YWCA staff, volunteers and leaders. The YWCA speaks of itself as 'we' in the same way in many documents, such as its Annual Council Reports (ACRs). In English-speaking contexts, individual members of institutions, organizations or groups regularly use 'we' in precisely this way (Linde 2000). This use of the first-person plural indicates a level of personal identification between each research participant and the Association to which they belong, and allows them to claim authority to speak on its behalf. Ontological narratives explain 'our' existence and connect what 'we' do to who 'we' are, and vice versa.

Unlike ontological narratives, public narratives do not necessarily make explicit references to 'who we are', but they are integral to narrative constructions of shared identity. Public narratives are those which tell of 'cultural and institutional formations larger than the single individual' whether these are smaller stories of particular events like the foundation of the YWCA, of larger social phenomena like British colonization of eastern Africa or of shared origins such as creation myths (Somers 1994: 619). They explain and give context to the connections people have to the institutions, relationships, practices and norms that surround them. In other words, public narratives insert us as minor characters in the stories of our wider contexts, or tell us our position in a shared story or history of our nation, community, institution or family. Like Somers, I emphasize the material *context* as central to the argument that identity is *relational*: that is, social forces, public narratives and other people, and their narratives, all interact with one another, with material effects as well as consequences for the stories we can tell about ourselves and others (Somers 1994: 622–7). The material context within which narrative and identity are produced is relational in that people exist only by virtue of their relationships with one another – an insight regularly placed at the centre of African ethics as *Ubuntu* (Mangena 2009). We negotiate our identities in personal and institutional relationships, and in historical settings of time and place, which distribute different types of power unevenly, and these relationships are 'constantly in flux' (Somers 1994: 621). In other words, identities are dynamic and can be unpredictable even when the narratives that construct them present them as permanent and static.

People and institutions construct and sustain their identities by (re)telling their own origin, identity or biographical stories in ways that utilize these public narratives, and moreover, doing so then influences their conduct. As people tell of 'what they do' they also represent themselves and co-construct their identity; and with each retelling comes the possibility of telling different versions of the story. To whatever degree these narrations are consistent, they influence our behaviour – since identity is inherently related to behaviour. What we say about ourselves can expand or restrict what it is intelligible or reasonable for us to subsequently stand for, or against. For instance, when the YWCA was established as an evangelical Protestant movement in Victorian England, it incorporated narratives of mission and imperialistic metaphors to define its purpose. These narratives were used subsequently to justify its expansion throughout the British Empire. The narrative constitution of identity is therefore not only historical but also a projection of future conduct. Narrating identity influences behaviour, which in turn produces new narratives of identity that differ from and concur with previous narratives, creating new possibilities and/or (re)confirming existing norms. Thus, doing and being, or behaviour and identity, are mutually constitutive elements in a narrative spiral of which the subject is not the sole author.

Biographical storytelling and the stories of others addressing 'you' (second-person narratives) are necessary for the development of a personal identity because they add information that the subject could not otherwise know. In this view, we learn who we are and our connections to the people around us through the biographical narrative interventions of those who bring us up through infancy into childhood and adolescence – learning our own life story through others' stories of our life (Cavarero 2000: 14–15). We form and communicate memories as stories, structuring our experiences in story form, as a plot, chronologically and relationally, since constituting an identity involves intersubjectively and collaboratively creating and sharing a biography. In the psychoanalytic-feminist philosophy of Adriana Cavarero, the relational, self-disclosing subject narrates her own story and listens to those of others because 'biography and autobiography are bound together in a single desire' (Cavarero 2000: 33). This desire seems to provide the means and opportunity for the collaborative narration of shared identities, and suggests that the identities of others are implicated in the construction of our own. The notion of moral identity, to which I return shortly, is a reflection of this desire – in particular, the desire to hear one's story told in a way that recognizes one's ethical self.

A dialogue-centred model of relational self-narration foregrounds two aspects of narrative identity that emerged in my research with the YWCA. These are, first, the significance of collaborative storytelling over time, particularly within long-term relationships of responsibility such as the contributions to YWCA stories made by leaders and other committed YWCA members. The second aspect is the pleasures and rewards of being recognized and included by or in an identity, or the sanctions incurred as a result of deviating from it, such as being recognized as a 'staunch' Christian, or defined according to the stereotypes that circulate in moral narratives. There are multiple narratives which sit alongside and contribute to the YWCA's ontological or identity narrative, including a 'return-to-origins' story that contributes to the practices of 'Christian emphasis'. The YWCA's Christian emphasis narratives establish a deviation from the standards or norms of Christianity in order to tell a story of redemption, in which Christianity has been reaffirmed as the central focus of the organization and its work. These narratives sit alongside an origins story that claims the YWCA has been consistently, staunchly Christian since 1912. The Christian foundations of the organization are identified as significant and through repeated reference to them, they continue to provide the narrative of the present-day YWCA with a source for its identity. I specifically discuss the YWCA's narrative 'Christian emphasis' efforts in Chapters 5 and 6, but Christianity and its relevance or meaning for the YWCA crops up regularly throughout my account of the organization's history in Chapters 2–4.

Narrative identity is very closely related to, and reliant upon, memory. An organization like the YWCA 'remembers' through the efforts of the people who make use of its artefacts, buildings and texts as occasions and prompts to give an account of its history (Linde 2009). Staff, leaders and others 'within' an organization learn and record its processes, structures, ethos and its stories, and pass these on to newcomers, often with revisions, additions and omissions. Some stories come to have the status of 'collective memories' which are (re)produced through 'retold tales' – narratives available to be learned and recounted by those who joined the organization after the events in the story (Linde 2000: 608–13; Linde 2009: 72). Retold institutional tales bridge the gap between personal experience and institutional identity by allowing members of an institution to access collective memories and incorporate them into their own life stories. Learning organizational stories happens as/in a process of 'narrative induction', as described by Charlotte Linde (2000). The concept of 'narrative induction' refers to the assimilation of new recruits by institutional narratives, and the corresponding utilization of those narratives by members of the institution in constructing their own identities in ways that connect them to the institution as constituent parts of a whole. Relevant stories circulate through an institution via its personnel, finding expression when they are useful, initiating and orienting newcomers. As a person becomes fluent in this corpus of shared stories, they are recognized as a member of the organization (Linde 2000: 608–13). Points of similarity between one's own story and the stories of others can create a sense of shared identity, and through the process of narrative induction, people who belong to an institution learn and incorporate the same repertoire of stories into their own. For example, being able to retell a story about the YWCA's history can demonstrate active and committed YWCA membership, while being able to refer to the YWCA's stance as 'our stance', or the ability to say 'we', establishes the speaker as one who can speak for the YWCA and suggests that they share its commitments. Retold tales are not only expressions of the institution's culture; they also reflect and refer to the wider matrix of public narratives, which often position personal identity within social hierarchies as they intersect with the organization. For instance, widespread narratives of Christian identity offer models for the expression of a serious, staunch and/or pious personal faith – models that provide the YWCA with a way of emphasizing its Christianity, as I discuss in Chapter 6.

Shared or organizational identities can thus be shared unevenly; people in central or leadership positions may be more able, or willing, to adopt them – perhaps due to the greater incentives and rewards offered to them for doing so. Those in structurally marginal positions may be less inclined to adopt the practice of speaking for the organization or the group. In the case of the YWCA, the shared identity seems to be stronger and more persuasive for a large proportion of its staff and members, I think, because of the way in which it combines professional or vocational identities with personal faith and religious identities. Telling, integrating and solidifying an institution's stories of its history also provides models for the relationship between the member's personal life and the institution of which they are part. As stories emerge and are (re)told they begin to solidify as 'instance[s] of a normative pattern', such as the story of the exemplary staff member (Linde 2000: 621). This was especially evident when my research participants told me about their faith and their career trajectory, as I suggested in Nyaboke's case. My point here is that these elements of the narrative construction or constitution of identity can be drawn together to explain how the YWCA's Christian identity and ethical perspective are mutually constitutive and are co-constructed through narrative means.[1]

Narratively constructing and emphasizing the YWCA's Christian identity is, on one level, about making sure outsiders know what kind of organization it is, and thus functions to set up a contrast with other organizations. The terms of this comparison remain largely implied, as my research participants only occasionally referred to 'other organizations' and tended not to name them. One exception was Njeri, who specified that having a Christian identity distinguished the YWCA from the major institutions of the Kenyan women's movement: '[it] makes us different from Maendeleo ya Wanawake, from the National Council of Women of Kenya, from [the] League of Women Voters' (Njeri, interview,

2012). While my research participants seemed to rely implicitly on narratives of 'secularism' or 'secularization' to establish the difference made by the YWCA's Christianity, they rarely identified secularism directly. Nonetheless, there were moments when secularism clearly functioned, alongside feminism, as a point of comparison against which the YWCA was thought to favourably distinguish itself, or to which it risked succumbing: for instance, the idea that the YWCA 'has also been influenced by what is happening out in the secular world' (Joyce, interview, 2012). Referring to the 'secular' world as 'outside' the YWCA functioned as a way for Joyce to explain the influence of technical, instrumental development rationales on the Association since the 1990s. This tension is ameliorated through a commitment to incorporating explicit Christian worship into the day-to-day activities of the Association: 'What makes [the YWCA] different from another organisation is that we are able to engage churches, and because we are from a Christian organisation then the reception is better ... of course we pray ... we do the meetings and after we have devotions. So there is a spiritual component' (Wandia, interview, 2012). The 'spiritual component' was evident to me as an outsider, including memorable occasions when delegates at a meeting sang a hymn to greet a guest from the World YWCA.

By ensuring that the Association's activities provide opportunities for staff and members to express and perform their Christian identities, the YWCA offers the chance to reinforce a personal moral identity as the right kind of 'staunch' Christian. Two further significant implications of organizational identity constitution are implied by the YWCA's emphasis of its Christianity: to exclude those who cannot count themselves under the named identity and to avoid being attributed an unwanted identity. Both of these seemed to be captured in the YWCA's sense of 'not being feminists', to which my research participants gave explicit attention on a number of occasions.

> You will just hear some people say, 'No, but we are not feminists!' OK? We are not feminists. 'We are Christian women, and so we are not feminists' ... the understanding of that terminology may differ from person to person ... a number of [World] YWCA staff have taken specific stands ... [but] as you get down to the grassroots, everybody's orientation, and background, and socialisation is different. So, we have not really had a clear-cut stand on that. We say, 'Yes we work on women's issues, but we are not feminists.' (Njeri, interview, 2012)

The World YWCA has historically described itself as 'a global movement working for women's empowerment, leadership and rights', as opposed to a feminist organization, but accommodates feminist convictions

(Seymour-Jones 1994: 315–38). Njeri recognized that Christianity and feminism are not necessarily mutually exclusive categories, but she described intrinsic and instrumental reasons for the YWCA to refuse the label 'feminist'. First, the anti-feminist attitudes of unspecified others were considered to require maintaining a neat distinction between feminism, as something foreign to the YWCA, and 'work on women's issues' which is apparently compatible with a Christian organizational identity. Second, the attitudes of YWCA members required eschewing 'feminism' including at the 'grassroots' both among members and programme beneficiaries. In both cases there is a possibility that identifying the YWCA as feminist could be counterproductive. Third, YWCA identity narratives do not offer a compelling basis on which to establish a claim that it is or ever was a feminist organization. The YWCA's continual invocation of its origins in order to emphasize its Christian identity and underline its legitimacy would stand in tension with any attempts to revise the organization's identity as 'feminist'.

Generally speaking, Kenyan women's organizations have not consistently, publicly self-applied the label 'feminist', and there are good reasons why many African women's rights activists may reject feminist politics. Racism and coloniality have been constitutive of white women's movements since their emergence in the nineteenth century. The YWCA excluded African women until 1955, and then reinforced its white identity in the 'multiracial' logic of its subsequent attempts to 'include' them, as I explore in Chapter 2.[2] This dynamic was repeated in explicitly feminist movements and organizations that grew out of northern/European contexts. Postcolonial and anti-racist gender theorists and women's rights activists have pointed out in detail how feminist theory and praxis has often been indistinguishable from white colonial logics, and racism more generally (Mohanty 1988; Oyěwùmí 1997; Ware 1992). Instead of attempting to reform these hegemonic white feminisms, African scholars and activists have developed womanisms, motherisms and African feminisms starting from different premises and assumptions. While it is not clear that the full scope of this history is accessible to women at the grassroots in Kenya, its implications seem to be. The irrelevance or inapplicability of feminism to African realities is a strong current in discourses of gender inequality.[3] Contrary to Njeri's description of the YWCA's approach as 'not clear cut', I think that to separate out 'work on women's issues' from feminism reflects a very clear line of reasoning, for the aforementioned reasons. Finally, I consider the way in which this refusal of feminism is made to be significant. The YWCA says 'we are Christians' first and most frequently, and then it says 'we are not feminists', but it does not say 'we stand opposed to feminism'. The YWCA articulates its identity and ethos with reference to Christianity, because it offers an established and respectable position from which to launch gender-equality projects and 'work on women's issues'. It additionally deflects potential suspicions about feminism by virtue of the popular assumption that feminism and Christianity are mutually exclusive. It presents the YWCA as a partner of the churches, rather than antagonistic to them, even if it offers resistance to some of their teachings.

1.3 Narrative and ethics

Stories perform and constitute the meanings of who we are and the world we live in, and they are vehicles for ethics and modes of ethical reasoning. In recent liberal political philosophy, social identity, including religious identity, has been claimed as a site for the assertion of ethics. In *The Ethics of Identity*, Kwame Appiah discusses the ways in which claiming a collective identity can limit what is thought or done, by associating that identity with particular 'modes of behavior' (Appiah 2005: 108–10). Appiah refers to Charles Taylor's related notions of the 'politics of recognition' (Taylor 1994: 24) and the dialogical construction of the self within 'webs of interlocution' (Taylor 2006: 36). In these accounts, identity and its 'constitutive attachments' are recognized as the starting point for ethical deliberation (Benhabib 1992: 70–4). Where feminist narrative theories of self-making differ to this body of philosophy is by offering narrative as a communicative or dialogic method through which identity is constructed. In this perspective, the subject is relational, interdependent, divided and non-rational, constructed and constrained by her position within structures of power (Frazer and Lacey 1993; Somers 1994). For Judith Butler (2001), drawing on Adriana Cavarero (2000), narratives of identity create the appearance of solidity around this fragmentary subject, and she argues that this fact reveals the necessity of 'an ethics based on our shared, and invariable, partial blindness about ourselves' (Butler 2001: 27). Our identities thus emerge from collaborative storytelling efforts and generate a sense of trajectory, connecting our past, present and future in a more or less 'unified' story of a life that implies pursuing particular projects and ways of living (Atkins 2008: 3).

Whether fictional or otherwise, narratives have an intrinsic moral quality that facilitates value judgements, even if not communicating an explicit ethical message. An ethical point of view depends on underlying assumptions about who counts as a person and what people are like. The capacity of stories to convey ethical messages and ideas is expressed in the identification of the 'moral narrative', as Dina Ligaga (2020) has explored in relation to Kenyan popular media. The loose genre of moral narrative refers to those stories that function primarily to facilitate moral evaluation and offer more or less explicit moral lessons. Stories are worth telling if and when they convey a 'moral meaning' or judgement 'about the way the world is' (Linde 2009: 179). Although the genre includes stories that do not announce themselves as moral narratives, many subgenres or types of narrative do offer more straightforward or obvious judgements, the moral of the story; 'stories inform people's sense of what counts as good and bad, of how to act and how not to act ... [and] teach what counts as good and bad by linking characters' actions to consequences that listeners feel are good or bad' (Frank 2010: 36). Moral narratives are usually pedagogical on some level: they impart a certain kind of ethical knowledge, and they also model appropriate and inappropriate ways of behaving. Cautionary tales, found in diverse forms such as mythology, children's literature and gossip, are among the most common and directly pedagogical moral narratives.[4] Soap operas, comic strips and other forms of popular media are highly conducive to be interpreted for ethical messages, especially when they centre on melodrama and scandal. The lessons they offer are exaggerated, broad illustrations of good and bad conduct, making clean moral distinctions that enable the listener to follow suit (Ligaga 2020: 14–16). Building on Ligaga's insights, I think that moral and narrative go together in a more fundamental way, because stories are a form of ethical reasoning: 'Narrative is the discourse unit that presents both what happened, that is, events in the past, and what they mean, that is, the evaluation of the moral significance of these events' (Linde 2009: 221). When people learn and talk about ethics, inside and outside of academic spaces, they use a range of narrative methods. In other words, they tell stories in order not only to sketch hypothetical situations and relate cautionary tales but also to establish an identity and an associated range of commitments.

Ligaga argues that the genre of moral narrative has a long history in African oral literature and that it has recently been reinforced and influenced by Western 'morality tales' that have arrived in Kenya through coloniality and Christianity. The moral stories that address matters related to gender and sexuality in Kenyan popular media employ a range of distinct plots, characters and storylines. The characters that populate these stories are often the result of stereotypes which they in turn reinforce. Referring to 'ubiquitous and recognizable' figures such as these bypasses the need for characterization as might be seen in longer-form narratives (Ligaga 2020: 25). Potent gendered stereotypes offer models of respectable femininity in the figure of the dutiful daughter and the 'mother Africa' trope. These are constructed in opposition to models of deviant femininity – the 'barren woman', the 'wicked city woman' and the 'good-time girl' (Ligaga 2020: 16–17). The attributes that are sanctioned or encouraged through these plots, and the characters that inhabit them, reinforce a distinction between 'good' and 'bad' women and girls. 'Respectable femininity' is located in a narrow range of roles, whereas there are many ways in which a woman's behaviour or character can be deemed transgressive and dangerous.

These stereotypes have found expression in popular fiction, but these figures also enter popular discourse through other routes, including news media and social media, gossip and urban legends. Development interventions also make use of similarly one-dimensional figures to facilitate the telling of moral narratives, for example, the method of 'education-entertainment', which has been used to disseminate messages around HIV prevention and AIDS care in African contexts (Singhal and Rogers 2003: 287–316). The use of narrative for development communication demonstrates how its power to influence has been recognized and instrumentalized to 'overcome resistance' in situations when the audience are aware of the 'persuasive intent' of the communication (Hinyard and Kreuter 2007: 779–85). By avoiding analytical or argumentative form and content, such messaging relies on established understanding and common-sense views. Ultimately, in relation to gender and sexuality, it risks buying uncritical assent to the 'development' lesson imparted at the expense of women and other already-marginalized groups. In such narratives, the 'cut' girl, the regretful teenage mother, the HIV-positive woman or the girl coerced into sex feature in narratives to illustrate the negative consequences of targeted behaviour (Win 2004). As I show in my analysis of a YWCA's pamphlet *My Youth, My Pride*, even organizations that 'work on women's issues' like the YWCA can end up reinforcing harmful stereotypes. Such publications regularly feature success stories featuring the reformed sex worker or the widow who becomes an entrepreneur. Ligaga's analysis of gender and sexuality in moral narratives in Kenya illustrates critical aspects of the context in which the YWCA's assertion of 'controversial faith issues' makes sense. These moral narratives are part of the matrix of public narratives from which the YWCA borrows themes, characters and plots.

When we engage with ethically oriented narratives, their identity-constituting effects are implicitly involved, and I also think the reverse is true: when we engage with identity narratives, their ethical dimensions are implicitly involved. I argue that this is the case for the YWCA by analysing my research participants' accounts of the Association's history, ecumenism and piety in the service of naming and reinforcing its Christian identity and ethics. As suggested by theorizations of 'ordinary ethics', ethics should be studied where it is found, in everyday social life (Das 2015; Fassin 2012; Lambek 2010). Furthermore, ethics is largely based on tacit assumptions, often framed by claims to common sense, and practiced quietly without naming itself as 'ethics' or 'ethical conduct'. However, in this book there are numerous examples of people and institutions explicitly articulating ethical rules and values – a phenomenon encountered regularly in the study of Christianity. When I refer to 'Christian ethics' it is not to name a coherent field but the ethical dimensions of the lives and understandings of Christians, as these are expressed, contested and applied in the messy reality of life. Critiques of Christian sexual ethics often assume that a focus on the institutional positions taken by churches is justified because these indicate Christians' beliefs and dictate their practices. The question is rather, as Beth Maina Ahlberg and her co-authors ask in relation to sexuality, 'How do individuals and groups interpret and act on ... Christian moral scripts ... [a]nd do their actions in turn influence the discourses or scripts and in what ways?' (Ahlberg et al. 2009: 107). In fact, Christian ethics are plural, malleable and articulated in response to their historical, cultural and political context. Any articulation of Christian ethics is a claim to have authority to interpret revelation, tradition and doctrine, and often a claim to have privileged access to the truth. Christian ethical deliberation is not necessarily constrained by doctrine and tradition, but rather doctrine and tradition constitute the narrative contexts within which individuals and groups are positioned. They provide the resources on which Christians can draw to authorize their decisions and judgements. In other words, the official stances of Christian churches are relevant not because they dictate the content and conclusions of Christian ethics. They are relevant because they provide the narrative and discursive matrix in which Christians evaluate and employ principles and ideas in ways that sometimes align with, and at other times contradict, hegemonic Christian positions. By identifying these narrative identity constructions and the everyday ethics they support, I investigate the explicit negotiations and implicit themes pervading the YWCA's sexual health programmes.

1.4 Moral narratives in the development industry

In Western Christian imaginaries, mothers have occupied a paradoxical position as the bearers of ultimate virtue and value, and objects of love, partly because of the religious significance of the Virgin Mary, the mother of Jesus

(Kwok 2005: 11). However, since the nineteenth century, motherhood has simultaneously been defined according to narrow classed and racialized norms of middle-class whiteness, deprived of political power and socially marginalized in the 'private sphere'. The theory of the 'feminization of religion' has been used to explain the coterminous development in Europe of the private home as the domain of women's agency and authority as wives and mothers, and the retreat of Christianity into 'private' life in the nineteenth century (Pasture, Art and Buerman 2012). This connection between the feminine private sphere, motherhood, wifehood and Christian piety informed the YWCA movement from its inception, as it capitalized on these connections to enable and encourage affluent middle-aged women to assert their maternalistic authority in efforts to protect the welfare of young, poor and working women. The colonization of eastern Africa involved the application of this 'knowledge' about women, which informed racist misinterpretations of African societies and motivated the colonial and missionary imposition of ideals and norms of white femininity, wifehood, motherhood and domesticity.

This does not imply that mothers, or the labour they perform, are unimportant. On a basic level, human life revolves around relationships of care and intimacy between parents and children – equally between lovers, spouses, grandparents, wider families and communities formed of chosen and unchosen connections and responsibilities. Life is literally and figuratively reproduced by and in these relationships, as people have children (or not) and bring them up according to – or, less often, at odds with – the norms and practices particular to their time, place, family and community. Feminists have long analysed how the physical and social production and support of life have become 'women's work': partly through doing this work of procreation and mothering, people are gendered and recognized as women. The things women do (statistically and stereotypically) have been systematically devalued through their association with women, while simultaneously being held up as constitutive of womanhood. These include caring activities of all kinds: mothering, childcare, cleaning, elder care and nursing. Historically, these have not been the focus of academic work or ethical theory, so our knowledge of them comes from personal experience and feminist knowledge production. Care ethics attempts a reversal of values, emphasizing the necessity of caring practices for the material, biological maintenance of life and its social reproduction. In its feminist forms, care ethics demonstrates that these practices have been globalized and racialized throughout the twentieth century so that global 'chains of care' have emerged, linking the exploitation of people from former colonies to the maintenance of life in their roles as migrant care labourers in the north (Narayan 1995; Robinson 2015; Tronto 1993).

For these reasons, feminist activism and advocacy has long focused on analysing and improving the material realities in which women work, have sex, give birth and raise children, and to make space for those who do not. Some feminist activists have capitalized on the openings offered by international legal and development structures, such as the UN Decade for Women (1975–85), to establish women's rights instruments, like the Convention on the Elimination of All Forms of Discrimination against Women (CEDAW, adopted 1979). This approach has been successful by its own standards, to the degree that aspects of a feminist agenda (like sexual and reproductive health and rights) have been incorporated into development industry policy and targets, like the Millennium Development Goals (MDGs) and Sustainable Development Goals (SDGs). These platforms recognize the significance of educating girls, maternal health care and sexual and reproductive health and rights. However desirable education and maternal health care are, they have entered development discourse divorced from feminist analysis as part of efforts towards 'gender mainstreaming'. This is an appropriation of feminist positions and critiques, reduced to ameliorative gender equality measures that separate them from political analyses of the links between racism, capitalism, colonialism and sexism that cause and perpetuate inequality (Mama 2011). Desiree Lewis (2008b: 78–9) has critiqued this trend as the tokenization of gender transformation – as evident, for instance, in exclusively rights-based approaches (Okech 2016: 4–5) and instrumentalizing the 'girl-child' as the ultimate object of development (Switzer 2013: 347). Thus 'gender' language, and not feminist politics, marks the ways in which inequalities between men, women, boys and girls can be addressed as part of development industry interventions (Okech 2009: 30–5). These critical perspectives on the uses of gender language and moral narratives in the development industry are threads that reappear throughout my exploration of the YWCA's work.

The international development industry sustains a 'complex of unequal material relationships and processes which structure engagement' between Africa and the West, and 'the primary discursive framework within which these relationships have been constructed', one deeply invested in capitalism and imperialism (Wilson 2015: 804). In African contexts, international development discourses have become embedded in some legal instruments and policies, particularly the New Partnership for Africa's Development (NEPAD), an African Union project which has guided national development policies. NEPAD has come under criticism from feminists/women's rights activists and others for its failure to challenge the neoliberal hegemony of the international development industry, for instance acquiescing to the imposition of structural adjustment policies (SAPs) and generally promoting gender-blind and economic approaches to development (Muhibbu-Din 2011; Okeke and Onu 2006; Sewpaul 2005: 108–9). This 'gender mainstreaming' of quasi-feminist values instrumentalizes women and girls; for instance, by valuing education on the basis that 'literate mothers have better fed children who are more likely to attend school' (Momsen 2003: 9). In this view, instead of valuing women's rights to education in their own right, they are a means to producing healthy and educated children. This approach has often deepened gender inequalities by instrumentalizing girls' and women's bodies and labour in ways that presume and reinforce existing gender norms and inequalities (Wilson 2015: 818).

Development industry applications of 'gender' draw on popular rhetorical uses of 'women' and 'gender' in wider political discourse. Sara Farris describes the appropriation of white feminist narratives, like the 'harms' of veiling or sex segregation, by (primarily) Western states to claim that women are liberated 'here', in contrast to the 'oppression' of women by Islam, a phenomenon she names 'femonationalism' (Farris 2017). Using women's alleged freedom and unfreedom to make and justify a range of distinctions between 'us' and 'them' facilitates Islamophobia and racism, and it props up the imperialist claims that Western, Christian/secular gender relations are innately better for women. This is a reiteration and reinvention of the familiar trope in colonial narratives, 'white men ... saving brown women from brown men', the analysis of which has been foundational for postcolonial feminist theory (Spivak 2010: 49). Feminist philosopher Serene Khader describes what she names 'missionary feminism' that posits white Western/Northern feminists as the only ones 'who can make change' towards this Western, modern 'form of life [that] "other" cultures should ultimately be changed to' (Khader 2019: 23). This is an ongoing expression of the same hierarchical colonial worldview established by white women's movements at the height of European mission and colonization. One result of this hierarchy is that 'good white women' take up the saviour's mantle in the form of working in charity, philanthropy and/or the development industry. The dominant Western narrative of 'development' allows ordinary white citizens in the north to establish a moral identity as the 'saviour' of Africans, especially of African children. The aptly named 'White Savior Industrial Complex' achieves this effect by presenting war, poverty and famine in abstraction from their structural causes and contexts – thereby encouraging the illusion that they can be solved by goodwill or 'sentiment' (Cole 2012, para 20). This critical perspective has been widely cited but has been unevenly recognized in the development industry. More often, it is a point emphasized in opposition to the activities of international development and missionary agencies by local movements and activists seeking to protect their communities from well-meaning interference by 'voluntourists', whose efforts are at best ineffective and at worst deadly.[5]

In these cases of femonationalism, missionary feminism and white saviourism, the exercise of power is facilitated by the availability of positive moral identities through narratives that secure Western 'progress' in comparison with people and places deemed 'behind', and in need of 'saving'. The notion of 'moral identity' is a positive self-image associated with one's vocation, career or other labour: 'Any identity that testifies to a person's good character can be a moral identity, such as mother, Christian, breadwinner, or feminist' (Kleinman 1996: 5). Moral identities, like other relational identities, are achieved and reinforced through narrative practices – stories, biographies, and histories that demonstrate 'the mutuality and reciprocity of character and action' (Atkins 2008: 88). As pointed out by many postcolonial and decolonial feminist critics, international development is a primary arena in which this conduct is facilitated and rewarded (see, e.g., Ali and Syed 2011: 356–61; Pailey 2019). Natalia Deeb-Sossa's (2007) analysis of healthcare workers at a community clinic in the US revealed that their moral identities as 'good feminists' could obscure their failures to act in ways consistent with their ethical claims. She specifically points out that the workers treated Latina women and Black women differently, revealing an anti-Black racism covered up and enabled by their moral identities (Deeb-Sossa 2007: 753). The existing power of the global north and former colonial powers, and their white citizens, is enhanced and reinforced by narratives such as these. On the microscale, the grammatical structures of narratives of development establish those who act, the saviours, and those who are acted upon, the saved. The explicit messages delivered, and above all the conduct they authorize, centre the benevolence, generosity or lawfulness of aid agencies and the states they represent or donors who fund them.

The development industry has its own moral identity: the only, or most efficient, means by which to address global inequality and suffering. It is in fact a primary means through which these circumstances are upheld, because it has been co-opted by states and corporations that are invested in the continuing success of colonial capitalism, which necessitates the exploitation of workers and the environment. When local, grassroots activist groups develop structural analyses and practical solutions specific to their circumstances, these are often taken up by development discourse. For example, the concept of 'reproductive justice' was conceived by women of colour scholar-activists, to describe how structural sexism, classism, racism and ableism, and their intersections, produce inequalities that manifest in the sexual and reproductive lives of Black women and others who live beyond white, cis-heterosexual, middle-class norms (Price 2010).[6]

> The right to have children, not have children, and to parent the children we have in safe and healthy environments – is based on the human right to make personal decisions about one's life, and the obligation of government and society to ensure that the conditions are suitable for implementing one's decisions ... reproductive rights + social justice = reproductive justice. (Sistersong 2015: para 4)

This formulation, based on advocacy organization Sistersong's many years of activism and collective struggle, builds on the shared communal and/or social experiences of obstacles to bodily autonomy that are raised by structural oppressions. It demonstrates how the legal right to abortion does not, on its own, represent the achievement of reproductive freedom, because sexual and reproductive dimensions of inequality are inseparable from the surrounding socio-cultural, religious, economic and political context. I have found reproductive justice to be a useful way to frame and analyse the structural and discursive constraints on girls' and women's sexual and reproductive lives in postcolonial Kenya. However, it is important to remember that this concept was formulated in and for a specific constituency in the US. As a concept or theory travels outside its original context, it can be taken up by those who do not share the commitments of its authors, creating the potential for it to be distorted. Despite its original connection to Black and transnational feminisms, in the instruments of the development industry reproductive justice has been reduced to maternal health care, as discussed above (Garita 2014: 2; Harcourt 2009: 42–57).

1.5 Sexuality and scandal

In 2012 a scandal emerged in Kenya's news media – the moral panic surrounding 'Campus Divas for Rich Men', a Facebook page claiming to be an escort agency connecting female university students with older men in Nairobi. The young women at the centre of the scandal were earning money, as many do, from various forms of sex work, or the acquisition of a single 'sugar daddy' to support them financially through university or simply to maintain a middle-class lifestyle. The dominant narrative of the Campus Divas positioned this as women's exploitation of their sexuality, of taking an easy route by accepting money or gifts in exchange for sex. The construction of 'young, wayward university women' in the Divas' behaviour was interpreted as evidence of the moral vacuum in which these young women lived 'away from [the] normalizing structures of family, church, and school' (Ligaga 2020: 107). At the same time as the Campus Divas were made into a scandal in Kenya's popular media, several hundred pupils at Rwathia Girls' School staged a protest against their school uniform of ankle-length skirts. The girls wanted to wear shorter skirts than their uniform currently allowed, and the then-minister of education, Mutula Kilonzo, made some brief comments in support of their demand. However, the media reported that the girls had demanded to wear miniskirts, and that Kilonzo had agreed, leading some clergy to state their opposition to miniskirts (Barasa et al. 2012). In public reactions to the Campus Divas and the schoolgirls' skirts, education was construed as a threat to ways of organizing life that are constructed in this discourse as 'traditional' and 'African' (Switzer 2010: 142–52). Modern, urban, consumerist lifestyles are the background against which these 'wayward' women can be made out. Women were reminded of their responsibility for performing respectable femininity, and the state played a role in policing this performance, supported by the churches, both often pointing to 'cultural' norms for reinforcement.

These themes were rehearsed again in narratives of the murder of Sharon Otieno, a twenty-six-year-old student who was killed in 2018 apparently by, or on behalf of, her 'sugar daddy', Okoth Obado, the governor of Migori County. Like the 'Campus Divas' scandal, Ms Otieno's murder was translated into the terms of the dominant moral narrative of young, educated, urban women's 'wayward sexualities'. Ms Otieno's life and death were interpreted through the narrative of modern girls, especially female students in cities, who are considered to have 'loose morals', and thereby victim-blamed for her own brutal murder. Critically, Ms Otieno was seven months pregnant when she was murdered, and this was widely taken as evidence that she had brought on this act in retaliation for deliberately becoming pregnant by a married man. Even though it seems this was a wanted pregnancy, the fact that it occurred outside of a heterosexual monogamous marriage made it evidence of immorality. Here can be seen the influence of the stereotypical figures of good mothers and bad city women in moral narratives: it is not enough to have a child; in fact, the identity 'mother' is strictly policed. After flag independence, 'mothering' and 'motherhood' were conflated with 'respectable femininity' and made 'central to the nation' through manifesting the reproduction of culture (Okech 2019: 15). Simultaneously, women's sexualities were relegated to the 'private' realm, policed using pronatalism, while full citizenship was defined along masculinist lines. In both cases, 'the problem lay squarely with women whose sexualities and bodies needed to be policed' (Ligaga 2020: 113–14; Okech 2019: 19).

Some of these tropes were evident in the occasional mention of sex work by my interlocutors at the YWCA. Winnie, who had received theological training, described how she felt that sex work diminished women's sense of being 'in charge of' their bodies. She claimed, 'Your sexuality is God-given … it must not be abused, it is not a source of income … It is much more sacred than that and you can't just … give it away because you need food for your belly.' Her approach was certainly not the same as the popular moral horror at the Campus Divas, as she described that she would encourage young women to look at themselves 'differently to what … a male-dominated society has brought them to believe', rather than reinforcing modernity and materialism, as represented by the university campus, as corrupting influences (Winnie, interview, 2012). Occasionally, my research participants at the YWCA did cite the connection between social change, Westernisation and sexuality: 'When such topics [as LGBTQ rights] come up, you can clearly see that these are foreign … we know some things are not acceptable in the society, so when suddenly you have a few people shouting here and there, they are shouting for somebody who is not Kenyan. That is the truth' (Wandia, interview, 2012). In making these connections, sexual liberation and its markers – including gender equality and LGBTQ rights – are positioned both as a cause and a result of secularization (Scott 2009: 1–2; Shorter and Onyancha 1997: 104–9). Framing issues of sexuality and gender in terms of African Christianity and Western secularism informs many assertions of Christian moral positions in Kenya. This tendency is similar to, and often appears in combination with, a postcolonial political strategy of reappraising local norms and traditions as 'authentic' in opposition to the norms and traditions of the missionary or the colonizer (Lewis 2005: 384). This can be performed as a rejection of coloniality, but it can also undergird the rejection of LGBTQ rights in the name of 'African' culture (Chanika, Lwanda and Muula 2013). The story presented is that 'the African way of life rejects completely' LGBTQ relationships, identities and desires, and that in Africa these are 'a remnant of a colonial past … [or] a neo-colonial attempt at cultural imperialism' (Mwikya 2014: 99). Narratives of secularization, urbanization and Westernisation tend to additionally suggest that feminism is a feature of the social changes they describe.

1.6 Summary

In this chapter I have summarized my major theoretical and thematic concerns in this book, outlining the ways in which narrative, identity and ethics are connected in institutional practices, personal identity and pedagogical stories. Consciously held personal and institutional identities are constructed through biographical storytelling practices, and in institutions one of the most common genres of story is the ontological narrative through which a connection is established between identity and conduct. Moral narratives and moral identities are two facets of the imbrication of ethics and/in narrative – the former being pedagogical stories and the latter the result of self-making enterprises that frame the subject as morally good, interpreting their donations, voluntary work or career as proof. The existence of multiple overlapping moral identities from which the YWCA can speak and from which its members and staff can construct moral identities is especially significant. In the chapters that follow I show how these (African, Christian, feminist/developmental) have been produced through the interaction of material power relations, as represented, remembered, justified and legitimized in narrative. A narrative approach to ethics and identity allows me to pinpoint the circulation and expression of ethics in everyday life and trace its influence on the YWCA.

Part 2

2

Imperial maternalism, 1855–1965

The emergence of the YWCA movement in England in the mid-nineteenth century reflects the various influences of Protestant revivalism in Europe, the social gospel and the cult of domesticity. The YWCA has its origin in the parallel efforts of two British women: an aristocrat, Mary Jane Kinnaird, and a middle-class woman, Emma Robarts. In 1855 these women each began working on behalf of young women, independently of one another, but equally motivated by their Christian faith and the social changes instigated by the role played by women as nurses during the Crimean War. Emma Robarts engaged in letter writing with other women around Britain, encouraging them to 'pray for the young women of the world' (Duguid 1955: 12). Meanwhile, Mary Jane Kinnaird opened hostels to provide accommodation and refuge for nurses and other working women – the first being in London. In 1877 the two incipient organizations merged to form the first YWCA. The decision to name the movement as such reflected a desire to mirror the purpose, and success, of the YMCA, thereby beginning a relationship which has ongoing significance for the identity and activities of the YWCA (Duguid 1955: 7–12; Seymour-Jones 1994: 5–7). The YWCA's position in relation to the social issues affecting young women and its divergence from nascent feminisms demonstrates that it was aligned with, and not opposed to, the theological anthropology of mainstream Protestant Christianity. The YWCA preferred non-confrontational interventions for social change – providing hostel accommodation for women, organizing prayer circles and encouraging middle-class women to support their sisters through charity (Seymour-Jones 1994: 1–3).

By outlining the Victorian, British origins of the YWCA movement, I sketch the character and direction of the Kenyan Association from its inception in 1912 until the departure of its last white leader, Vera Harley. The historical narrative I present relies on Harley's *Rickshaws to Jets*, a self-published book based partly on its author's own experiences as the YWCA's National General Secretary (NGS) from 1958 to 1965 (Harley 1995). Since its publication, it has served as a major point of reference and source from which YWCA identity narratives have been drawn. Many of the events described therein have risen to the status of collective memory and its version of the YWCA's history has eclipsed other possible versions, as I discuss at length in Chapter 6. In *Rickshaws to Jets*, Harley avoids explicitly addressing the racist history of the YWCA despite having to account for it in several places, as I suggest in my reading of the YWCA's process of becoming 'multiracial'. Thus, the historical growth and change of the YWCA in Kenya is not straightforwardly recorded, either in *Rickshaws to Jets* or in my retelling here; rather, it is told according to a specific set of interests and filters that influence its content and tone.

Framing my study with an acknowledgement of Kenya's and the YWCA's colonial past introduces a tension into my analysis because my research participants did not explicitly refer to coloniality or racism in their narrations of YWCA history. The account I give is not the only possible narrative; it is a critical and self-consciously scholarly narrative in which the voices of the women who have constituted the YWCA are subordinated to my own analysis, which implicitly privileges my point of view and my voice (Bannerji 1998: 288, 292). The absences and visibilities in the YWCA history I analyse herein reflect and reinforce colonial ideologies, epistemologies and power relations that excluded the voices of African women almost entirely from the record. Each (re)telling of colonial history provides opportunities to repeat themes of nostalgia and apologia for colonization or resist and critique them. To this end, I point out these structures of power, and the effects they have had on the writing and remembering of YWCA history, but, in doing so, I directly contradict the version of history told to me by my research participants. One expression of the colonial power under analysis in this chapter is addressed under the heading of 'imperial maternalism'. This is a moral identity based on the construction of Christianity as white, and of European culture as superior. It enabled white colonizer women to adopt a distinctive ethical stance towards African women, and a point from which they could increase and leverage their limited social power as women. Later in the YWCA's history the structure established during the colonial period continued to enable a hierarchy of age and class.

2.1 'The extension of his kingdom', 1855–1912

The YMCA offered a blueprint for the early development of the YWCA and often provided material support; the first YWCA meeting in Nairobi was held in the YMCA's premises. The evangelical revival that had swept through Europe in the eighteenth and nineteenth centuries catalysed the development of both the YWCA and the YMCA. The YMCA was founded in Britain in 1844, just eleven years before the YWCA in 1855. With a desire to respond to perceived threats to young men's moral and social well-being posed by modernization and secularization, the YMCA movement spread from the UK to Germany and the United States by the 1850s (Wignall 2014: 21–2). The YMCA was conceived as a membership organization for men who could demonstrate, through church membership or otherwise, their personal faith (Fretheim 2008: 118). With the rapid growth of the YMCA movement, the World Alliance of YMCAs was formed in 1855 in Paris with the adoption of what has become known as the 'Paris Basis'. The Paris Basis became the defining statement of the movement's purpose and identity, directing its constituent Associations to

> unite those young men who, regarding Jesus Christ as their God and Saviour ... desire to be his disciples in their faith and in their life, and to associate their efforts for the extension of his Kingdom ... Any differences of opinion on other subjects, however important in themselves, shall not interfere with ... harmonious relations. (World YMCA 2013)

Each National YMCA additionally asserted their unity of 'principle and operation' but also their 'complete independence' from one another, further guaranteeing the ability of Associations to hold different positions, and mitigating against the development of a comprehensive YMCA theology or ethics (Fretheim 2008: 119–20). However, this insistence on independence also facilitated the gradual expression of the movement's ecumenical character, particularly in the interwar period when YMCAs were established in Orthodox Christian and Catholic contexts (Fretheim 2008: 123). The 'Paris Basis' later served as the template upon which the World's YWCA would construct its own constitution (Fretheim 2008: 117; Seymour-Jones 1994: 12–13). In 1883 the YWCA of Great Britain set out its aims and identity as follows:

> Work among Young Women of all Classes, by all means that are in accordance with God's word ... To unite them for mutual help, sympathy and instruction ... To seek to win the knowledge of Christ our sisters all around us ... To provide Christian friends for all Young Women, especially those who come from the country into the towns ... To promote the moral and social wellbeing of all ... To afford protection to those who need it, and thus help them to avoid the dangers and temptations which they may meet. (Duguid 1955: 30)

The YWCA of Great Britain seems to have had a much more explicitly evangelical outlook in its orientation towards 'rescuing' young women from 'a world that was using them harshly' (Duguid 1955: 32). During these early years, the YWCA sought to intervene in the lives of Jewish and Catholic women, 'criminals' and 'fallen' women through prayer, and to support working women and nurses by providing hostel accommodation in cities. The concern about the threat posed by urbanization towards young women appears again in the rationale for the work of the nascent YWCA of Kenya, as discussed below. These objectives were clearly filtered through a particular theological conceptualization of human nature and of gender. The YWCA's work expressed a central contention of the social gospel: to 'Christianize society by applying the Biblical principles of love and justice to such institutions as the family, the state and the economy' (Brauer 1971: 775). Again paralleling the YMCA's growth and spread across national borders, the YWCA movement spread from Britain to the United States, Norway, Spain, Australia, Sweden, Italy and India, and between these Associations the World's YWCA was founded in 1898, headquartered in London until 1930 when it moved to Geneva (Seymour-Jones 1994: 13). An impulse towards ecumenism and territorial expansion can be seen in the adaptation of the YMCA's Paris Basis as the foundational text for the World's YWCA's object and basis:

> The object of the Association shall be the federation, development, and extension of Young Women's Christian Associations in all lands ... The World's YWCA seeks to unite those young women who, regarding the Lord Jesus Christ as their God and Saviour, according to the Holy Scriptures, are vitally united to him through the love of God shed abroad in their hearts by the Holy Spirit, and desire to associate their efforts for the extension of His Kingdom among all young women by such means as are in accordance with the Word of God. (Seymour-Jones 1994: 12)

In the Paris Basis and the World's YWCA's foundational texts, colonial and imperial metaphors were used to describe its evangelical mandate 'the extension of His kingdom'. The World YWCA (as it is now called) continues to operate with a Constitution document, reproduced in part below, that resembles the Paris Basis in several key respects. The similarities can be clearly seen in the orientation towards 'uniting' young women who share a common faith as Christians. There remains an emphasis on the unity of the member associations under the relatively broad stipulations of the Constitution, namely the centrality of Christian faith to the work of the organization and its wide-ranging, ambitious aims.

Founded by women from Christian traditions around the world ... [the World YWCA] is based on faith in God the Almighty, Jesus Christ and the Holy Spirit. Its vision is of a fully inclusive world where justice, peace, health, human dignity, freedom and care for the environment are promoted and sustained by women's leadership. The World YWCA recognises the equal value of all human beings ... The World YWCA is founded on and inspired by the Christian faith ... The purpose of the World YWCA is to develop the leadership and collective power of women and girls around the world to achieve justice, peace, health, human dignity, freedom and a sustainable environment for all people. (World YWCA 2015: 9–10)

In more than a century since the original World YWCA constitution was drafted, much has changed; but significantly, the focus on the organization's Christian identity remains. However, the implications of this Christian identity are now confined to providing the motivation and justification for its development, social justice and welfare work, being that upon which the World YWCA 'is based', 'is founded' and 'inspired by'. Unity in difference continues to be a useful dimension of YWCA identity and practice, an issue to which I return in Chapter 6. With the YWCA movement well-established, it spread throughout British colonies in Africa; it took root in Egypt in 1876, South Africa in 1886, Ghana in 1899, Kenya in 1912 and Sierra Leone in 1915 (Seymour-Jones 1994: 507–10).

2.2 Imperial maternalism, 1912–55

The Imperial British East Africa Company claimed the territory that would later be called Kenya as the Protectorate of British East Africa in 1885, and in 1920 these lands were annexed to the British crown as 'Kenya Colony'. British colonization of eastern Africa throughout this period involved physically redistributing the population through educational and medical services at mission compounds, the concentration of economic opportunities in towns and large-scale migration to Nairobi. These were accompanied by a range of adjustments in local social hierarchies and structures. Gender was always implied in such changes. Binary gender categories and roles ('man' and 'woman') were redefined and imposed on colonized peoples through the introduction of the English language, British naming conventions and dress codes, formal schooling, institutionalized medicine, employment and missionary Christianity (Shaw 1995). Tabitha Kanogo (2005) provides a critical historical contextualization of the multiple and often contradictory processes by which the women of colonized eastern

Africa became recognized, constituted and interpellated as 'African women' through British colonization and Christian mission.[1] This was achieved through explicit attempts to construct 'African womanhood' as such, as well as various unforeseen consequences of colonial interventions in gender, religion, culture and economy. The evidence provided by Kanogo's research into maternity, sexuality, education and initiation during British colonization of the region suggests that it is necessary to move beyond the question of how 'African women' were treated by colonizers – although this remains extremely pertinent – to question gender's role in the establishment and maintenance of imperial control. Gendered categories and systems gave foundational support to imperialism and colonization (Kwok 2005: 7; Lugones 2008).

A committee of fifteen British women had founded the YWCA in Nairobi in 1912, and it officially became part of the World YWCA movement six years later in 1918. During its early years, it was in fact the Nairobi branch of the YWCA of Great Britain, and therefore not a completely independent organization. It received staff and funding from the British organization, and approval for major decisions was granted by its London office. The YWCA recruited new members from among the young women emigrating to the colony from Britain to work (Harley 1995: 9–11). These young women were perceived as vulnerable to the pressures and temptations of colonial city life by virtue of their whiteness, youth and working-class and lower-middle-class status. Thus, the YWCA considered these newly arrived nurses and 'business girls' to be in 'great need' of protection and guidance and considered itself the ideal venue for this effort (Harley 1995: 10). In this way, like many other organizations in British colonies, the YWCA ensured the continuation of British 'Christian' culture and etiquette, a significant proportion of which involved maintaining norms of white middle-class womanhood (Higgs 2016).

The YWCA's work in early colonial Nairobi was entirely based on the needs of colonizer women, functioning primarily as a social club and a hostel for those who worked in Nairobi, for example as secretaries. During this period the YWCA was more similar to other women's clubs in the city than it was to a church or mission society, despite the 'Christian' in its name. The decidedly spiritual concerns of the movement's founders in Britain remained part of the YWCA's identity and activities, but apparently they were not the main attraction for its members. For example, in 1912 it was not yet standard practice to close YWCA social events 'with prayer and praise', and a 'difference of opinion' prevented consensus on the question (Harley 1995: 6). Bible study classes were a fixed item on the YWCA's programme of activities, but in 1917 some of its leaders were concerned that so few members were attending them, while French, shorthand and typing classes were popular (Harley 1995: 16). For much of the 1920s and 1930s the YWCA worked closely with the East African Women's League (EAWL), another organization for colonizer women based in Nairobi (Van Tol 2015: 444). The EAWL claimed no religious identity, yet the two organizations were so similar that they were on occasion mistaken for one another (Harley 1995: 32–3).

Along with other women's organizations and Christian institutions, the YWCA was a relatively visible and active part of social life in Kenya colony. This privileged position partly stemmed from the class of the founding members of the YWCA, who were part of a tight-knit social circle in and near Nairobi. The patterns of interconnection between YWCA members, missionaries and other prominent members of colonial society greatly benefited the Association throughout the colonial period. In the case of the YWCA, the nexus of whiteness, middle-class status, middle-age, and Christianity dominated the internal structure of the organization from 1912 until it was interrupted by the decolonial revolt of Mau Mau in the mid-1950s. I consider the early YWCA as an example of what might be called 'maternalism' for its reliance on essentializing (white, upper and middle class, British) women as maternal, and its deployment of motherhood as a source of authority (Ware 1992; Woollacott 1998). In colonial Kenya, this maternalism allowed middle-class and upper-class white women to claim a social, moral and religious authority over other women, and over colonized peoples. While they may or may not have been biological parents themselves, they capitalized on the social position of 'mother' available to them through their participation in voluntary associations, church groups and social clubs, including the YWCA, as married and 'senior' women both in age and experience, as well as class and social standing.

2.3 Conceptualizing whiteness and Christianity

Racial and religious subjectivities, social positions and identities are co-constitutive: 'The category of religion is always already a racialized category' (Vial 2016: 1). Specifically, in British imperial history, the racialization of religion has relied in part on the definition of Christianity as white (Nye 2018: 17, 19–20). These identities/positions exist together; nobody is *only* a Christian, and nobody is *only* white. During the early colonial era in Kenya, a 'Christian' identity was practically synonymous with whiteness. Furthermore, Christianity was so closely associated with whiteness that each also signified 'civilized', 'modern', 'European' and/or 'Western'. In this religion-race construct, wherein 'Christian' was a white, and not necessarily a 'religious', position, 'womanhood' was a white-Christian gender construct. While colonizer women benefited from the social position afforded to them by motherhood (albeit an idealized and sometimes metaphorical motherhood), the material conditions in which colonized African communities raised their children were destabilized and degraded by the systematic destruction of their bodily autonomy and the devaluation of non-Christian cultures. All dimensions of colonization, from legislation to ecocide, relied on these conceptual connections to justify and make sense of the ways in which it treated the people it assumed authority over, and to redefine them as less than people. The point of highlighting the co-constitutive nature of gender and race is that this dynamic was a core building block of British colonization in which the YWCA participated (Muhonja 2018: xi; Nye 2018: 17–18; Shadle 2015: 27). In the early twentieth century YWCA membership was closed to Black African women because they could not be conceived as women, or 'Christian', in the same way as white women.

Theorists of gender in historical and contemporary colonial contexts have identified the role of gender and sexuality in colonial power relations, expressed by María Lugones as the 'coloniality of gender' (Lugones 2008). Coloniality describes the power relations that uphold white supremacy, neocolonialism, Western hegemony and imperialism and the logics that justify those relations. Coloniality, as a relational concept, finds a variety of local expressions, but it extends to a global scale as 'the most general form of domination in the world today' (Quijano 2007: 170). Coloniality is reproduced through Eurocentrism, whiteness and heteronormativity, all of which have been aided by Christianity and by scientific/scholarly 'modern Western rationality', as anthropological and scientific 'discovery' was advanced by opportunities presented by colonization (Maldonado-Torres et al. 2018: 66–7). Colonization additionally involved restructuring social and economic life for colonized African people by exerting control over their bodies, communities and labour. People in colonized eastern Africa were instrumentalized, jointly and severally approached as bodies, largely reduced to their physical contributions to the colonial economy as labourers and servants. This effect was, somewhat paradoxically, achieved by the partial destruction of their cultures, social structures and associated epistemologies (Ndolvu-Gatsheni 2013: 7–8). The denial of the spiritual, emotional, psychological and relational lives of people in colonized eastern Africa paradoxically relied on identifying precisely these dimensions of their lives and targeting them for explicit devaluation. A redefinition of gender and sexuality according to the colonizers' sociocultural norms was a significant result of the aforementioned destruction of cultures in combination with missionary Christianity.

The breadth of colonial transformations of eastern African world views and lifestyles is summarized by Kenda Mutongi as 'practical Christianity'. Missionary education was total, encompassing how the home should be constructed and organized, hygiene, clothing and etiquette, alongside schooling in literacy and religion (Mutongi 2007: 45–7). That Christianity was a primary tool used in this project was not an inevitable outcome of Christianity but reflects dominant missionary and colonial interpretations. The versions of missionary colonial Christianity that were introduced to colonized eastern Africa were suited to the task. The model of god as 'vertically transcendent', physically distant from and above 'His' creation, has legitimized and facilitated a human hierarchy of power and authority expressed in European colonization and imperialism (Rivera 2007). The co-constitution of mission and colonization is clear in the conflation of the 'extension' of 'god's kingdom' and the extension of the British Empire, particularly since the monarch is the head of both the state and the Church of England. Such power relations were supported by the assumption that colonial Christianity denoted whiteness. Under colonial relations of white domination in the past, such as the British Empire, and in the present, this has significant and frequently violent effects for members of racialized minority religious groups (Grosfoguel 2016: 11–12; Nye 2018: 4).

The YWCA was not different from this wider tendency. For the YWCA and other women's organizations and missionary societies, African peoples were positioned as beneficiaries of white benevolence, and therefore essential to the construction of their moral identities. When the YWCA and other white women's movements arrived in African territories that had been colonized by European powers, they actively and passively reinforced the 'difference' between Africans and Europeans by excluding non-white people from their organizations, and approaching them as primitives in need of assistance. The incongruity of the YWCA's colonial lifestyle is captured by the contrasts in the YWCA's concerns until the mid-1930s; it invested in ballrooms, libraries and tennis courts, while relying on the labour of 'bath boys' and a 'rickshaw boy' as late as 1932 (Harley 1995: 36–7). The YWCA's Christian identity relied for its meaning on narratives that positioned the colony as a dangerous masculine space in which white women needed a safe 'home away from home', and associated Christianity with whiteness, 'civilization' and European identity in contrast to African 'backwardness'. The large-scale conversion of local populations to Christianity made it increasingly difficult for the YWCA to maintain its exclusive whiteness after the 1940s – particularly as it coincided with church discourses of 'Africanization', official discourses of 'multiracialism' and the growing anti-racist critique in the African-led parts of the Kenyan women's movement (Aubrey 1997; Likimani 2005; Maathai 2008; Oduol and Kabira 1995; Van Tol 2015).

Far from being a singular entity, 'Christianity' has taken many different forms and has been deployed with different effects at different times. Missionary and 'mainline' churches were vectors for multiple colonial interventions and mechanisms of control, from health care, to education, to the learning and translation of local languages into English (often through the translation of the Bible). Later forms of Christianity that were led by Black African Christians, such as revival movements and African Instituted Churches (AICs), offered opportunities to oppose imperialism, such as the resistance of Gĩkũyũ independent churches to the colonial government's interference in 'female genital practices' (Njambi 2007). Thus, Christian identities have been constructed using a wide range of narratives, interacting with, and reinforcing, both British imperialism and anti-colonial resistance to it. The YWCA has displayed both tendencies at different points in its history, as a colonial Christian organization with origins in Britain that was comprehensively 'Africanized' in the latter part of the twentieth century.

The whiteness of Christianity and the coloniality of gender reinforced one another in the colonial YWCA. Through missionary work and through less formal interventions, implicitly white Christian constructions of women's sexuality were promoted as a model for colonized African women. This model was developed through a constellation of religious, literary and sociopolitical representations of maternity and female sexuality in Britain in the long eighteenth century. From its inception, the YWCA approached women with the repronormative assumption that they should, and would, be mothers above all else. To be a 'mother' for an upper- and middle-class white British woman was more than the mere fact of having children. It was a moral identity which relied upon an oppositional dynamic whereby her sexual desires were denied and externalized onto her class and racial others. The settlement of the North American 'West' and British imperial interests in the 'Orient' provided images and stories that could be used to anticipate and make sense of later British experiences of colonizing Africa. Britain's invasion and settlement of various African territories, including Kenya, made use of these. The 'prostitute', the 'Oriental' woman of the harem, the African 'tribeswoman' and the enslaved woman on the plantation, all figured prominently in literary representations of womanhood in the eighteenth century, and demonstrate that British imperialism relied upon gendered othering, while gendered social structures 'at home' relied on racialized imperialism (Nussbaum 1995; Stoler 1992: 521; Ware 1992: 37; Webster 1998: 45-7). Constructions of female sex/gender actually varied within Britain during this period, with the heterosexuality of proper womanhood established by contrasting an image of her 'pure', chaste monogamy with the ambiguous gender and transgressive sexuality of working women, particularly sex workers and colonized women. That the construction of motherhood as a moral identity belied the material realities of many (or most) women and/as mothers does not diminish the power it wielded as the model of womanhood. It became a singular avenue for women to access and exercise social power. The connection between middle-class (and often middle-aged) women's exercise of moral and maternal authority is especially significant for my analysis here.

Motherhood was thus highly significant as a moral identity in the Victorian social context out of which the YWCA grew; it intersected with class to construct upper- and middle-class white British wives and mothers as morally superior to other women, and to men. This phenomenon was expressed in women's performance of 'genteel essential femininity', which throughout the nineteenth and early twentieth centuries was demonstrated in pious Christian faith and voluntary service (Woollacott 1998: 86). Throughout the British Empire, middle-class British women's assumed position of moral scrupulousness facilitated many, like the well-known anti-prostitution campaigner Josephine Butler (1828-1906) in India, to promote a vision of women's fulfilment and dignity through Christianity, education and domesticity. The features of this trend have been thoroughly described and analysed elsewhere, most notably by Vron Ware (1992), but the role of the YWCA in this hierarchy of colonizer women's age, class and race remains understudied.

2.4 Sex work and public health in colonial Nairobi

Eastern African women's sexual and reproductive lives were subject to multiple, often contradictory, interventions during British colonization of the region. Colonizers were interested in birth rates and intervened liberally to increase and decrease the number of births; considering that children would ensure the future growth of the colony, as labourers and taxpayers. Abortion, 'female circumcision', sex work, maternal health care and marriage were all sites where colonial lawmakers and Christian missionaries sought to 'improve' the conditions of life for African women, through restricting and changing the options available to them (Booth 2004; Boulanger 2008; Kanogo 2005; Njambi 2007; Thomas 2003;

Ware 1992). The architects of these interventions often invoked a Christian moral schema to justify their actions, but were motivated at least in part by the instrumental value of these interventions for the maintenance of colonial control or the growth of the colonial economy. Many such interventions began and ended many decades ago, but they continue to echo in the present through, for instance, the culture and instruments of the legal system, and the country's public Christianity and moral narratives associating the city with danger. This is not to imply that every part of Kenya's postcolonial condition can be neatly and fully explained with reference to a self-evident colonial antecedent. Rather, I want to note the continuing significance of colonial history for understanding the moral narratives of gender and sexuality in the postcolonial era, which have shaped the context in which the YWCA has intervened. In this regard, the co-optation and manipulation of women's bodies by colonial powers in 1920s and 1930s Kenya is a significant reality against which a pro-natal and heteronormative sexual regime constitutes a Kenyan nationalist position (Aniekwu 2006: 152–3). Postcolonial histories feed into the narrative matrix out of which the YWCA draws themes for its own narrative moral identity. With this intertextuality in mind, in this section I provide a brief overview of the parallels and continuities between the postcolonial past and the situation in contemporary Kenya, to which I turn my attention in the subsequent section. This history shows how women's sexual and reproductive lives have often been identified as a battleground on which nationalist projects and Western imperialism fight for dominance (Yuval Davis 1998: 30–1).

The development of Nairobi catalysed the migration of single women to cities alongside industrialization, giving rise to similar gender and class concerns to those that had spurred the development of the YWCA in mid-nineteenth-century Britain. With the movement into Nairobi of African workers and white settlers, by 1917 the YWCA became concerned about 'urbanization problems' accompanying the growth of the city – namely the presence of colonized African women understood to be 'prostitutes' (Harley 1995: 24–7). Early colonial Nairobi was a nascent city constructed by the multiple, overlapping and sometimes contradictory attempts of colonial administrators to establish a British stronghold from which to govern eastern Africa. So, although the history of colonial attempts to control African women's sexual and reproductive lives is traceable to multiple locations and events, for the purposes of the present discussion, I will focus on the racial and gendered spatial organization of early colonial Nairobi as a 'contact zone' where the messy relations between colonizers and colonized smouldered (Booth 2004; Muchomba 2014; White 1990). The sexual-racial spatial division of Nairobi was an effort to preserve white racial and cultural purity, considered to be at risk of dilution or interruption by close contact with Africans. In the 1910s and 1920s Nairobi was already structured by racial segregation, and additionally considered by colonists and Africans alike to be a place for men, not women (Booth 2004; Harley 1995: 2; Kanogo 2005: 165). The small numbers of white women who had settled in the region were unlikely to be seen in public in Nairobi; indeed, it was this sense of men's access to city spaces, and women's vulnerability within them, that underwrote the nascent YWCA's provision of hostel accommodation for many colonizer women who would otherwise have arrived in Nairobi alone. In Britain, widespread concern about single women in cities had focused on their moral rectitude and the threats posed by being alone in public, on the street. It comes as no surprise that the logic of sexism meant that responses to this perceived risk were centred on bringing these women back into private, closed and gender-segregated spaces.

The introduction of a capitalist economic system to colonized eastern Africa shaped women's reproductive and sexual lives by presenting them with new obstacles and opportunities, to which they responded in a variety of novel ways, including but not limited to transactional sex (Omosa 1995: 63). By the early 1920s, contrary to the expectations of colonial administrators, and often going against the wishes of their communities, African women were migrating to Nairobi. Colonizers offered no formal employment to African women in the city at the time, but female migrants improvised various forms of self-employment catering to the male migrants among whom they lived (White 1990: 40–5). Providing cleaning and cooking services, as well as producing alcoholic beverages, formed a large part of their work, but most significantly for the present discussion, a large proportion of these migrant women in colonial Nairobi was also thought to be engaged in 'transactional sex' (Muchomba 2014: 83). The colonists' moralizing attitudes towards sex workers mixed with their racist dismissal of African women in such a way as to categorize (almost) all African women in Nairobi as 'prostitutes' (Kanogo 2005: 33–4). The growing number of these 'prostitutes' (read: seemingly unmarried African women) in Nairobi coincided with a marked rise in syphilis among colonizers and Africans, which confirmed the association of African women's bodies with immorality, illicit sexual activity and disease. Colonial administrators responded by reinforcing the racialized geography of the city, attempting to segregate its inhabitants (White 1990: 46).

Sexualized violence was a common feature of colonization. In Kenya there were many stories of colonizer men sexually exploiting African women and children, with apparent impunity (Shadle 2015: 101–2; Shaw 1995: 215; Wilson 2012: 33). The arrival in the 1920s and 1930s of large numbers of white women was credited with having a 'domesticating influence' and changing the tone of interracial relationships in Nairobi. This story suggests that their arrival precipitated a decrease in the rate at which colonizer men were committing sexualized violence against Africans. This is not a claim that can be easily verified, but it shows that white women were considered responsible for white men's behaviour both in terms of their availability as sexual partners and their supposedly elevating moral influence (Muchomba 2014: 86). The arrival of more white women further justified the racial segregation of the city, as the mingling of African men and colonizer women was considered undesirable, placing white women at risk. There were, of course, notable exceptions to this rule, including colonizers' widespread employment of African men as personal servants (derisorily called 'boys'). Women living at the YWCA hostel in Nairobi were permitted to employ 'personal boys' until 1923 (Harley 1995: 29), while the Association itself employed male Africans as cooks, gardeners and servants until at least the 1940s (Harley 1995: 45). The delineation of 'safe' and 'dangerous' spaces for white women in colonial Nairobi was more complex than the segregation of the city.

Throughout the colonial period African men migrated to the city to work but after 1921 they were permitted to live only in certain peripheral areas, the so-called 'African Locations' or 'Native Locations' (Booth 2004: 23–4; Kanogo 2005: 7; Likimani 1985: 75). Typically, these migrant workers left their wives, sisters, mothers, daughters and other female relatives 'at home' in the rural communities to which the men themselves remained fundamentally attached. Having been confined to living on 'swampy' land at the margins of the city, with public health measures such as sanitation largely neglected, and overcrowding an increasing problem, communicable diseases began to spread among the African migrant workers. Widespread pneumonia, malaria, tuberculosis and syphilis outbreaks were caused and exacerbated by lack of suitable housing, pervasive malnutrition, stress and harsh working conditions (Booth 2004: 24–5). These public health crises were not incidental; they were an inevitable result of colonization (Ramugondo 2018). They reinforced the colonists' existing prejudices about the 'unhygienic habits' of Africans, which rationalized the segregation of the city and offered further 'evidence' of the dangers posed by contact with 'contagious' Africans.

In the 1920s and 1930s, colonists' attempts to control the Africans living in Nairobi were a reflection of the perceived needs of the colony. Africans were present in Nairobi primarily because they were compelled to perform wage labour in order to pay the taxes that had been imposed by the colonial state in 1926 (Oduol and Kabira 1995: 194). From the perspective of colonial administrators, African workers were essential for economic growth and the generation of tax income. African women who were thought to be 'prostitutes', the supply of alcohol they provided and the syphilis they were thought to be spreading disrupted the colonizers' plans (Booth 2004: 28–9). The imposition of a variety of legislation and policy exerted a more direct influence to control the size and distribution of the African population – both in Nairobi as in the case of 'prostitutes' and further afield in the case of the 'female circumcision crisis' of the same period.

2.5 The 'female circumcision' crisis

The 'female circumcision crisis' began during the 1910s at a time when British control was already firmly established, and a large number of missionary societies were an active presence in eastern Africa. A diverse range of initiation rituals that included differing types and degrees of genital cutting existed in many but not all of the indigenous cultures in colonized eastern Africa.[2] Female genital cutting is a harmful practice like others found around the world, such as skin lightening, foot binding, diet culture and surgical interventions on intersex infants. In this vein, any analysis of 'female circumcision' should take into account its various meanings, as part of a longer process of physical, mental and cultural preparation for marriage, sex, pregnancy and childbirth. Colonizers and missionaries largely ignored the significance of circumcision as initiation rituals constitutive of adulthood and ethnic identity for men and women of many communities in Kenya. Rather, they came to consider all such practices a 'cosmetic surgery' which was nevertheless interpreted as proof that Africans were 'barbaric', 'heathen' and 'evil' (Boulanger 2008: 63–8). Concerns about health, hygiene and the pain involved in the procedure itself do seem to have been part of some missionaries' opposition to these practices. On the whole, however, this rejection of 'female circumcision' was not predicated on a concern for girls' bodily autonomy, their health or their right to sexual pleasure.

Many missions attempted to eradicate 'female circumcision' locally, including in Gĩkũyũ communities, which is where the female circumcision crisis took place. These attempts at eradication were usually resisted by Gĩkũyũ women, men and community leaders. However, neither the missionaries nor the populations to whom they ministered were united on the issue of 'female circumcision' (Boulanger 2008: 67–8; Njambi 2007: 691; Presley 1988: 504; Stanley 1990: 152; Thomas 1998: 122). At one Church of Scotland Mission station, an attempted compromise between the missionaries' opposition to 'female circumcision' and Gĩkũyũ attachment to it led to the cutting or 'circumcision' element of the Gĩkũyũ *irua ria atumia* ritual being performed at the mission compound. These kinds of compromises were widespread but ultimately unsuccessful, because European surveillance of the cutting itself reinforced the idea that 'female circumcision' was 'revolting', 'unhygienic' and cruel (Boulanger 2008: 64). On this basis, in 1916 mission churches began explicitly to forbid female genital practices, meaning that many Christian parents and their daughters were caught between the demands of their culture and the stipulations of white missionaries and priests (Boulanger 2008: 61–74). Protestant missionaries began emphasizing the health risks associated with 'female circumcision' in an attempt to deter congregants from 'circumcising' their daughters, and by the mid-1920s girls were allowed access to mission schools only if they 'denounced' the practice (Boulanger 2008: 66).

The crisis took hold in March 1929, when the Protestant churches called on all African Christians to sign a pledge to repudiate 'female circumcision', with those who refused to do so being expelled from their churches (Boulanger 2008: 67–8). In other words, while converts were constantly reduced to a stereotype of their 'African' identity by the colonial state, missionaries made the abandonment of practices marked as 'African', such as 'female circumcision' and polygyny, into a measure of Christians' commitment to their faith. News of the crisis presumably reached the World YWCA, since in 1930 it wrote to the Nairobi office 'suggest[ing] that the YWCA should take up the matter of mutilation of women in Kenya', but at this time the YWCA 'had no contact at all with Africans', so it did not intervene (Harley 1995: 35) Missionaries and their congregations had complicated and uneven investments in and entanglements with local cultures, British culture, missionary education, formal schooling and health care. In response to interventions against 'female circumcision', large numbers of African Christians left the mission churches and took their children out of mission schools. Gĩkũyũ Christians founded their own independent schools and churches that allowed the continuation of Gĩkũyũ cultural practices that had been problematized or banned alongside Christian worship, and generally held strongly anti-colonial views (Boulanger 2008: 70; Njambi 2007: 698).

The 'female circumcision' crisis is a narrative that has been read in opposing ways; to colonial authorities it represented the difficulty of governing a rural

African population, while to missionaries it was a more acutely moral problem of defining acceptable Christian conduct (Boulanger 2008; Njambi 2007; Shaw 1995; Thomas 2003). The crisis was a major way (certainly not the only way) in which rural African girls' and women's bodies and choices were constrained by colonial administrators, missionaries, community elders and their families (Boulanger 2008: 73). Competing regimes attempted to instrumentalize girls' and women's bodies to serve further ends – namely, to change African cultures towards a Eurocentric Christian ideal, to exploit Africans as labourers or to maintain cultures, identities, practices in resistance to colonial interventions. Women and girls were active in each of these projects, as daughters, mothers, circumcisers, Christians, Gĩkũyũs and workers, inhabiting multiple roles simultaneously. From these positions African women and girls negotiated their ways through the crisis, not usually by achieving a complete break from their community but through 'shifts, straddling, adoption of [a] new religious affiliation', learning new skills and strategies and facing down many contradictions in the process (Kanogo 2005: 245). Thus, the women and girls who survived this crisis did so between the competing demands of the institutions and cultures and narratives to which they belonged and which claimed them.

For colonizers and missionaries, the 'crisis' surrounding 'female circumcision' manifested in African resistance to their attempts to control female genital practices. These attempts drove converts away from mission churches and stoked anti-colonial sentiment. Imagining the crisis from the point of view of adolescent Gĩkũyũ Christian girls, the 'crisis' seems to have been one of a contradiction between their (new) faith and their ethnic identity. They often faced a choice of whether to undergo the 'cutting' portion of their initiation into adulthood, or not – and the implications of this choice for their status at church, at home and at school. Furthermore, of course, their bodies would bear the immediate and lifelong marks of their decision and its impact on their identity and social status (Boulanger 2008: 70; Kanogo 2005: 81–2). Some girls responded by running away from their parents to a mission compound in order to escape 'female circumcision'. Other girls ran away from their mission schools in order to undertake the ritual and become a recognizable adult member of their community. The crisis was generated in part by an ethics of benevolent condescension that focused not on the well-being of the colonized but on bolstering the narratively constituted moral identity of missionaries. The logic of imperialism denigrated 'African' cultural practices, but the instrumental use of intervening in female genital practices was to guarantee a large and able-bodied workforce. In many Kenyan cultures, the initiation ceremonies at which the 'cutting' took place were always held at a certain time of year, and involved all the girls from an entire age group at once. This often meant that large numbers of young women were away from their work on farms for several months at a time (Boulanger 2008: 71; Njambi 2007: 697). The instrumental value of African women's bodies is clear when Lynn Thomas describes how colonial authorities at one time decided to enforce a mass 'female circumcision' in Meru, central Kenya (Thomas 1998: 121).

Colonizers, missionaries and local patriarchs each drew very different conclusions about what practices were appropriate for the construction of moral authority, adulthood and proper ethnic identity and group membership (Thomas 2003: 15–17). In the 1930s, the colonial government determined that the birth rate in Kenya was 'too low'. Maintaining a large population was necessary for the extraction of resources and the generation of wealth, including through agriculture and other industry which required labourers. The missionaries' interruption of female circumcisions unintentionally impacted upon this by interrupting the graduation of a whole generation into adulthood. The colonial interpretation of this situation was that there were now an increased number of older adolescents who were still considered 'girls', not adults. The colonial government 'knew' that among some ethnic groups, including the Meru, the community would not allow uncircumcised adolescent girls to become mothers (Thomas 2003: 27–41). They thought that this would mean high levels of abortion and infanticide, thus lower rates of population growth and fewer workers. The colonizers' solution was to perform a 'female circumcision' on all uncircumcised girls in Meru. This was an effort to ensure that all the girls would become adults in the eyes of their communities. In turn, they would be allowed to marry and any pregnancies would be carried to term, and thereby the birth rate would increase, to the benefit of the colony.

This project was carried out through mass circumcisions known by the Meru girls as *kiwagrie*, 'the one for which we were not prepared' or 'the one which was unexpected' (Thomas 1998: 139; Thomas 2003: 44–51). These 'circumcisions' were performed by persons who lacked the proper authority, possibly by male police officers. Many girls in Meru were therefore later 'circumcised' a second time by female elders who were able to observe the correct ritual procedure (Boulanger 2008: 72; Thomas 1998: 140–1). Abortion, and the colonizers' attempts to guarantee higher birth rates, was thereby implicated in the complex tangle of interventions and negotiations between missionaries, circumcisers, girls and the colonial economy. The story of *kiwagrie* was not known by anti-FGM (female genital mutilation) campaigners I met in Nairobi in 2012 (both at the YWCA and outside it), perhaps because it complicates the narrative of crisis and resolution, problematizes the role of the state in development and muddies the notion of progress implied in so many development projects. Regardless of whether and how this historical antecedent is actively remembered in relation to contemporary anti-FGM campaigns, I think it is useful to understand this nexus of interest in and control over African women's and girls' bodies and reproductive capacities.

Looking at these dynamics underlines how central gender was to the articulation of colonial power with the explicit intention of imparting 'civilization'. Thus, moral, legal and medical perspectives on abortion all inform its position of significance for nationalism, Christianity, colonialism, development and women's movements. White colonizer women were implicated in imperial interventions in sexuality and reproduction. The colonial women's organizations that existed at the time of the 'female circumcision crisis', including the YWCA, explicitly accepted and contributed to the rhetorical construction of African women as lesser-than. The YWCA's activities were part of a range of official and unofficial strategies supported by this colonial gender construction. Furthermore, these efforts to regulate African sexuality and procreation reflected the Christian-colonial claim to authority on the basis of moral superiority. These dimensions of the 'crises' around 'circumcision' and abortion are crucial elements of the historical context in which the YWCA articulated a Christian ethical perspective on 'controversial faith issues' in the twenty-first century.

2.6 Becoming 'multiracial', 1955–65

The YWCA's identity and activities throughout the colonial period reinforced classed, raced and gendered standards of behaviour that privileged white colonizer women, while reinforcing prevailing racist assumptions about African women. While white women in colonial Kenya overwhelmingly remained in favour of informal segregation and white rule, the stance of the YWCA began to change in the mid-1950s when it included African women as members for the first time. During this period, considerable pressure was brought to bear on the YWCA to remain relevant and active in a rapidly changing country. The extent of the racial segregation that persisted at the YWCA at the end of the 1950s is evident, as Harley felt 'disappointed not to meet any African members' of Mombasa YWCA when she paid a short visit there in December 1958, shortly after her appointment as NGS (Harley 1995: 77–8). This period was defined by the 'State of Emergency' declared by the colonial government in October 1952, during which it effectively waged a civil war against the so-called 'Mau Mau' anti-colonial uprising (Furedi 1989: 117–18). By 1955, the British colonial government had defeated Mau Mau. The colonizers brutally repressed the Gĩkũyũ communities from which the rebels came, including imprisoning and torturing Gĩkũyũs in what amounted to concentration camps. The clash left thousands dead. The exact figures are disputed, but estimates range from eleven thousand to three hundred thousand including both Gĩkũyũ civilians killed by the British and by Mau Mau and Mau Mau fighters executed by the British (Anderson 2005; Blacker 2007; Elkins 2005). By comparison, it is thought that thirty-two European settlers lost their lives at the hands of Mau Mau (Newsinger 1981: 80–1). There was considerable uncertainty about the future of Kenya as a British colony, and an explicit political strategy of 'multiracialism' was launched as part of de-colonization.[3] 'Multiracialism', as the name suggests, did not involve a deconstruction of 'race' or racism, nor was it based on a recognition of the moral equality of 'races'. Rather, it was the strategic removal of certain barriers to enable African men to participate in local and national politics, deployed to mediate between the forces of African nationalism and white supremacy (Gordon 1986: 125–9). The YWCA's adoption of the language of 'multiracialism' suggests that it saw its efforts as part of wider British efforts to mete out certain kinds of power and access, in order to re-establish the legitimacy of British colonial rule.

Among the British responses to Mau Mau was the Community Development Department, founded in 1952, 'whose policies and programs were directed specifically to wean women away from Mau Mau' (Presley 1988: 503–4). The colonial government also sought to exploit women's participation in Mau Mau to their own ends, through the newly formed *Maendeleo Ya Wanawake* (MYW) organization.[4] MYW was founded by colonizer women in 1952 and described its activities as providing training to African women in skills for a life of homemaking and domesticity (Aubrey 1997: 45–7). From the outset MYW was different from other colonial women's organizations in one key respect: its primary focus was African women. It reached out to them by incorporating existing informal African women's groups into its structure, offering classes in sewing, cooking, child welfare, hygiene, singing and dancing (Aubrey 1997: 47). When the YWCA began to 'include' African women, it did so on much the same terms. Its activities stood in continuity with, if not directly in support of, wider late-colonial efforts to co-opt and pacify African women in response to Mau Mau. In fact, Harley identifies Mau Mau as a direct influence on the YWCA's work in the late 1950s, as the colonial government considered the Association to be in a good position to 'rehabilitate' Gĩkũyũ youth (Harley 1995: 74–5).

The YWCA explicitly excluded African women and girls from core services and membership until 1955 (Harley 1995: 41–2). Racist exclusionary practices to define and control 'white' spaces were intrinsic to the colonization of Kenya, and common throughout the British Empire (Shadle 2015: 11; Stoler 1989: 154). In the case of the YWCA, its exclusion of African (and Indian) women also reflects the influence of the Anglican Church in the colony, which in 1913 stipulated that its material support for the organization would depend on the restriction of the YWCA's hostel to 'young white girls' (Harley 1995: 9). Although African women were not eligible for YWCA membership until after 1955, the labour of African men in their roles as servants had always been essential to its operations – including five 'bath boys' whose job was to fetch hot water and carry it up to the bathrooms for the hostel's residents to bathe (Harley 1995: 37). As hostel residents, non-British whites were largely welcomed as equals, but the YWCA maintained a particularly British, Protestant character.[5] There is evidence to suggest that the total refusal to include African women was specific to the Kenyan YWCA, as other colonial YWCAs of the same period were oriented towards evangelical, interracial and cross-cultural work. For example, at the turn of the century in China, a YWCA was established with a focus on responding to the (perceived) 'spiritual needs' of (Chinese) women working in factories (Seymour-Jones 1994: 15). However, the grammar of 'working with' and 'for' local and indigenous women was typical, indicating that in colonial situations the YWCA conceived of itself as distinct from the 'Other' women who remained outside it (Harley 1995: 53). Since the 1940s, the World YWCA had considered the Kenyan Association to be in need of significant reform, and began encouraging it to abandon its practices of racist exclusion (Harley 1995: 51; Seymour-Jones 1994: 217). As part of this effort the World YWCA appointed Vera Harley, white British woman, as NGS of Kenya YWCA in 1958. Harley had the explicit mandate to 'work with' African women (Harley 1995: 73). The prevailing social context of colonial Kenya was characterized by deep divisions not only between Africans and colonizers but over the future of Kenya and in whose interests that future ought to be decided.

The first African women to be enrolled as YWCA members were admitted in Nairobi and Mombasa in 1955. However, a network of local, rural, semi-formal, women's groups that facilitated cooperation for mutual benefit had already been gradually absorbed by the YWCA, missions and other national women's groups since the advent of colonization. These women's groups were usually temporary and formed for very specific aims, such as the organization and division of women's labour at harvest time (Mathangani 1995; Stamp 1986; Von Bülow 1992). Under colonization, the power of these groups was recognized and harnessed, with missions, churches, schools and the women's groups themselves recognizing the benefits of formalizing and associating with other larger institutions. In the 1950s this trend accelerated, and many women's groups became affiliated to the YWCA, and MYW. The YWCA approached these groups with literacy programmes, and other explicit attempts at propagating domesticity; their members were not full members of the YWCA. The YWCA's first African members were given their own sub-branch in Nairobi, which effectively kept them segregated from the rest of the Association. Pioneering Kenyan author and businesswoman Muthoni Likimani was among the first African women to become a member of the YWCA. Mrs Likimani remembers that the so-called 'African YWCA group' was 'not allowed to meet at the YWCA headquarters ... We were given an old building of iron sheets and wooden floor' (Likimani 2005: 337–8). This old building was a 'hut' that had previously been used as a clubhouse for the Boy Scouts, but that YWCA rented in 1955 specifically to serve as 'the meeting place for all African and multi-racial activities' (Harley 1995: 59). Indeed, the YWCA 'had not been willing to consider' making the headquarters into a 'multi-racial building' (Harley 1995: 75).

Racism was embedded in the education and vocational training courses the YWCA provided for African women. Noticing that educational and employment opportunities for African girls were few, Harley resolved to ensure that 'the current educational needs of African girls might, in some small way, be met by the YWCA' (Harley 1995: 76). The training offered seems to have been interpreted differently by YWCA staff according to their political sympathies. Harley stressed that the two years' training offered to school leavers would enable young women to 'take up a wide range of occupations', while others on the YWCA's Executive Committee expected the project to train African girls to work as servants (Harley 1995: 78–9). The content of the training offered was 'child care, first aid, home nursing, nutrition and hygiene', use of a sewing machine and 'English for Foreigners', during which time the African women 'assisted with' the cooking, cleaning and laundry at the YWCA hostels, where the majority of guests were white and European (Harley 1995: 78–81). While this did serve as vocational training through which young women were able to gain experience for future employment, it hardly challenged prevailing assumptions about the kinds of employment to which African women were suited. Moreover, African women were clearly approached primarily as the passive recipients of colonizer women's instruction and benevolence. This attitude of condescension was not unique to the YWCA in colonial contexts. In fact it was the first impulse of the Association at the point it was founded in London in 1855. The early YWCA's role in facilitating the tutelage of young, white working-class women by older, white middle-class women was transformed through the colonial period. The British class system incorporated the colonial racial hierarchy to offer lower-class white women a superior position to African women, particularly as teachers (Ware 1992: 126–8). This marked a shift in the YWCA's attitude from what might be considered maternalism to a specifically imperial form of maternalism (Higgs 2019).

In her tenure as NGS, Vera Harley had two main aims: to recruit and train an African YWCA leadership and, in the shorter term, to extend YWCA services to African women and girls: 'to create a national movement and train African [women] to run it' (Harley 1995: 73–4). By the beginning of the 1960s, Harley had achieved some success as 'working with African women' had been established as the undisputed focus of the YWCA. However, as revealed by the phrase 'working with', the YWCA continued to be identified with white women and African women were approached as an external, separate group. White women inside and outside the YWCA displayed a general unwillingness to approach African women on fully equal terms, reflecting among other things the almost complete overlap of race and class. Nevertheless in 1960 Margaret Kariuki, daughter of the first Gĩkũyũ Anglican Bishop, became the first African woman to hold 'a senior post' at the YWCA, when she became the Deputy Warden of the hostel and Assistant Headmistress of the YWCA's vocational training school (Harley 1995: 93). Although Kariuki's position was not a particularly pivotal one within the organization, her appointment was a major step towards recognizing the capability of African women. The YWCA was by this time moving in step with other Christian institutions, as throughout the early 1960s African men were beginning to take up leadership positions within the Anglican, Presbyterian and Methodist Churches (Barrett et al. 1973: 37), although locally, African men were being ordained to act as members of the clergy in mission churches from at least 1910.

By the mid-1960s the handover of leadership power from colonizer women to African women was well underway. In July 1963 Ernestine Kiano became the first Black woman to hold a leadership position at the YWCA, when she was appointed as National President – this was not a full-time job but rather a voluntary position as chairperson of the YWCA's national Executive Committee. Mrs Kiano was from the United States and Kenyan by marriage, so she did not straightforwardly meet the YWCA's stipulation that the new President should be 'of the country' (Harley 1995: 130), suggesting that such changes were not undertaken as a result of a commitment specifically to African women's leadership. However, at the 1963 Annual Council meeting of the YWCA, for the first time the number of African and colonizer women on the Executive Committee became equal (Harley 1995: 131).

The Association's shift away from the exclusion of African women coincided with wider sociopolitical changes that preceded Kenya's independence from Britain. The YWCA attended the 1957 Convention of Women's Societies held in Nairobi, along with white women representing twenty-six women's organizations, including the EAWL and MYW (Van Tol 2015: 455). At this meeting, the white women's organizations decided to start 'including' African women. The YWCA's initial move towards 'multiracial' work precedes the Convention by two years, but that should not be interpreted as evidence of a progressive stance on the part of the YWCA. In many ways, white settler women used the Convention and the idea of 'multiracial' work to cement their own place in the soon-to-be independent Kenya (Van Tol 2015: 442). At the fourth Convention in 1961, six African women including Muthoni Likimani explicitly levelled this charge at white women's organizations, and protested against what they described as their 'domination' (Likimani 2005: 331–2). Some white women were still being brought into Kenya from elsewhere to take up senior positions at the YWCA, illustrated particularly by the request for a 'European General Secretary' to be sent to Mombasa Branch (Harley 1995: 140). This approach – of white women holding onto their power in the late-colonial period by strictly controlling the entry of African women into their organizations – would be repeated with the appointment of Margaret Mugo as the first Black African NGS.[6]

Vera Harley's interventions set a course towards the full racial integration of the YWCA, even if that was something not all its white members could imagine, predict or welcome at the time. When Kenya became independent from Britain on 29 December 1963, the YWCA had changed the racial make-up of its leaders and membership base just enough to justify its continued presence in Kenya. In 1963 Margaret Mugo, who was known to some YWCA leaders but was not herself involved in the organization, was chosen as the first African woman to lead the YWCA in Kenya. Harley recalls that the process began when, in August that year, she unofficially enquired to see whether Mrs Mugo would consider joining the YWCA as NGS, and that Mrs Mugo agreed (Harley 1995: 132). Soon after this, Mrs Mugo left Kenya to prepare for her new role by undertaking YWCA training programmes in the United States, Switzerland, the UK and Greece, before returning to Nairobi to take office in the summer of 1964 (Harley 1995: 139). Mrs Mugo was appointed with some fanfare – as Harley writes that 'KBC [Kenya Broadcasting Company] broadcast in the news that the Kenya YWCA had appointed an African National General Secretary' (Harley 1995: 141). By this time, the number of white women on the YWCA's Executive Board dropped to nine out of twenty-eight, giving African women the clear majority for the first time (Harley 1995: 141). After Mrs Mugo took over as leader, Harley nevertheless remained at the YWCA as a 'consultant' for a further six months, leaving for good in January 1965. Harley made a highly significant address to the YWCA at the National Convention in Mombasa in January 1965, her final act as NGS to which I return my attention in Chapter 6. The complete removal of colonizer women from all positions of power at the YWCA was an ongoing process which would not be complete until the beginning of the 1970s. The turn towards 'multiracial' integration was achieved with, and partly camouflaged by, the Association's self-representation as a Christian organization despite its record of defining its identity as a 'home away from home' for white British women. These changes were reflected and codified in the organization's identity narrative, which helped the YWCA survive as a 'Christian women's organization' in an independent African country – albeit one in which its former colonizers were explicitly invited to remain and participate. The longer-term effects of this turn in the YWCA's identity, and the intervention Harley made in order to secure it, are the focus of narrative analysis later in Chapter 6.

2.7 Summary

The YWCA arrived in colonized eastern Africa as one of several white women's groups catering to the interests of the colonizing population and cooperated with Christian missionary efforts. In colonized eastern Africa, girls and women were normatively expected to have children regardless of their racialized position, and Christianity deepened and changed existing stigmas attached to sex and sexual health topics while introducing new ones. Colonization, economic exploitation and missionary interventions all contributed towards sexual ill health, infant and maternal mortality, but they also imposed a racist and moralizing interpretive frame that redefined 'African' sexual/reproductive decisions and behaviours as unhealthy, irresponsible and/or immoral. The 'female circumcision crisis' illustrates the interrelated nature of the aspects of sexuality, health and the coloniality of gender under study in this book, demonstrating the long and complex history of Christian and imperial interventions in women's (sexual) health in Kenya and the multiple interventions and stakes involved. Christian institutions at times aligned themselves with the interests of the colonial government and at other times against it, and many oppositions emerged between missionary organizations, individual missionaries and their denominations – illustrating that an ostensible shared Christian basis for the ethical evaluation of apparently harmful practices did not produce a uniform Christian stance, neither among colonizers nor among the colonized. This internal differentiation of Christian ethical thought, which ranges from a lack of consensus through to virulent disagreement, is a thread that will re-emerge later in my argument. That female genital practices have survived into the present is partly a legacy of colonial interventions like those constituting the 'female circumcision' crisis, which contributed to the significance these practices took on as symbols of anti-colonial resistance (Njambi 2007; Shaw 1995). In the YWCA's later history female genital practices reappear, renamed 'FGM', and embedded in discourses of the development industry.

3

From welfare to development, 1965–2000

The colonial missionary and women's organizations of the early twentieth century, like the YWCA, were in some ways the forerunners of the development industry. These phenomena and their histories are anchored in binary logics that equate modernity, Christianity and civilization against African traditions and practices defined in advance as antiquated and inferior. This set of binaries is in fact a construction achieved in narratives of progress that were explicit in rationales for colonization, and remain as largely implicit, embedded assumptions in development discourse. In this chapter I outline the emergence of development in the wake of decolonization, to provide context for the YWCA's later shift towards programmatic interventions for sexual and reproductive health and rights. In Kenya in the latter half of the twentieth century, gender and sexuality were addressed within competing and overlapping worldviews: the development industry promoted women's empowerment and maternal health, in contrast to the state that officially denied that gender inequality existed. Churches and other Christian institutions provided health care, but simultaneously contributed to the stigmatization of contraception and sexuality. The emergence of HIV in the 1980s pushed these concerns to the forefront of international concern and increased development interest in and attention to sex and sexuality. I echo postcolonial feminist critiques of the development industry, illustrating its imperialism and neocolonialism (Dossa 2007; Pailey 2019; Rodney 2018; Saunders 2002; Wilson 2012). An instrumentalist 'developmental paradigm' has been highly influential in the study of women and gender in Africa, subordinating critical educational and intellectual work to 'economic and donor-related' interests (Lewis 2005: 386–8). In other words, changes that benefit women and girls are apt to be included in development interventions if they are thought to serve further development goals, by contributing to economic growth or raising employment figures. They are not necessarily sought and included because they are considered to be important in their own right. I begin my discussion with an outline of development as an illustration of the impact of colonial power structures and narratives after formal end of empire. This leads into an overview of development in Kenya specifically, and the YWCA's place within that as its activities shifted from domesticity in the colonial era, to welfare, and towards development.

3.1 International development industry

On the large scale, international development is an industrial complex invested in the maintenance of a global network of investment and trade that immediately benefits a transnational elite class of bureaucrats, politicians and oligarchs (Dossa 2007; Wilson 2012). It upholds the hierarchies and hegemonies established by (mostly European) colonizations of the majority world and facilitates the continued capitalist economic exploitation of (formerly) colonized peoples as workers (Rodney 2018). The concept of 'development' can be traced from Western/European processes of change via industrial capitalism in the eighteenth and nineteenth centuries. Capitalism and colonization instigated a range of changes, processes of expansion and accumulation, upon which it was considered necessary for the ruling classes, acting as 'trustees', to impose order and control. As a symptom of social change, urbanization caused anxiety, as people conceived of as ' "dangerous classes" … were drawn to the industrialising cities but were yet to be disciplined by capital' (Wilson 2012: 18). The YWCA's position in this nexus of power relations and anxieties, its interest in urbanization and its maternalist orientation suggests that it was closely involved in the conceptualization of development from a Christian point of view at this early stage, although as was clear in the previous chapter, it did not yet use this language.

Development was interpreted as change according to a linear model that suggested 'progress', established in part by a comparison of European modernity to 'Africa' as unchanging (Wilson 2012: 18–19). Development contains an implicit orientation towards an imagined future that aligns change towards European modernity as progress, thus closely mirroring colonial interventions by promoting a specific set of understandings of what is good for human life. It connotes a 'teleological complex', and not merely a neutral descriptor of change towards any given goal, but rather produces and reinforces 'our present single and westernized world system' (Wynter 1996: 299–300). In the latter half of the twentieth century, 'cultural differences' have permeated the language of development and replaced explicit appeals to 'racial' difference (Wilson 2012: 208). The notion of cultural difference 'sustains' the idea of the 'developed' world as 'modern', and the 'developing' world as 'traditional' (Kothari 2006: 13). This 'developmentalism' undergirds the aforementioned dichotomies, and facilitates the continued extraction of wealth, labour and resources from African nations. Now independent, they were coerced into allowing relations of exploitation to continue (Wilson 2012: 212). The 'development industry' includes the Bretton Woods institutions – the World Bank (WB) and International Monetary Fund (IMF) – as well as other agencies like the national aid branches of Western governments (for instance, UKAID and USAID). Large international NGOs (INGOs), philanthropic projects (like the Bill and Melinda Gates Foundation) and charitable organizations are part of the development industry precisely to the degree that their activities facilitate the objectives of the aforementioned institutions.

The specific interventions and initiatives of the development industry rely on a set of narratives about white compassion, expertise and agency, in contrast to 'Third World' incapacity. These narratives simultaneously obscure the ways in which development initiatives perpetuate the relations and structures that impoverish, disempower and kill people in the majority world. If the development industry perpetuates the structural inequalities caused by colonization, then development interventions cannot address the effects of a global capitalist economy; they are invested in upholding it. They ignore the ways in which development by Western/Northern agents stands in continuity with the earlier deprivations of colonization. Colonizer states that enriched themselves by extracting resources and wealth from the territories they colonized now return a small fraction of that wealth in the form of aid. At the same time, multinational corporations based in the North/West conduct business like mining and agriculture, which impoverish their own employees while polluting the environment and avoiding the payment of taxes (Wilson 2012: 17). For example, individual citizens of the North, such as myself, donate money to charitable and relief organizations that address the effects of poverty. But at the same time, we benefit exponentially from the resources provided to us by those actors that impoverish people in the first place. This illustrates the systemic nature of the forces that create 'poverty' and the comparatively individualistic scale of the 'solutions' offered in response.

Poverty is identified and measured using a wide range of tools and thresholds, many of which have been criticized for their implicit basis in Eurocentric conceptions of the 'good life' or for overemphasizing income over other determinants of well-being. Following these critiques, it is necessary to name the specific dimensions of poverty at issue in any given context or development intervention. In Kenya, 'poverty' comprises various consequences of colonization, transnational and local economic exploitation and the practices of global financial and political institutions. All of these interfere with individuals' and communities' ability to meet their survival needs in terms of, for instance, the availability of goods and services, and access to infrastructure or political representation (Chant 2010; Kabeer 2015; Mohanty 1999). Poverty is in this way 'multidimensional', and intersects with other causes and effects of (dis)advantage and oppression – so that not all Kenyans are at risk of living in poverty, and poverty manifests in different ways in different communities (AWID 2004: 6; Oluoko-Odingo 2009: 327–8). For similar reasons, Kenyan women's access to sexual and reproductive health services is differentiated according to location and class, as well as race and religion.

The narratives and networks of the development industry are related to those of humanitarian aid, charity and 'voluntourism', and sharply differentiated from resistant and revolutionary social movements. However, there is an area of overlap in which advocacy and activism that aims at social justice and transformation utilizes mechanisms in the development industry while not being part of it (Bernal and Grewal 2014: 3–6; Roy 2014). As activists and professionals, African women have provided leadership and innovation in many areas of development thought and practice, including as part of transnational feminist, women's and girls' and gender equality campaigns and organizations. When 'development' has been articulated and pursued outside the confines of global institutions and in opposition to imperialism, it has presented feminists and women's rights activists with opportunities to form transnational alliances that challenge the global networks of power embedded therein (Bose 2012: 69–71; Lewis 2005: 390–2; Mama 2011: e5–e7). As will become clear throughout this chapter, the YWCA, as a Christian membership organization, is more similar to African feminist interventions in development, not a development agency; but ultimately, it is neither. I refer to the YWCA as doing 'gender work', to mark its position as an organization that declines the label 'feminist', and works 'on women's issues' in the gender and development (GAD) paradigm outlined in this chapter.

Development, as suggested above, requires a narrative of 'the African past' that supplies theoretical and empirical 'evidence' and examples of that which must be improved or abandoned. 'Africa' is constructed, homogenized and represented as hopeless, poor, huge, war-torn and so on in the popular Western imagination. This dominant representation of 'Africa' can be traced back to

Joseph Conrad's *Heart of Darkness* (1902). Chinua Achebe argues that Conrad imagined Africa 'as "the other world," the antithesis of Europe and therefore of civilization' (Achebe 2010: 1785). Indeed, the hegemonic Western vision of 'Africa' is of a homogeneous yet enormous territory that is filled only with that which is opposite to an idealized version of Europe – at one and the same time an exotic landscape full of wildlife and a desolate place full of poverty, war and 'harmful cultural traditions'. Kenyan writer Binyavanga Wainaina was moved to critique the persistence of these representations in his satirical essay 'How to Write about Africa', in which he sarcastically advised,

> In your text, treat Africa as if it were one country. It is hot and dusty with rolling grasslands and huge herds of animals and tall, thin people who are starving. Or it is hot and steamy with very short people who eat primates. Don't get bogged down with precise descriptions. Africa is big, fifty-four countries, 900-million people who are too busy starving and dying and warring and emigrating to read your book. (Wainaina 2005: 92)

Such representations of 'Africa' remain ubiquitous, raising the troubling question of how knowledge about 'Africa' is produced, disseminated and interpreted in a context characterized by such misrepresentations.[1] Edward Said's (1978) articulation of orientalism was partly premised on a similar question in relation to knowledge production about the Middle East and its relationship to the project of European identity construction. European processes of knowledge production and interrelated dynamics of identity formation, disciplinary traditions and institutional racism have forged both 'the Orient' and the monolithic 'Africa' in the Western imagination. This does not mean that the truth is in the reversal of this discourse, in which 'Africa' is idealized. As Desiree Lewis puts it, there has been a postcolonial tendency to reject 'the West' as a monolith and assert a reified 'Africanness' in terms of unchanging cultural and religious practices and norms (Lewis 2005: 384). This is problematic to the extent that it can serve to justify, romanticize and promote sexist or otherwise harmful practices and ideas under the guise that they are 'authentically' precolonial, and therefore anti-colonial (Lugones 2003: 156–9). African feminists have pointed out that it is possible and necessary to reject both home-grown and colonial misogyny and homophobia.

As a generalization, Kenyans have not enjoyed good access to sexual, reproductive and maternal health care and services. One of the most recent causes of this lack is the SAPs that were introduced in the 1980s, consisting of loans from the WB with conditions and advice attached to them by the IMF. Serving these institutions' overall remit of promoting 'global' economic stability and growth, but 'driven by the collective will of the G-7', SAPs required recipient states to reduce public spending, instead prioritizing loan repayments alongside other changes, including the privatization and removal or weakening of state controls over investment and trade (Stiglitz 2002: 14–17). In Kenya, SAPs became a direct cause of public health crises, as spending on health and other public services was decreased. Other impacts of SAPs, including high interest rates and the collapse of local production due to the availability of cheap imported goods, compounded existing processes of impoverishment (Rodney 2018: 190–2). The effects of SAPs were felt deeply at the personal level, as services disappeared and women took on the burden of meeting the gaps in social care, childcare and health care: 'When a national government is ordered to cut back expenditure ... it is *this* mother who cannot afford to send her child to school, and it is *this* mother who cannot prevent her child from dying' (Sewpaul 2005: 109, emphasis in the original). The gaps created by these interventions created a huge unmet need for health care, as well as education, to which churches and Christian organizations responded by taking on more responsibility for providing these (Gifford 2015; Hofer 2003; Kamaara 1999: 16–17; Sabar-Friedman 1996: 383).

Development, taken separately from its predominant expression in the development industry, offers a means of articulating and working towards ameliorating the material conditions in which people live. This project cannot be fully identified with the capitalist and colonial interests that I have outlined so far. It remains part of the vocabulary of many African scholars and activists despite the anti-imperial and anti-colonial critiques it has attracted (Rodney 2018: 2). The dilemmas of development centre not on whether it is desirable to for people to improve the material conditions in which they live but on the questions of who defines and makes those interventions, whether they lead to sustainable and desirable changes and who benefits from them. The concept of development, in the sense of growth, improvement and change, was deployed by Jomo Kenyatta's government in newly independent Kenya to attempt to solve many of the problems left behind by the now-departed colonial government. The conceptualization of 'development' in Kenya requires attention to the *harambee* philosophy introduced into political discourse by Kenyatta when he became prime minister in May 1963. *Harambee* (Kiswahili, which roughly translates as 'let us pull together') was a way to mobilize anti-colonial and nationalist sentiments towards 'developing' the country. Functioning somewhat like an informal means of taxation, *harambee* was a means for eliciting donations from individuals towards a project whose benefits would be shared by the community, and ultimately the nation as a whole. It was also a legitimizing discourse, framing state interventions as support for and facilitation of necessary projects such as building schools and roads, or installing power lines, and creating employment in the process (Maloba 2017: 249-50; Mbithi and Rasmusson 1977). The YWCA's sense of its activities as 'developing the country' mirrors the ways *harambee* was initially constructed as a nationalistic duty for individuals and grassroots organizations in the wake of colonial exploitation and destruction.

Harambee seems to have modified the relationships between churches and the state in Kenya during the first years after flag independence. In 1963, around 90 per cent of Kenya's schools, health services, vocational training programmes and development projects were run by the 'mainline' churches.[2] The government invited the churches to 'work alongside' the state in meeting the needs of a widely dispersed population in a country that lacked infrastructure – particularly by providing healthcare services. The Catholic and Protestant mission-planted churches responded positively and, initially, uncritically to this invitation (Sabar 2002: 68-9). Churches and women's groups participated in *harambee* projects, and partially incorporated the *harambee* philosophy into their own ways of working. The context of *harambee* is significant because it connected the concept of 'development' with postcolonial nationalism, and facilitated the continuation of Christian institutions' exercise of power in education and health in such a way that benefited the YWCA. For many people in Kenya the concept of *harambee* has remained a potent expression of public spirit and community action (Ngunjiri 2009: 14; Wane 2013: 98). Well into the 1990s, women's organizations in Kenya drew on the template provided by their historical participation in *harambee* (Udvardy 1998: 1757). *Harambee* was routinely used by women's groups as a method known to effectively 'mobiliz[e] women throughout Kenya, especially those in the rural areas' (Nzomo 1989: 10). Thus, the work of women's groups has often been incorporated into the development discourse that has structured large-scale social action in Kenya. The involvement of Kenyan women's groups in the discourse of *harambee* cemented their position in the constellation of non-state actors providing services and infrastructure, particularly in rural areas. Shifting attention within the development industry subsequently recentred women's organizations in 'developing countries' like Kenya as desirable partners for the achievement of various programmes with goals such as the 'empowerment' of women.

3.2 Welfare and development, 1965–2000

As the YWCA moved away from white leadership, its activities changed only slightly. The formation of the World YWCA and the expansion of the movement through British colonies connected the YWCA's concerns about urbanization and social change with colonial discourses of the 'civilizing mission'. A distinctive style of Christian maternalism that had developed during the first century of YWCA work all around the world persisted in Kenya, now broad enough to include middle-class African women. As the YWCA's former colonial identity was dropped, a new explanatory framework emerged to underwrite the YWCA's continuing involvement in the education, welfare and accommodation of young women: 'development'. This shifting motivation was led and materially supported in large part by the World YWCA, which had become increasingly 'NGO-ized' and became involved in development discourse. The YWCA, as a constituent member association of the World YWCA, was part of an international women's movement, which ran parallel to the influence of women- and gender-focused, technocratic interventions in development (Garner 2007). The YWCA adopted a position in line with the World YWCA's commitment to working with rural women, established since the 1947 World Council, to guide its welfare and development-oriented work (World YWCA 2007: 23). The World YWCA began explicitly to engage in the language of the development industry in the 1980s, when it established the Women and Development Fund for the material support of small-scale and participatory projects (Seymour-Jones 1994: 437). Throughout the latter half of the twentieth century, the World YWCA was formally included in several UN bodies, beginning with being granted Consultative Status at the UN Economic and Social Council (ECOSOC) in 1948. It has routinely participated in Commission on the Status of Women (CSW) meetings, and it was a prominent participant at UN meetings in Nairobi in 1985, Cairo in 1994 and Beijing in 1995. This focus supported Kenya YWCA's long-standing concern with women's experiences of rural poverty, interventions in which comprised a range of highly practical projects of the sort typically considered under the label 'welfare'. These were largely translated into a development framework by the end of the century, under the YWCA's focus on 'economic empowerment' (Abok 2004: 91). The specific goals and interests to which these programmes responded were without question driven by YWCA staff and members.

3.2a Women's welfare, 1964–78

The beginning of this era was characterized by significant changes inaugurated by Kenya's independence from Britain and Jomo Kenyatta's premiership until his death in 1978.[3] The YWCA maintained a familiar range of programmes and activities for about decade after independence. During this time the World YWCA was particularly focused on supporting YWCAs in newly independent African countries, including Kenya (Seymour-Jones 1994: 136–234). In the 1960s and early 1970s, the YWCA's activities were characterized by a continuing commitment to a vision established in the 1950s. Its activities shifted slightly in their inclusion of African women, but still centred on picnics, netball, arts and crafts and Bible study, alongside cookery classes and adult literacy programmes. Its vocational training schools in Mombasa and Limuru now addressed an increase in youth unemployment. The courses they offered in 'domestic science', dressmaking and secretarial skills were very popular, attracting hundreds of applicants for its one- or two-year programmes aimed at school-leavers (Sheffield and Diejomoah 1972: 3).

The National Council of Women of Kenya (NCWK) was founded in 1964 to replace the colonial-era, white-dominated Convention of Women's Societies and coordinate the efforts of the women's movement (Oduol and Kabira 1995: 201). The YWCA was a member of both. However, the NCWK and other women's organizations were relatively quiet during the 1960s and 1970s, with no 'significant women's voice' heard during this time (Nzomo 1993: 136). The YWCA's response to rural women's poverty began in the 1960s with a focus on increasing women's income and sustainability at the household level, for example, by facilitating beekeeping. In urban areas, the YWCA introduced childcare in the form of subsidized nursery schools for the benefit of working mothers. By 1975, local concerns about rural women's experiences of poverty were reinforced by the World YWCA, which expressed its interest in supporting 'rural development' at its annual World Council meeting that year (Abok 2004: 91). The leaders of the women's movement the 1970s were 'generally elite and urban' but they were not completely removed from the realities of rural women's lives – not least because 'the rural areas were where [their] mothers and sisters still lived' (Maathai 2008: 120–4). Through its growing branch network, the YWCA was not as distinctly separate from the grassroots as some of the other Nairobi-based organizations. The YWCA offered agricultural training programmes to aid women to cultivate subsistence crops, and disseminated information about nutrition to help the many families who were finding it increasingly hard to survive on small-scale farming. It also reached out to rural women's groups, building hostels and community centres for the local branches, and establishing water supply and income-generation projects. Women's groups remained a major part of the YWCA, but their relationships with the national Association were minimal. They were the grassroots and the periphery where all the work was conducted, but their activities were not formalized, and were undertaken on the groups' initiative. Numerous healthcare programmes, nurseries and vegetable-growing projects were supported by funds from development agencies, indicating that any changes and compromises entailed in processes of formalization were expanding the YWCA's ability to intervene to alleviate women's experiences of poverty.

By the mid-1970s, the YWCA's activities were constrained by a lack of funding which manifested in a shortage of staff, and consequently the organization's programmes suffered. Members' complaints that the programmes were sometimes half-hearted and that their leaders lacked the necessary materials could only have made that reality more pressing for the National Headquarters staff, as the YWCA continued to rely on income from membership fees. After Kenyatta's government had effectively established single-party rule, it created the Women's Bureau in 1975. This was partly in response to the UN Decade for Women, 1975–85, which brought the final Conference of the Women's Decade to Nairobi in 1985. As a branch of government, the Women's Bureau was given the responsibility of coordinating the activities of all the women's groups in the country, a remit that completely undermined the work of the NCWK. The Women's Bureau performed the same tasks as NCWK, but on behalf of the government, to allow the state to closely monitor the activities of the women's movement (Nzomo 1993: 137). The mid-1970s thus represented the real beginning of the 'NGO-ization' of the YWCA, and of the other large institutions of the Kenyan women's movement (Omosa 1995: 78–80; Wipper 1995: 183–5). From this time on, the YWCA's activities increasingly tended to be highly formal programmatic interventions, with specific aims and objectives, informed by research, and supported by donors and partner organizations. The 1975 conference also inaugurated the height of women in development ('WID') discourse, as the development industry acted on the reformist imperative of dominant strands of Western feminism. Women in 'developing' countries were consciously reframed from their previous status as 'needy beneficiaries' to 'productive members of society' (Miller and Razavi 1995: 1–3). Women were thus approached as targets for development on the basis of the economic efficiency of doing so.

3.2b 'Self-reliance', 1979-89

These years were marked by the authoritarian regime led by President Daniel arap Moi from 1978 until 2002, who strengthened Kenya African National Union's (KANU's) hold on Kenya as a single-party state. The repressive atmosphere cultivated by Moi in the 1980s severely constrained the activities of the women's movement, civil society and social justice organizations throughout the country. Moi presented himself as 'a God-fearing leader', reflecting and reinforcing the utility of a public Christian identity and leaning on an implicit conflation of Kenyan state authority with 'Christian' morality (Bakari 2013: 17-18; Gez 2018: 99-101). The Moi government stuck to the position that the Kenyatta government before it had established: that women in Kenya were 'not discriminated against', and it continued to use the Women's Bureau to monitor and curtail the activities of organizations it could not control (Nzomo 1993: 136-7). MYW was absorbed into the state by being co-opted as the 'women's wing' of KANU, which took upon itself the power to censor, define or reject any MYW activity, locally or nationally. Its interference included rigging MYW's leadership contests to ensure the 'right' women were elected (Aubrey 1997: 71-9; House-Midamba 1990: 43). This tendency has been identified as 'femocracy', in which a combination of colonial and postcolonial patriarchal leadership styles has been able to instrumentalize women's groups in African contexts. A femocratic regime is one in which elite men monopolize power by 'exploit[ing] the commitments of the international movement for greater gender equality' to appoint their wives and daughters to, for example, positions in MYW, disenfranchising ordinary women in the process (Mama 1995: 41). For the YWCA, the worst effects of the Moi era's repression of women's organizations were avoided partly by foregrounding its Christian identity and its relationship to the churches, rather than its status as part of the women's movement. The YWCA, as an active partner of NCCK, regularly participated in its training workshops, including 'family life education', and partnered with it to work on specific projects.[4]

By the 1970s, African women occupied positions once reserved for colonizer women at all points in the structure of the YWCA, but the structure itself remained relatively unchanged from the 1950s. Mrs Mugo retired in 1981 after seventeen years in post as NGS, and Alice Mwajuma Abok was hired in 1983 as a member of staff at Mombasa Branch, responsible for programmes. Trained as a teacher, within a couple of years she had been promoted to work as the National Programmes Coordinator at the YWCA's headquarters in Nairobi. Dr Abok was only the third member of paid staff working at the National level, in addition to the NGS and an accountant (Dr Abok, interview, 2012). Hiring Dr Abok to this position reflected an institutionalization of the YWCA's shift away from welfare, towards development pursued through programmatic interventions. However, the YWCA continued to work with women's groups through programmes that had begun in the 1970s under the banner of 'rural development'. The localized focus of the branches on the needs of women within their areas allowed the Association to develop and support a diverse and context-specific range of activities, such as the provision of materials to reroof houses, and organizing lectures on agricultural techniques. The majority of the centrally administered programmes (those organized through the headquarters and implemented at two or more branches) focused on employability and life-skills training for impoverished women, for example through improving literacy or teaching vocational skills like dressmaking.

Other dimensions of the YWCA's work deserve a brief mention, including the splitting of the YWCA's presence in Nairobi in 1985. The compound on Mamlaka Road was maintained as the national headquarters, but the Nairobi Branch was redefined as a separate entity, and relocated at its own premises in Eastlands on the other side of the city. This programme of expansion included a new branch in Kisii, established in 1986, and a setting up a holiday and conference centre at Mombasa Branch (Abok 2004: 92). Between 1981 and 1986 under the repressive regime of Idi Amin, Uganda YWCA was the only women's organization that was able to operate in that country. During this period the YWCA cooperated with, and provided material support to, its Ugandan sister organization by delivering supplies via night-time border crossings (Seymour-Jones 1994: 224). The political situation in Kenya was by no means as severe as in Uganda, but the atmosphere was nonetheless repressive (James 1990: 93, interview with Micere Mugo).

The shift from WID to GAD can be illustrated in the contrasts and continuities between two YWCA projects in the 1980s: water and FGM. A water and sanitation project known as 'Maguna B' began in 1976 when a women's group in Rwanyange, Meru, decided to create a water channel to bring fresh water to the community, hoping to reduce the workload associated with daily water collection from four kilometres away. The plan responded to local realities when a herd of elephants destroyed the channel, so the women's group decided instead to install a pipe to connect the village directly to the source. The involvement of the YWCA was facilitated by the Branch Secretary of Meru YWCA, Harriet Gichiva, who lived in the area to be served by the proposed pipe. This cooperation starting in 1985 drew the attention of a staff member from the

World YWCA and Kenya YWCA's Programmes Secretary, who assisted in the formalization of the 'Water Committee' tasked with putting together a formal project proposal. A University of Nairobi professor produced a 'feasibility study', which was successful in aiding the World YWCA to secure donor funding for the project from international agencies. This funding covered 90 per cent of the costs, while the remainder was supplemented with significant community contributions raised partly through *harambee*, as well as a sponsored walk, raising a total of $10,000 (10 per cent of costs). In 1987, eight years after the women's group initiated the project, construction work began on the pipe, with portions of the manual labour undertaken by volunteers from the community.

This success inspired the women's group to pursue further community improvements, including the construction of two ventilated improved pit ('VIP') latrines for the local primary school, and others installed them at their homes. By 1992 the Maguna B project had provided water and sanitation for a small community that previously had neither. It became one of the YWCA's success stories, one which it expanded by replicating it in other communities (Owiti 1992: 85; Seymour-Jones 1994: 434–5). The power relations illustrated by this project are instructive; the YWCA became involved in and assisted in formalizing a project that was already underway at the initiative of a local women's group. The World YWCA acted as a facilitator, connecting the women's group with experts who could assist them in accessing funding and to plan the project in a professional manner. Clearly, in the late twentieth century the YWCA was responding to the locally defined needs of women at the grassroots, thanks in part to being in and of those communities, and being invested to their well-being. However, given the level of community involvement and the leadership of the women's group in fundraising, planning and organizing labour, it seems possible that the Maguna B project could have been completed without the YWCA's involvement.

The YWCA began running anti-FGM workshops in affected regions of Kenya in the 1980s, but it was the late 1990s before any first large-scale projects were attempted in order to address the issue. The YWCA first identified the problems surrounding practices of what it referred to at that time as 'women circumcision' in 1980. The minutes of the National Programmes Committee from that year note that the 'circumcision of women ... [was] ... again rampant in some tribes'. Whether or not female genital-cutting practices had previously been thought to be eliminated, it is clear that the YWCA had to some degree bought into the narrative of 'progress' associated with the abandonment of the practice. Observing its presence in some communities was therefore interpreted in terms of a regression. The minutes record that the YWCA considered the 'sensitivity' of this issue to present a particular challenge: 'We are trying to make them join the YWCA so that we can educate them on this subject slowly ... this is not an easy issue.' In 1984, former National YWCA Chairperson Wanjiku Chiuri drafted a research paper that was circulated throughout the branch network for staff and members to have their input. The result was an anti-'women circumcision' information leaflet that was translated into local languages for distribution at the grassroots level. National Headquarters allocated a small sum of money to develop and deploy educational projects on the topic with a particular focus on northern Kenya, where the practice was deemed to be more prevalent. The YWCA framed its work on FGM as a point of continuity with the international women's movement, as international attention had been drawn to FGM at the UN Women's Decade Mid-Decade Conference in Copenhagen, attended by representatives of the YWCA. The YWCA was evidently navigating a continued commitment to grassroots women's organizing, while seeking to make interventions from its vantage point as a national and internationally connected NGO. The Maguna B project received support from the World YWCA in part because it aligned with its established interest in rural women's development. FGM was identified by the YWCA through its contact with and embeddedness in local communities, but both projects were facilitated by the rise and visibility of women as legitimate targets for the development industry's attention.

3.2c Gender and development, 1990–2000

In the thirty-five years between the 'multiracial' moment and the end of the twentieth century, the YWCA changed considerably. It weathered numerous changes to the Kenyan social and political context in part by adapting itself to meeting the needs of women at the grassroots. However, it also remained formal and bureaucratic in its structure, and this strong institutional framework eased its transition into gender work on the periphery of the development industry. During the second period of Moi's presidency, from 1992 to 2002, the YWCA was defined by four major concerns: physical expansion, the reorientation of the Association's activities towards development, financial sustainability and the beginnings of a more comprehensive approach to sex education including HIV. It was in the mid-1980s that HIV emerged in Kenya, and elsewhere in Africa, and was met with denial, confusion and accusations. President Moi declared that there were insignificant numbers of HIV infections in Kenya, and claimed that AIDS was the fault of immoral westerners, especially 'homosexuals' (Booth

2004: 51–2). Once the disease was recognized, government response was slow, and the development industry soon addressed itself to the issue.

The 1990s began with historic elections that returned Kenya to multiparty politics. The YWCA participated alongside the churches and many other civil society organizations in the campaign for the repeal of Section 2A of the Kenyan constitution, which had made Kenya a *de jure* one-party state. In particular, during the active years of this campaign between 1988 and 1991, the YWCA's contribution was running civic education for women throughout the country (Oduol and Kabira 1995: 200–1). The programme consisted of 'Women/Youth Democratisation Seminars', the main objective of which was to 'educate women and youth on their rights as voters', undertaken in partnership with Federation of Women Lawyers Kenya (FIDA-K), Association of African Women for Research and Development (AAWORD), the League of Kenya Women Voters (LKWV) and the NCCK, among others. The expansion of the YWCA's branch network was achieved through establishing two new branches, first in Tana River county in 1992 and then in Siaya in 1996 (Abok 2004: 92). Dr Abok was appointed as NGS in 1996, and under her leadership in the latter half of the 1990s, the organization invested further in major infrastructural improvements, primarily the expansion of its hostels in central Nairobi.[5] The expansion and improvement of the hostel buildings was intended to 'develop' the YWCA by increasing its overall income. Thus, their purpose had shifted from being the primary focus of the YWCA to a source of income to support its other work.

In the 1990s, the YWCA also completed its move away from 'welfare' projects, towards 'development' programmes (Joyce, interview, 2012; Edith, interview, 2012). 'Welfare' was the language the YWCA used to refer to its programmes focusing on the provision of 'shelter, food, water, clothing, health', and the general material amelioration of women's lives that had formed the basis of its cooperative projects with women's groups at the grassroots since the 1960s (Abok 2004: 93). Internationally, 'welfare' discourse gave way to 'development' with the articulation of WID during the 1970s (Miller and Razavi 1995: 3–4). However, the YWCA sought to maintain welfare projects alongside development programmes, and introduced a distinction between the two approaches within its own work, such as Maguna B which was ongoing throughout the first half of the decade. Welfare incorporated efforts to meet women's daily needs, while development was considered to denote any large-scale interventions. The oversight of these programmes was largely transferred to the branches rather than necessarily being coordinated and administered by National Headquarters staff. The considerable overlap of content between earlier welfare projects and the development activities of the 1990s indicates that the distinction between welfare and development might not be as straightforward as my research participants sometimes implied. The WID to GAD shift in development was the result of debates within the development industry about what development should entail. Liberal feminist interventions had put 'women' into focus as valuable targets for development, but a subsequent change in language to 'gender' represented a reconstruction of this area of focus as a 'wing' of the development industry, enabling processes of 'mainstreaming' gender (Harcourt 2009: 28). Switching from language of women to gender seems to have been a reflection of feminist critiques of how the development industry approached 'difference'. Under GAD, rather than explicit attempts to impose Western norms, local and 'specific patriarchal structures, institutions and ideologies' were accepted on two fronts (Wilson 2012: 49). First, because they constituted the conditions under which women were understood to be efficient 'productive members of society' and thereby represent a rational investment of development funds. Second, that cultural change of the type pursued by feminists is, by definition, 'alien' to developing countries; for example, that 'concepts of emancipation are always external impositions' (Wilson 2012: 49). This has the effect of fixing cultural difference and assuming that dominant narratives represent the entirety of women's engagements with their social context.

In 1992, the World YWCA defined development as 'forward' and 'upward' movement, and 'the redistribution and equalisation of power' (Seymour-Jones 1994: 449). The World YWCA Deputy General Secretary in 1993 is reported to have characterized the dilemma of development for the YWCA as: how 'to move away from [culture and tradition] to what we call development' while remaining respectful of programme beneficiaries' existing practices and beliefs (Seymour-Jones 1994: 436). 'Progress' and the 'upward' movement, here, are strongly reminiscent of the colonial YWCA's perspective, and suggest leaving the past behind in favour of the methods, values and objectives promoted by 'modern' development 'experts'. A tension is clear in the YWCA's vision of development: it affirmed its commitment to participatory approaches and explicitly rejected 'top-down' development interventions, while relying on the same binary conceptual framework of modernity/tradition that justified colonial racism and missionary interventions.

The meaning of the term 'development' was something Edith engaged with directly when I interviewed her: 'As a development organisation, we are developing the individual, we are developing the country, we are developing the organisation itself' (Edith, interview, 2012). These three senses of development are evident in the YWCA's archival records from this period. 'Developing' individual women has in many ways been a constant theme of YWCA work since the first iteration of the organization in Britain in the mid-nineteenth century. In the early years of the YWCA, the emphasis of education, training and social activities was to 'develop' young women in culturally specific gender-, race- and class-appropriate ways. By the 1990s, the YWCA's focus on 'developing' women had expanded to encompass notions of individual human rights as measures of values such as 'dignity' and 'empowerment' (Abok 2004: 93). A slightly different perspective was offered by Joyce, who suggested that the YWCA's turn away from 'welfare' and towards 'development' aligned with the shift from 'women and development' to 'gender and development' in the 1980s (Joyce, interview, 2012). In development studies, this shift is typically understood as a reflection of gender conceptualized in terms of social power relations, thereby casting doubt on the efficacy of initiatives that sought to simply 'add women and stir' (Okech 2009: 36). With the shift to the language of development, and the eventual lifting of Moi's repression of women's organizations, since the early 1990s women's organizations in Kenya have had the opportunity to partner with Western donors, which further professionalized and NGO-ized many Kenyan women's organizations as agents of development.

The YWCA could not stage interventions for social change purely on the basis of its members' shared understanding of Christianity, or its assessment of the harm caused by particular gender norms and practices. It also responded to the interests of donors and partners, and the World YWCA, within the overarching context of Christian expectations of the scope of voluntary social action. An increase in reliance on external donors necessitated a new emphasis on producing substantive reports of the Association's programme activities and the standardization of its practices for the purposes of 'accountability'. The YWCA's newly established focus on 'development' led it to begin microfinance programmes, through which the Association facilitated the provision of loans to women's groups. Narrowly 'moral' questions like controversial faith issues and broader ethical ones like the influence of donors were engaged within the organization's repertoire of narratives of Christian identity. By 1993 the YWCA had become increasingly concerned with ensuring its financial stability in view of the difficulty of securing enough suitable funding from donors and partner organizations. The tendency for donor funding to be conditional meant that securing additional income would increase the Association's independence. The situation was complicated by the reluctance of the YWCA to enter partnerships with donors whose values might clash with its Christian ethos, and the similar reluctance of some donor organizations to support a faith-based organization like the YWCA (Wandia, interview, 2012). Any increase in the availability of funds was intended to be spread across all its major areas of work, as well as contributing to the ongoing infrastructural improvements and raising staff salaries. As an organization based on the participation of fee-paying members, the primary means through which income could be increased was through the recruitment of new members, and therefore this became a major focus of the YWCA's energies throughout the decade.

As the HIV epidemic worsened, it significantly increased the burdens on Kenya's healthcare services. The state relied on charitable and church-based health projects to cover gaps in its own provision of health care, following a pattern that has persisted since the colonial era (Sabar 2002). The YWCA was beginning to place more focus on sexual health, including HIV prevention. In 1999, the YWCA and YMCA organized a joint reproductive health programme in which thirty young people from both organizations participated. They came up with three recommendations aimed at guiding future interventions in the sex education of Kenyan youth. These were 'parents educate your children about sexuality', 'abortion: think twice' and 'talk to the youth about sex'. These overlapping themes reflect and reinforce the impression of sexuality as a taboo topic that was beginning to be dragged into mainstream health discourse in light of the HIV epidemic. In common with youth demands in other contexts, these recommendations emphasize bringing the youth into a conversation instead of preaching to them. Perhaps the most significant event for my account of the YWCA was Vera Harley's decision to write and publish a 'history and anecdotes' of the organization in 1995. I return to analyse this intervention and its wide-ranging effects in detail in Chapter 6.

3.3 Postcolonial feminist critique of sexuality in development

HIV and AIDS became enormously significant dimensions of the development industry's focus on Africa, gender and sexuality. Responses to the epidemic have hinged on the established narratives of racialized and pathologized sexualities of the colonial furore over 'prostitutes' (Wilson 2012: 97–115). Simultaneously, women's bodies maternal health and FGM have been addressed as mainstream 'gender' objectives within development, which has increasingly foregrounded 'choice' as a major component of women's empowerment and gender equality. Women were considered at higher risk of HIV infection than men, and tended to contract the virus at an earlier average age. Structural issues contributed to this vulnerability: widespread poverty and economic dependence, lack of access to education and health care, the prevalence of sexualized violence against women and girls and gender roles that reduced women's sexual agency (Kamau 2009; Kemboi, Onkware and Ntabo 2011).

Since the mid-1990s, the overriding international context of development interventions in reproductive health has been the 1994 International Conference on Population and Development (ICPD) in Cairo, which resulted in what is known as the 'Cairo Consensus'. The Cairo Consensus achieved a significant change in approaches to development, beginning a tendency of 'recognizing women's reproductive autonomy and human rights' rather than focusing on population (Garita 2014: 1). The Beijing Platform for Action, agreed soon after the Cairo Consensus in 1995, asserts that women have the right 'to have control over and decide freely and responsibly on matters related to their sexuality' (United Nations 1996: para 96). These two shifts in the mid-1990s equally generated support for feminist organizing on SRHR and catalysed a 'conservative' religious backlash against it (Balchin 2008; Harcourt 2009: 41–50; Horn 2012; Sjørup 1997). Internationally, the majority of funding for SRHR initiatives under the auspices of the development industry is provided by the Global Fund to Fight AIDS, TB and Malaria, the UN Family Planning Authority, the WB, UKAID, USAID and various philanthropic foundations (Garita 2014: 2–3; Seims 2011). This increases the risk that sexual health interventions are, and are perceived to be, launched primarily to complement the foreign policy and economic interests of the G-7 states.

Much contemporary development discourse treats sexuality and reproduction according to the precedent set by colonial interventions (Pigg and Adams 2005: 12–13). African women's social and cultural roles continue to be viewed by development agencies and white feminists – misled by Eurocentric conceptualizations of gender – as uniformly mired in 'archaic' traditions (Aniekwu 2006: 145; Mohanty 1988; Oyěwùmí 1997). This tendency is intimately linked to and reinforced by the maintenance of a distinction between 'tradition' and 'modernity' in order to define and defend the latter as a central element of white Western identity (Pigg 2005: 49). Sexuality and health, as writ upon the bodies of African people(s), have been a focal point for this distinction between traditional Africanness and modern Europeanness, as illustrated in Chapter 2. Among the consequences of this dynamic is the development industry's perpetuation of a largely 'biologized' conception of African peoples' bodies (Arnfred 2004: 66–7; Pigg 2005: 43). This has in turn led to the preponderance of medical and/or instrumental representations of/approaches to African women's sexual lives, to the neglect of feminist politics, emotion, desire, pleasure and the 'erotic' in Audre Lorde's (1984) sense (Ahlberg et al. 2009: 107, Machera 2003: 160-3). Many feminist critics have argued that development has translated feminist demands for sexual health and rights into a focus on 'maternal healthcare' in a way that depoliticizes SRHR; for instance, the Millennium Development Goals reduce the Cairo Consensus to simply 'improving maternal health' (Garita 2014: 2). In fact, decisions around funding, providing, promoting and researching maternal health and sexual health are inherently political.

Rachel Spronk (2005) has adopted a deliberately pleasure- and person-centred attitude towards the study of sexuality. She describes her understanding of sexuality as 'relational' as opposed to 'instrumental' in her research with young professional women in Nairobi. She writes,

> When it comes to women's sexuality, much HIV/AIDS-related research tends to place sexuality in a negative perspective: seeing sexuality as the 'problem' that results in HIV infection. Moreover, sexuality tends to be used in an instrumental and self-evident way ... [which results in] defining African women's sexuality as not just complex but above all, flawed. (Spronk 2005: 269)

Spronk's research focuses instead on women's 'sexual biographies', allowing her to centre their experiences of 'feeling sexy' and their negotiations with contradictory sexual norms of respectable virginity, 'modern' urban femininity and reproduction/motherhood (Spronk 2005: 270-6). The instrumental and scientistic definition of African women's sexual lives has been central to the international medical response to HIV on the continent and elsewhere. Indeed, European and North American medical and scientific progress and the scientistic epistemologies on which they are based are not merely coincidental with the colonization of Africa. Scientific research has been the complicit partner of colonization, depending on it for a steady supply of objects for study (Booth 2004: 83-7). By objectifying African women as vectors of disease, colonial attitudes presaged later medical-scientific isolation of African women's sexual behaviour as a site for intervention to control population growth, the spread of HIV and other sexually transmitted infections (STIs) and reinforce Western self-perception as modern and benevolent, through the distribution (and sometimes enforced use) of contraceptive technologies.

The continuing relevance of the colonial past, often mediated through the concepts of urbanization and instrumentalization, has been particularly evident in HIV research and prevention programmes. HIV researchers have studied

Nairobi's sex workers for decades, but their research is based on a number of assumptions which are racist, sexist and perpetuate a colonial hierarchy, globally and locally. Some developmental/medical narratives still represent the spread of HIV in Kenya in ways practically identical to the colonial discourse by which responsibility for the health of the colony was placed on the 'prostitutes' of Nairobi, as discussed above (Booth 2004: 88). Nairobi's sex workers have been studied because medical researchers have identified them as a 'reservoir' of HIV and other STIs, just as the colonial government identified 'prostitutes' as the primary source of syphilis in the region (Booth 2004: 27–8). Sex workers are represented as the transmitters of HIV infection to their (presumed male) clients, while how these women themselves became infected is not considered (Booth 2004: 87). Moreover, in striking conformity with the well-worn and oft-critiqued virgin/whore dichotomy, this story divides Kenya's women into two discrete categories: rural wives and mothers whose husbands may infect them with HIV and urban 'prostitutes' from whom they were infected. The likelihood that sex workers are also parents, or that married women may have sex with people other than their husbands, is ignored (Booth 2004: 88–99; NEPHAK, BHESP, KESWA and GNP+ 2015). The narrative conveys an implicit moral judgement about these two kinds of women, with a putative chain of cause and effect in which HIV is transmitted from sex worker to married man to his wife to her baby (Booth 2004: 105–7). Sex workers are thus constructed as a homogeneous bloc which poses a threat to the health of the nation and future generations.

This understanding of sex work and its relationship to the HIV epidemic goes hand in hand with the popular (and, I emphasize, inaccurate) stereotype of African men's sexuality as rampant – their behaviour somehow beyond the influence of either medical intervention or their sexual partners, presumed, of course, to be girls and women (Brouwers and Pala 2004: 14; Lewis 2011: 203–5). Under this understanding of the HIV epidemic, no interventions would target men to consistently use condoms, no sex workers would be approached as parents and HIV is fundamentally a moral problem resulting from sexual behaviour, such as some women's decision to be 'prostitutes' (Booth 2004: 106–7). As a result, it is 'African women' – constituted as a homogeneous group, as Chandra Mohanty noted of the construction of 'third world women' (Mohanty 1988: 66) – who are targeted for SRHR interventions by development agencies. For example, Esther Wangari observes that African women's fertility is often scapegoated as the cause of poverty (2002: 303). Poor women in Kenya are routinely assumed to be irresponsible and ignorant due to a lack of education, with various interventions justified on the grounds that African women's fertility requires externally imposed 'control' – for example, to slow population growth (Wangari 2002: 309, see also Harcourt 2009: 56–60). Similarly, women's apparent inability to insist on their male partners using condoms, or to prevent their babies being infected with HIV, is conceived as the cause of the HIV epidemic; in mainstream development discourse, African women's sexual lives are positioned as problems to be solved.

Wandia identified the instrumentalization of African women's reproductive health needs, as she described pressure on the YWCA and other organizations to promote a certain type of contraceptive technology:

> They are talking about population and ... push to show you that this contraceptive is what is good for you, and then sell it to Kenya as a market ... people are not interested in that type of contraceptive, and yet so much money has gone into that. So we are being used as a market, as a market for some foreign companies ... This contraception has been bought [but] these women don't even know about it, [so we ask] is there another cheaper and different way? We can still communicate the same message, without insisting that that has to be the contraceptive they must use. (Wandia, interview, 2012)

Wandia clearly articulates her sense of development as an avenue through which 'foreign' companies could make money out of the Kenyan 'market', alluding to the promotion by development agents of long-acting reversible contraceptives Norplant and Depo Provera (Bradley, Dwyer and Levin 2001). This unease about the vested interests of global institutions and corporations intervening particularly in sexual health is commonly seen in Anglophone Christian and nationalist discourses around the continent. This sense of suspicion about the real motives behind these interventions is reinforced by the fact that international structures and the legacies of colonization continue to impoverish African nations, preserve the power and wealth of the Global North and restrict access to anti-retroviral drugs (ARVs) and other pharmaceuticals (Oxfam 2012). Insufficient and unreliable supplies of condoms (Ahlberg et al. 2009: 114), lack of access to sexual and maternal health care within an overstretched and underfunded health service (FIDA-K and CRR 2007; Griffith 2014) and repeated abuses of power by healthcare professionals (CRR 2010) have thus combined to encourage a general mistrust of reproductive technologies as risky, and as instruments of imperialist control of African lives. These phenomena contribute to increased numbers of HIV infections developing into AIDS, among other effects, all of which demonstrate how global power dynamics are played out on the most intimate, personal scale.

3.4 Summary: Sexuality and Christianity in development

The tangled relationships between the state, women's movement, churches and development organizations in Kenya in the mid- to late-twentieth century created the context in which some SRHR issues became particularly 'controversial' for the YWCA. The conceptual frame and the practices I have outlined are generally reliant on, and have the effect of maintaining connections between whiteness, modernity and beneficence established under colonization and mission. After flag independence, Kenya's churches have continued to provide healthcare services, including running hospitals and providing specific care for people with HIV and AIDS (Gifford 2009: 47–9). Paul Gifford has argued that as a result of Christian institutions' aid and development work in Kenya, churches have become 'secularized', that is, somewhat separated from questions of faith, worship and salvation (Gifford 2009: 50; Gifford 2015: 103; Sabar-Friedman 1996: 393). However, Christian social action in Kenya is different in churches and organizations aligned with different denominations. Many AICs, Evangelical and Pentecostal churches do not seem to be 'secularized' in this way, despite many offering a range of similar services (Gitau 2018; Parsitau 2009). Ecumenical organizations, like the YWCA, have positioned their Christianity as justification for involvement in social action and development projects, even if the connection between them is complicated, as I discuss in Chapters 4 and 5. The outline of development I have offered in this chapter provides grounds for questioning the implicit assertion that development is 'secular'. The explicit motivation for development throughout the twentieth century rested on aspects of long-standing Christian and colonial assumptions and norms out of which it partially grew (Carbonnier 2013: 1; Salemink 2015: 38–40; Selinger 2004: 528). This is the case for the YWCA, which was explicitly established on the basis of an obligation for Christians to intervene in (perceived) contemporary social problems, as an expression of the social gospel (Izzo 2018: 46–51). However, the connection between secularization and 'development' does seem to describe YWCA's sense of becoming, or risking becoming, 'less' Christian as a result of its SRHR programmes, as I discuss in further detail in Chapters 5 and 6. Such concerns seem similar to the anxieties generated by narratives that position modernization and urbanization as necessarily morally compromising.

As I have already suggested, 'family life education' and sex education have been a concern of the YWCA since at least 1968. At that time, the YWCA's National Programmes Committee minutes record that staff 'all saw the need' for programmatic intervention in sexual health through education but were unsure of 'the best way to go about it'. From these first instances of YWCA attention to sex education, in the 1960s and 1970s, progress was initially quite slow. It would not be until the mid-1980s that serious attention was given to the idea of sex education on a large scale. In 1986 it ran a 'Family Life Education workshop' in partnership with the International Planned Parenthood Foundation (IPPF). The language the YWCA used to name this area of intervention seems significant, and it has changed over time reflecting shifts in its position in relation to imperatives of Christianity and development. From the 1960s to the 1990s, the YWCA used the terminology of 'family planning' and 'family life education', suggesting a continuity with this orientation towards integrating explicit moral messages about sexuality into its projects. The language of 'youth reproductive health' emerged as part of a wider effort towards 'Young Women's Health and Integrated Services' programme in the mid-1990s, funded by the Centre for Development and Population Activities (CEDPA) with a grant of $25,000. This was followed by a 'Youth Health and Sexuality Management Counselling' training workshop for YWCA Programmes staff, in an attempt to facilitate the 'integration of family planning into YWCA's activities'. These semantic changes are in line with the shifts in development and transnational feminist discourse brought about by the Cairo Consensus, as described above (Garita 2014: para 1). After this point, gender work was cemented as a primary focus for the YWCA, and it started talking in terms of 'reproductive health' with only a couple of instances of 'family planning' in the archival record, which was in turn replaced by SRHR in about 2005.

Since at least the 1970s, 'family life education' has been a popular euphemism for sex education. It typically implies a more holistic approach incorporating broad themes of personal, social and health education. Demonstrating this dual meaning, in Kenya the NCCK has been among the most prominent proponents and critics of family life education from a Christian point of view. On its website in 2014, it described its family life education as addressing 'the deteriorating condition of the family institution … [which NCCK has] identified as one of the most critical challenges facing Christians … The [NCCK] will therefore facilitate communities with information and education to enable them build better families' (NCCK 2014). Thus, the NCCK identifies the need for 'family life education' but then suggests the wrong kind of education has directly contributed to the 'deterioration' of the family (Kangara 2007: 9–11). It is not always made clear what constitutes a threat to the fabric of the family; but 'family' is so deeply connected with gender and sexual norms that are used to mark social changes in the status of women and sexual minorities. In contemporary Christian discourse in Kenya, social change continues to be associated with urbanization, in continuity with earlier colonial discourses linking migration to the city for work with the breakdown of gender norms and the relationships they sustain. The risks of urban life are contrasted with an idealized rural idyll in which 'African' traditions ameliorated by a non-specific, Christian, monogamous, heteropatriarchy in perfect isolation from non-normative sexualities, abortion, HIV, consumerism and mainstream media. When connected to women, this set of associations coalesces in the 'mother Africa' figure in moral narratives of respectable femininity (Ligaga 2020). As such, anxiety about urbanization can be an 'African' version of respectability politics, played out on a stage set by postcolonial critique.

A recent description of this discourse in use within a Christian community in Nairobi is given by Wanjiru Gitau (2018) in her discussion of a Nairobi-based Mavuno megachurch. Mavuno's relationship curricula, named *Ndoa* (marriage) and *Lea* (parenting), were conceived as responses to the 'high rates of divorce and poorly parented children' among middle-class Nairobians (Gitau 2018: 60). The church apparently attributes these trends to a generational shift it observes particularly among urban millennial university graduates defined by the dislocation and 'social homelessness' in which they grew up.[6] This generation is thought to be more likely to participate in a consumerist lifestyle enabled by urban life, with an attendant set of materialist, individualist values that encourage 'moral laxity' and 'promiscuous living'. In echoing some of the same concerns as evangelical organizations which identify 'secular values' and non-Christian practices as a threat to 'the family', the NCCK also signals attention to the recent, marginal gains made by sexual minorities in Kenya in the promulgation of the new constitution in 2010. This is line with the trend many observers have noted of the rhetorical use of the 'family' in the construction and defence of (hetero-) nationalist projects in African contexts (Kaoma 2009; Lewis 2008a; Van Klinken 2014). Women who fall outside the boundaries of heteronormativity are not considered to be part of, or wish to have, a family; they are instead positioned as a 'threat' to the institution of the family, and are excluded from any expectation to need or want 'family life education'.

In the context of Kenyan discourses on women's sexuality, urbanization narratives identify the city and modernity with a range of 'new' threats, a concentration of temptations that are thought to encourage behaviours evaluated as immoral or sinful. The early YWCA's concern for the well-being of young women in Nairobi – articulated in terms of their vulnerability to the threats posed by being in the city unsupervised – parallels the perception of threat of 'secularization' that frames some Kenyan Christian commentators' association of urbanization with materialism, liberalism, individualism and Westernization (Getui 2003: 66–71; Shorter and Onyancha 1997: 123–6). This dichotomic thinking reinscribes rural, traditional home and community life as safe, authentic and moral by contrast. Despite the sociopolitical changes the region has witnessed in the intervening years, anxieties about urbanization and approaches dominated by instrumentalism have characterized the landscape of interventions surrounding sexual and reproductive health and rights in Kenya since the 1960s. Elements of the YWCA's programmes addressing HIV, FGM and sexual health more broadly represent continuations of this discourse.

In this chapter, I have addressed the nexus of imperialisms, Christianities and struggles for reproductive justice in Kenya with a methodological lens that reveals the construction of the tradition/modernity binary in narratives of Western progress. I reject 'the colonial medicalisation of African sexuality and [a] simultaneous reduction of its purpose to reproduction' (Tamale 2011: 16), and contest the instrumentalization and objectification of African women's bodies by white-feminist development projects, such as is characteristic of many international responses to 'population growth' and HIV (Adams and Pigg 2005; Arnfred 2004). The development discourse that emerged in the 1970s fixed African women to these roles in the Western imagination in order to motivate and justify various interventions aimed at 'empowerment' (Okech 2019: 12). The YWCA continues to rely on the material support of its partners and donors from the development industry, the global institutions of the ecumenical Christian movement and women's movements as well as within the women's movement in Kenya and transnationally across Africa. Thus, its activities cannot be considered to be representative of Kenyan Christian women's ethics, regardless of the representative decision-making procedures that are integrated into its structure and practices.

4

African, Christian, feminist? 2000–12

In this chapter I outline the YWCA's programmatic interventions during the period 2000 to 2012, with a focus on FGM, HIV and SRHR. This period was marked by myriad development industry and Christian institutional interventions into sexual health and family life, as well as recent moral panics over women's sex lives and non-normative sexualities in the overriding context of the HIV epidemic. The YWCA's gender work was refined and pursued through programmatic interventions under five 'thematic areas of focus': social empowerment, economic empowerment, health, HIV and justice, peace and human rights. The priorities and objectives of the YWCA reflect an ongoing concern for women and girls in impoverished rural and urban communities, as it has continued with welfare and development work that was already a well-established part of its repertoire. Notably, approximately 350 local women's groups were affiliated with the YWCA by 2011, and were mainly engaged in income-generation projects. In the latter part of this period the YWCA was extensively involved in implementing various projects to address issues related to sexual and maternal health, and microfinance and credit schemes, as well as women's engagement in national politics.

I consider the YWCA's interventions in each of these areas in terms of the ways they implicate different dimensions of its identity as a Christian women's organization that is involved in development. The YWCA's work on sexuality and reproduction at times aligns with, and at other times departs from, values that are widely considered to be 'African', 'traditional', 'Christian', 'Western' and 'secular'. The dominant narratives supporting a gender and development paradigm, for instance, imply a general affinity with feminism as outlined in Chapter 3, along with a rejection of 'traditional' norms and an antipathy towards religions for their role in reinforcing those norms. I show in this chapter that these dominant narratives connect identity x to ethical commitment y. This is significant because of the persuasive and explanatory power exerted by these narratives of identity and associated ethical positions. The alignments and departures within these narratives generate tensions for the YWCA in its gender work, as it responds to the hegemonies of Christian institutions and the development industry.

To understand the effect this positioning has on the YWCA, I critically read a range of texts associated with its programmatic interventions, including internal and external reports, educational leaflets and the minutes of National Programmes Committee meetings. These representations of the YWCA's interventions are assembled from the complex and often contradictory experiences of implementing planned interventions, and they are published for specific purposes: such as to report to donors and partners, to attract funding or for the use of programme beneficiaries. My analysis reflects how the YWCA represents its interventions around sexuality, including HIV, FGM and SRHR, in relation to the binaries of identity and ethical commitment that operate in wider discourses of Christian morality, women's rights and empowerment and 'African-ness'. Within each, the YWCA negotiates its organizational identity and its conduct in relation to the apparently mutually exclusive positions of feminism, Christianity and African-ness. This context is the narrative landscape and the material circumstances in which the YWCA identifies condoms, abortion and non-normative sexualities as 'controversial faith issues', as I discuss at length in Chapter 5. This chapter thus begins to explore some of the implications of the YWCA's identity as a non-feminist, Kenyan, ecumenical Christian women's organization, which is further analysed through the words of my research participants in Chapter 6.

4.1 Abortion and nationalism

My focus on SRHR places one small proportion of the YWCA's work under a microscope while sidelining a large number of other projects. Notably, the organization was involved in responding to post-election violence after the failed elections in December 2007. After conducting a 'rapid needs assessment', the YWCA proceeded to provide humanitarian relief for 'elderly women, pregnant women, and lactating mothers', counselling services and other forms of support at internally displaced persons (IDP) camps (YWCA 2008: 14–15). Throughout 2008 it repurposed aspects of its existing governance and civic education programmes, which had been ongoing since 2002, to offer peace-building workshops and 'enhance the capacities of women and youth as mediators, conflict managers, and peace ambassadors' (YWCA 2008: 15;

Zimbizi, Kopiyo and Owiti 2011). After its role responding to the aftermath of post-election violence, the YWCA retained a focus on issues of women's political participation. This primarily centred on the referendum on the new constitution in 2010, during which time Dr Abok, in her role as NGS, represented the YWCA on the Executive Committee of the NCCK. While the NCCK emerged as a prominent opponent of the draft constitution, the YWCA 'decided to be non-partisan ... if [we] took one stand, it would not augur well for the organisation ... We'd provide information to everybody, whether they were in the opposition or not ... [and] with that information, they would be able to make informed choices' (Dr Abok, interview, 2012). This effort to provide non-partisan information was channelled through its Civic Education programme, which was funded by UN Women. The education and sensitization activities at the grassroots level throughout its network of branches and women's groups included question-and-answer sessions in market places, 'advocacy caravans' for the promotion of peaceful voting and the use of local theatre, song and dance to educate communities about the proposed constitution. Above all, the YWCA wanted to encourage women to use their vote, based on the 'gains for women' the draft constitution offered (Dr Abok, interview, 2012). The YWCA

> focused on the gains for women and the promotion of peace ... we did not talk about who is saying this, who is saying that. It would be: 'here are copies of the constitution' and then 'we've come up with a small leaflet that focuses on the gains for women: you'll have more representation, you'll have better access to health' – you know, we didn't talk about those contentious issues at all. (Lavender, interview, 2012)

The constitution-drafting process was touted as a liberalizing and reforming moment. Input on the draft constitution was sought by Muslims to ensure legal recognition for *shari'a* mediation, by LGBTQ rights campaigners to gain equality under the law and the right to marry and by women's rights organizations to establish quotas for government positions and other gender equality measures. Popular political discourse generated controversies related to almost all progressive elements of this agenda: gender quotas, LGBTQ rights, the place of Muslims in Kenya and abortion – all topics that implicated deeply felt ethnic, religious and national identities, and their associated ethical commitments. When abortion was mentioned during my conversations with women at the YWCA, it was largely considered in terms of interpersonal ethical conduct. While it was identified as a 'controversial faith issue', it was approached in terms of the personal effects of the continuation or termination of a pregnancy, and its implications for the wider family, as I describe in greater detail in the next chapter. The YWCA's position was informed by the reality that a legal, medical abortion performed by a qualified health professional was beyond the reach of many in Kenya, since these services were accessible only through larger hospitals, often at an expensive personal cost. An unwanted pregnancy could be dealt with using non-medical methods to induce abortion, with potentially harmful side effects, making abortion a widespread cause of death. Estimates from 2012 suggest that approximately 450,000 abortions were carried out in Kenya every year, mostly not in medical settings. Despite the prevalence of abortion in Kenya, opposition to it is widespread. The education system and mainstream media have historically promoted sensationalist anti-abortion messages and churches have endorsed these as Christian (FIDA-K and CRR 2007: 14; Griffith 2014; KHRC and RHRA 2010: 23–34; Mantell et al. 2011; Marlow et al. 2014: 150–3; Mitchell et al. 2006: 517; Osur 2011; Ouko-Otieno 2009: 68).

I think it is critical to place the YWCA's point of view on abortion in the wider political, historical context of colonial interventions, and the public Christian opposition to the draft constitution that was based, in part, on an absolute rejection of abortion. The regulation and disapproval of abortion is clearly influenced by long-standing moral narratives of women's and girls' sexuality and bodily autonomy, which may be traced in terms of abortion from the *kiwagrie* reaction to the female circumcision crisis in the 1930s. The fact that abortion became a focal point of debates about the constitution is not incidental but rather demonstrates the long-standing and widespread connections between patriarchal control over reproduction, particularly norms of pro-natalism, with nationalisms and nation-building projects. In this case, it also testifies to global webs of connection and influence within and among Christian institutions and organizations. The NCCK exerted pressure on the parliamentary committee responsible for drafting the document, and took the opportunity to push for the illegalization of abortion. Apparently through unofficial channels, the NCCK persuaded the draft's authors to add a clause stating that the right to life begins at conception. Kenya's legal and medical professionals and some women's organizations, including FIDA-K, protested that the constitution was an inappropriate venue in which to legislate against abortion. Unable to exert enough influence to prevent abortion being included in the draft, a coalition of doctors and lawyers came together to modify the draft constitution through the same informal means (Anyangu-Amu 2010; Osur 2011: 34–40). Article 26 of the draft constitution therefore came to reflect a mixture of two opposing perspectives. Clauses stating that 'the life of a person begins at conception' and 'abortion is not permitted', apparently inserted by NCCK, were added to extend the constitutional right to life to include embryos and foetuses. Clause (d) was subsequently amended by the doctors in response, to specify that medically necessary induced abortions would be permitted. As a result, Article 26 legally defines the start of personhood and life at conception, attempting to settle an enormously complex and philosophically dense question for the sake of illegalizing abortion. The debate placed these theological questions firmly on the agenda of public discourse.

Kenya's major Christian institutions, including NCCK, formed a united Christian opposition to the proposed constitution, called the Kenya Christian Leaders Forum (KCLF). It strongly discouraged Christian voters from backing the constitution. In one communique, it declared that 'pro-abortionists' were motivated by making money from vulnerable women, and defined abortion as 'murder, the killing of the unborn innocents' (KCLF 2010). The NCCK similarly talked about 'protecting' Kenya's 'unborn children' from abortion. This misleading rhetoric and the repetition of the fact that life begins at conception were the pillars of mainstream Kenyan Christian institutions' position that abortion is immoral and that on these grounds Kenyan Christians should vote to reject the proposed constitution at the referendum. In a campaign leaflet outlining its position on the proposed constitution, the NCCK set out aspects of its opposition to abortion.

> If this draft constitution passes, then foreign laws, some which are un-Biblical and unethical, will be introduced ... These could undermine our sovereignty and are loopholes for the legalization of abortion and homosexuality ... doctors, nurses, clinical officers, mortuary attendants and even first aid attendants will be allowed ... to carry out abortions for all manner of reasons. Why should Kenyan children be killed so casually? Abortion is murder of children, and it contradicts Exodus 20:13 ('You shall not murder'). (NCCK and KCLF 2010: para 1-9)

In this statement, the NCCK suggested connections between the legal implications of Kenya's ratification of international instruments with concerns about Western cultural imperialism and Kenya's sovereignty, Kenyan nationalism and the presumption that Kenya ought to be governed according to 'biblical' principles.[1] This powerful rhetoric joined together a range of disparate issues to form a Christian-nationalist position from which to oppose the reforms implied by the proposed constitution. This is not unprecedented. Religious institutions have criticized the provision for abortion in the Maputo Protocol (Balchin

2008: 9), while appeals to Christian sexual ethics have also been identified in the construction of a Christian national identity in Zambia (Van Klinken 2014, 2015).

Throughout the pre-referendum period in Kenya, right-wing evangelical Christian organizations from the United States were taking advantage of the situation to campaign against abortion. Their messaging similarly focused on the moral status of 'unborn' children. The NCCK received funding from the East African Centre for Law and Justice (EALCJ), a subsidiary of the American Centre for Law and Justice (ACLJ), with the express intent to convince the Kenyan public to reject the legalization of abortion through the proposed constitution (Kaoma 2012; Osur 2011).[2] The proposed constitution's provision for Muslim *shari'a* councils was also opposed by the NCCK, and they misrepresented the new constitution as forcing Christians to live under *shari'a* law, demonstrating a striking continuity of strategic anti-Islam rhetoric between the Anglophone west and Kenya. The NCCK was nevertheless happy to insist that Kenya should be governed by Christian principles (Gez 2018: 103–4; Okech 2019: 17). Despite the uniformity of the churches' arguments against the draft constitution, their message did not necessarily convince Christians. The public debate ignored the real situations of women and girls who seek abortions, and women's voices were rarely heard on either side. Many women felt alienated by the arrogance of clergy who preferred doctrine and moralizing to listening to their congregants: 'Many people stopped going to church because they said, "These people are talking about abortion, they are church ministers, they don't live with daughters, and they don't live with wives who have abortions … so they cannot talk on our behalf." [Ministers] have not come to congregations and [asked] them, "what do you people think?"' (Lavender, interview, 2012). When it came to the referendum in 2010, the proposed constitution was largely supported by Kenyan citizens, and it was approved with 68 per cent of the vote. This implies that a majority of Christians voted in favour, as around 80 per cent of Kenya's population identifies as Christian. In reaction to the results of the referendum a spokesperson for NCCK, Canon Peter Karanja, thanked those who had voted 'No' and added, 'Those who have sinned [i.e. voted for the constitution] shall surely die' (Osur 2011: 159).

After the referendum went in favour of the new constitution, the YWCA shifted the focus of its Civic Education programme to explain the gains for women that would now be enacted. Some of these have direct implications for women's political participation, such as the requirement that 'not more than two-thirds of the members of elective public bodies shall be of the same gender'

(Constitution of Kenya, Art. 81.b). Additionally, the YWCA's Gender and Governance programme encouraged women to take advantage of these quotas, aiming to 'increas[e] women's participation in decision making and governance structures' from national to county level (YWCA 2011: 8; Zimbizi, Kopiyo and Owiti 2011). This programme was not limited to training for women but included 'voter mobilisation and registration', 'community sensitisation on women's leadership' and training in 'peace and conflict management' (YWCA 2011: 8) and the 'negative cultural beliefs and attitudes' that face women who are in, or seek, positions of political power in Kenya (YWCA 2011: 23). The YWCA thereby challenged local patriarchal hierarchies, in addition to preparing and supporting young women to achieve political and other leadership positions. Such programmes have far-reaching implications not only within a narrowly defined 'political sphere' but also more broadly, for instance in churches where women demand the right to be ordained and agitate for increased power within institutional structures. Many powerful people's interests were evidently challenged by Kenya's new constitution, which promised more equitable land rights alongside other reforms. It seems that the constitution itself, by promising a combination of a bill of rights, stronger democratic processes and gender quotas, was threatening to the 'ruling elite' (Murunga, Okello and Sjögren 2014: 6–7). Therefore, some commentators consider that abortion was merely a convenient, populist excuse for rejecting the constitution (Osur 2011). This was only possible because abortion was already a viable way to express specifically Kenyan, Christian anxieties about sexuality, secularism and national sovereignty in the context of ongoing Western imperialism. The value of women's bodies as a site for negotiating sexuality as part of the reproduction of the nation is evident in the abortion debates and other discourses of SRHR.

4.2 FGM: 'Harmful cultural traditions' and 'African' identities

At 9.00 am on 7 February 2012, I arrived at the YWCA's headquarters to attend a meeting billed as a 'Practice Review and Awareness Building on FGM Workshop'. Held in the large meeting room next door to Wandia's office, I took my seat at a neatly laid-out conference table covered in a white and blue YWCA-branded tablecloth. The purpose of the meeting was to gather branch staff to evaluate the FGM Programme to date and discuss its implementation throughout the coming year, particularly focusing on the message to be communicated. The YWCA has been implementing its 'Practice Reduction and Awareness Building on Female Genital Mutilation' Programme (hereafter, 'FGM Programme') since 2006, in Kisii, Meru and Kajiado. The meeting lasted all morning, with delegates from Meru, Kisii and Nairobi branches in attendance as well as Wandia and Lavender who took the lead in much of the workshop. Wandia opened the meeting by introducing the topic, explaining that the YWCA is concerned about FGM because it is a violation of women's human rights, and that girls are not given a choice about whether to undergo any kind of genital practices. Behind the label 'FGM' there are a range of female genital practices associated with coming-of-age rituals and other beliefs and religious/cultural practices of some ethnic groups (but not all) in Kenya (Njambi 2007). The YWCA is explicit about its belief that these practices constitute a form of mutilation, and thus uses the mainstream developmentalist terminology of 'FGM' to discuss them. The programmes staff were keen to discourage using the language of 'circumcision', as doing so encourages an unhelpful comparison with 'male' circumcision. Lavender argued that FGM was more like 'cutting off one-third of the penis', emphasizing the severity and invasiveness of these procedures rather than the relatively marginal effects of removing the foreskin.

The practices collected under the title 'FGM' are long-standing, and in many cases have persisted in private while being condemned in public. While the YWCA had been running anti-FGM workshops in the affected regions of Kenya since the 1980s, large-scale projects were developed only in the late 1990s. It took until the early 2000s before Kenyan women's rights activists and health workers had legislative tools with which to work. The impression given at the meeting was that FGM was a subject over which medical professionals and women's rights activists regularly clashed with parents and community leaders. The YWCA felt it had to contend with targeted communities' rejection of 'outside influence', which was strongly resisted. In 2002, FGM was illegalized in Kenyan law, and both circumcisers and parents are now punishable with fines and incarceration if found guilty of performing or procuring FGM for/on a minor. This legislation received widespread attention at the time it was passed, and has succeeded somewhat in steering public opinion towards eradicating FGM, although it is considered to be not well-enforced. The continuation of FGM despite its illegalization reflects the pervasiveness of the justifications offered to make sense of it. The YWCA observed that these were typically framed in terms of the undesirable consequences thought to follow from failing to perform it, which are not reasoned from a medical, biological perspective. Legal instruments are commonly cited in anti-FGM literature, used to lend support to their arguments with local patriarchal leaders (Ingdal, Umbima and Tysse 2008: 44; Oloo, Wanjiru and Newell-Jones 2001: 18). For example, a four-page leaflet that the YWCA was using in 2012 entitled *Know Your Facts about Female Genital Mutilation* emphasizes the illegality of FGM alongside its harmful effects.

The *Know Your Facts* leaflet outlines the YWCA's position on FGM, and offers information considered relevant to older adolescents and parents. For instance, the practices covered by the term FGM are acknowledged to be diverse, but are nevertheless opposed equally for three reasons: they are harmful to general health; they are a violation of women's and girls' rights; and they pose a threat to women's reproductive capacities. A list of reasons is given in answer to the question 'Why is FGM Practiced?', identifying a range of gendered constructions, for instance believing that genital alterations are necessary for successful pregnancy and childbirth. Next, a list of 'facts' about FGM is given, including general information intended to counterbalance the cultural justifications listed on the previous page, as well as details of the immediate and long-term health risks associated with FGM, from fatal blood loss to urinary tract infections. Finally, the leaflet lists six ways the reader can help 'stop' FGM, the overall thrust of which is to share the information presented in the leaflet as a means of changing the attitudes of those who continue to support the practice. Thus, the FGM Programme ultimately aims at providing information, on the assumption that new knowledge can facilitate social change. The delegates at the workshop I attended seemed unanimously to concur with the point of view outlined in the *Know Your Facts* leaflet.

Kisii Branch representatives described using local media, particularly radio, as a strategy for reaching the largest possible audience with an anti-FGM message. As a result, girls in Kisii 'know' they can 'run away' to the YWCA for protection from FGM. This awareness-raising effort to facilitate girls' resistance to FGM has been supported by efforts to 'retrain' girls and their mothers, that is, through workshops aiming to sensitize them to the dangers of FGM and give them tools for resistance. Meru Branch has used similar strategies, but the context presents different challenges. In the areas covered by this branch, FGM is practiced relatively secretly and only in a few localities. Identifying the women who carry out the genital-cutting element of coming-of-age ceremonies (known as 'circumcisers') is therefore made even more difficult given the now-illegal status of FGM. Where they can be identified, circumcisers are included in the campaign as much as possible as their role is central to the continuation of these practices. Many circumcisers are said to consider their role in purely economic terms, as they are paid by the girl's parents for their services. Therefore, a key strategy that the YWCA increasingly seeks to use is the testimony of former circumcisers, a couple of whom have been able to publicly decry their former employment and demonstrate to other circumcisers that they have been able to find reliable alternative sources of income. Here, biography is used within the programme itself, functioning as a moral narrative by offering a new figure of the 'reformed circumciser' as a viable identity and position. Alternative rites of passage (ARPs) for the transition from childhood to adulthood are another major element of the YWCA's strategy in Meru. This involves eliminating only the harmful cutting and modification of girls' genitalia, while continuing, and reinterpreting, meaningful rituals that mark the passage into adolescence. This strategy, usually combined with sex education or 'family life education', is not unique to the YWCA; many other bodies have suggested that this is the most effective way to reduce the incidence of FGM in culturally appropriate ways (Akin-Aina 2011: 83; Ingdal, Umbima and Tysse 2008: 17–19). The illegalization of FGM and its replacement with ARP has become a significant element of Kenyan (and African) constructions of modernity (Moore 2009: 212–16).

A public campaign including the distribution of leaflets was designed to run during school holidays in April, August and December, as circumcision ceremonies tend to be held when children are out of school to allow for them to recover before returning to class. Girls are considered to be at risk when they are out of the gaze and grasp of their teachers, and thus schools remain relatively powerless to intervene against FGM practices. The YWCA recognizes its position as one that allows it to reach and potentially protect children at a time when they are most vulnerable. By arranging ARP to take place at the same time during school holidays, the YWCA is able to use the facilities of local schools for the week-long camps, including involving teachers as facilitators (Ingdal, Umbima and Tysse 2008: 17, Oloo and Wanjiru 2011: 27). As of 2008, several hundred girls had been reached this way, with results being difficult to quantify but generally graduates of the ARP were thought to be good peer educators and keen to share their knowledge with other girls (Ingdal, Umbima and Tysse 2008: 14). Girls are often recruited to the programme's activities through schools and churches, although sometimes this causes tensions between the YWCA and parents who are said often to feel that their wishes have been disregarded when girls are recruited directly, rather than approached via their parents.

Nairobi Branch covers an area much larger than the city, including Kajiado County which stretches from the south of the city to the border with Tanzania. The targets of the FGM programme at Nairobi Branch are Maasai communities in Kajiado. In 2009 the YWCA conducted a survey in Kajiado to discover the prevalence of FGM and found that 'health workers' were performing the cutting in medicalized contexts, in an effort to avoid some of the risks associated with infection and scar tissue. The wide geographic spread of the Maasai across this region means it has a low population density, making it harder to reach these communities with the same kinds of group activities used in Meru and Kisii. In localities where the YWCA rarely works, including Kajiado, the YWCA was concerned not to become too closely associated with anti-FGM work and thus put off potential new members. Additionally, some staff were worried that the YWCA might be confused with MYW, because the latter is well known for its anti-FGM initiatives. This is an unusual example of concern about preserving the YWCA's identity that did not primarily foreground the loss or emphasis of its Christianity. The YWCA considered Maasai chiefs and community leaders to be highly controlling of their communities, enforcing patriarchal prerogatives where they could. Maasai women and men were understood to socialize in gender-segregated groups, and so the programme was modified to target these groups separately. Cultural sensitivity is of paramount importance to the YWCA and the success of its interventions, and a point was made of explaining that a local person knows how to talk to their neighbours, understands the culture better than outsiders and can act with due sensitivity. A primary fieldworker was a recent Maasai college graduate with ties to the targeted communities, as well as the required language skills and knowledge of the cultural context. This approach further aids the YWCA in avoiding any suggestions of criticizing or attempting to change Maasai culture from the outside. Nevertheless, the challenges of intervening in Maasai FGM practices were reported to be the most difficult to tackle, not least due to the restrictions of budget and the logistical requirements of a sparsely distributed target population.

The overall aim of 'reducing' support for and practice of FGM proved difficult for the YWCA to measure, and the evaluation of programme outcomes was complicated by the absence of hard statistics. Headquarters staff suggested a degree of pressure on them to justify to the Association's international donors how continued material support for the programme would translate into concrete results. Many girls who go through the ARP subsequently join the Association as members, and their FGM status is therefore more easily followed up. Girls who seek no further contact with the YWCA are far less easy to track and, as a result, it is not known for certain how many have been effectively 'reached' by the programme. These concerns notwithstanding, a programme evaluation report described the training, ARP, media outreach and information dissemination activities as 'relatively effective' (Ingdal, Umbima and Tysse 2008: 37). In Kisii, the YWCA felt it had been moderately successful because 'most of' the girls who have attended anti-FGM training activities also joined the YWCA as members.

There are those within the YWCA who, by virtue of their ethnicity and class, are positioned between the YWCA's support for the values enshrined in the Maputo Protocol and Christian rejection of FGM, and on the other hand the social pressure, norms and expectations of the community and/or culture of their family. Statistically, it is likely that there are members of rural YWCA-affiliated women's groups who continue to practice FGM. One of my research participants, Susan – a professional woman in a leadership position at the YWCA – confided in me that she had 'been cut' when she was young. While Susan explained that she had made sure her own daughters were not 'cut', it was still a common practice in her community. The involvement of women like Susan and Nyaboke gave the YWCA a powerful position from which to advocate for the abandonment of the cutting element of initiation ceremonies, especially among Christian communities. But it also illustrates how there are many people who remain to be convinced enough by these anti-FGM messages to not 'cut' their daughters, which may seem like a risk given the range of beliefs about the 'positive' effects of clitoridectomy and various degrees of infibulation and excision.

The YWCA did not refer to 'Christian' values to explain or support its opposition to FGM. Rather, women's human rights were the dominant conceptual framework within which the causes and consequences of FGM were addressed. This approach seems to be at least partly a response to the perception that the majority of those who practice FGM are themselves Christians, so according to Njeri it 'becomes difficult' to use Christian arguments to persuade them (Njeri, interview, 2012). Nonetheless, as discussed in Chapter 2, there is a historical precedent of Christian groups implementing anti-FGM projects in Kenya, and this pattern continues in the present day (Harcourt 2009: 198–9; Ingdal, Umbima and Tysse 2008: 7–8). In an evaluation of the FGM Programme, it was suggested that the YWCA's 'Christian values and relationship with churches' are instrumentally valuable, compared to 'many civil society organisations that do not have grass roots [sic] anchoring and a membership base' (Ingdal, Umbima and Tysse 2008: 40). In the development and women's rights discourse in which the YWCA is embedded, FGM is perhaps the topic on which there is greatest consensus, although there is a range of critical theoretical perspectives evident in academic literature on the topic (Bagnol and Mariano 2011; Gordon 1997;

Harcourt 2009; Njambi 2007; Pedwell 2007; Shell-Duncan 2008).[3] The status of 'African tradition' is more nuanced for the YWCA than the condemnation of missionaries during the 'female circumcision crisis', on one hand, or the uncritical reification in some postcolonial African efforts to recuperate it, on the other. However, it seems that FGM's status as an 'African tradition' helps the YWCA articulate a critique of it, while it does not approach many other SRHR issues as somehow specifically African. The YWCA focuses on girls' and women's rights to bodily autonomy and the absence of consent as the cornerstones of their opposition to FGM as a 'harmful cultural practice'. Presenting adolescent girls and their parents with a choice and encouraging individual resistance to FGM are therefore at the forefront of the message the YWCA communicates with its programme participants and beneficiaries. The discourse of women's and girls' rights in respect of their health, sexuality, reproductive lives and their bodies is paralleled and continued throughout the YWCA's related work on HIV.

4.3 HIV: Condoms, Christianity and maternalism

More ubiquitous even than FGM in discourses of gender and development in Africa, HIV is a defining context of the YWCA's interventions in sexual health. There is little need to describe the severity and extent of HIV across the African continent, but the specificities of the Kenyan context bear brief revision here. In 2011, it is reported that 49,126 Kenyans died as a result of AIDS-related illnesses (NACC and NASCOP 2012: 9). Approximately 6.2 per cent of the adult population of Kenya was HIV-positive, of whom more than half were women (NACC and NASCOP 2012: 6). These figures represent the whole country, but HIV and AIDS is unevenly distributed. Nyanza province was considered 'hyper-endemic' with an infection rate between 13 and 25 per cent (NACC and NASCOP 2012: 6). The YWCA's Kisii Branch, in Nyanza, reported in 2001 that it was becoming difficult to implement aspects of its other programmes, specifically a project focusing on youth economic empowerment, because of the impact HIV was having on its target demographic. From 2003 onwards, HIV awareness, prevention and care were permanent fixtures in the YWCA's work, with each branch running at least one HIV programme by 2004.[4] The very real dangers posed by the HIV epidemic necessitate incorporating it into almost every aspect of the work the YWCA does. As the risks of HIV infection immediately implicate sexual behaviour as a major route for the transmission of the virus, the YWCA has responded by integrating considerations of HIV into its sexual health programmes and launching new initiatives to target young people's sexual behaviour as a site for the prevention of HIV transmission. An awareness of gendered risks for HIV infection additionally directs attention towards sexualized violence against women and girls, as well as FGM which has been identified as a potential source of HIV infection through the use of one cutting implement on more than one girl (Yount and Abraham 2007).

The YWCA has taken the approach of helping young women to avoid HIV infection, partly through promoting abstinence and behaviour change, but also by introducing condoms as part of the solution. It has also tended to apply a maternal ethics by placing YWCA staff and members *in loco maternis* over its young members and beneficiaries. The YWCA's programmatic interventions in HIV reflect the position of condoms in Christian discourses of sexuality, including widespread moralizing about sexual behaviour and related heteropatriarchal and repronormative attitudes. A strongly Christian-inflected public discourse of moral and immoral sexual conduct further associated HIV with immoral behaviour, while a personal 'commitment to Christ' is thought to mitigate against HIV infection (Kamau 2009: 208–9; Spronk 2005: 268). This is a result of the narratively sustained, if largely implicit, connection between Christian identity and a sexual ethic of abstinence and monogamy. Resisting this discourse risks associating HIV transmission exclusively with sex, although there are other ways to become infected with HIV: mother–infant transmission during delivery or breastfeeding, blood transfusions and sharing needles.[5]

Just as FGM interventions plug the YWCA into a narrative legacy of white feminist perceptions of African misogyny, HIV discourses draw on a long-established history of stigmatization of sex, and of women's bodies in particular. The widespread tension between concerns of HIV infection, reasonable dislike of condom use and moralizing about sex contributes to an increased risk for those Kenyans who have a larger number of sexual partners. Sex work is criminalized in Kenya, and sex workers are widely discriminated against and stigmatized as immoral and dangerous. The colonial construction of 'prostitutes' in Nairobi serves as a background against which sex work is narratively positioned as sinful and a threat to the family. As a result, as many as 30–47 per cent of female Kenyan sex workers are estimated to be HIV-positive (Shannon et al. 2015: 63), a situation surely made worse by police practices that mitigate against the use of condoms. The illegal status of sex work allows police routinely to confiscate or destroy condoms they find on (suspected) sex workers. Conversely, potentially any woman who carries condoms on her person risks arrest since condoms are often interpreted as evidence of the intent to sell sex (Elmore-Meegan et al.

2004: 54; NEPHAK, KESWA, BHESP and GNP+ 2015: 25-31; Open Society 2012: 12-15). This situation has dire consequences for the health of sex workers themselves, and it reveals the widespread mistrust of and antipathy towards condoms.

This complex nexus of issues informed the YWCA's Youth Reproductive Health (YRH) Programme, initiated in 2006, and implemented across all seven branches until 2009, at which time it narrowed its focus to Mombasa, Tana River and Nairobi branches. The YRH Programme aimed to 'reduce the vulnerability of young people against HIV'. As critical as this work has been in the lives of thousands of women and youths across the YWCA's branch network, these programmes have been conceived and implemented under strict constraints of funding and minimal resources. One of the most widely used strategies is the appointment of community-based trainers, youth peer counsellors and peer educators, all of whom (ideally) absorb the relevant information about HIV from their training sessions at the YWCA, and then disseminate it among their peers. Training included a range of topics related to HIV including antiretroviral drugs (ARVs), the availability of voluntary counselling and testing (VCT) services, stigma, substance abuse, rape, other sexually transmitted infections and the importance of personal support networks. Peer education was intended to address the problem that many teenagers and young people lack guidance from older generations – particularly those who grew up in an era before HIV. As a method of outreach, it capitalizes on the tendency of youths to seek information from their peers rather than seeking the advice of medical professionals or adults who may be expected to punish them or otherwise respond negatively. The role of the peer educator is quite demanding, as these young people are expected to act as 'living examples to the[ir] fellow youth and the wider community in matters of HIV, [s]ex and sexuality, reproductive health and behaviour change ... [and to] be the ambassadors of responsible behaviour' (YWCA 2010: 16). Despite these high expectations, there seem to be significant numbers of young people willing to become peer educators: 39 'master' peer educators trained 134 peer educators who collectively reached 5,510 youths in Mombasa, Nairobi and Tana River in 2010.

Condoms are widely promoted by the state and NGOs as effective means of protecting oneself from HIV, but they come up against a pro-natal culture in which their contraceptive effect has negative symbolism (Baitu 2008: 98-9). It is not the prophylactic function of condoms but their contraceptive effect that is problematic, compounded by the general mistrust and dislike of condoms, especially among men (Booth 2004: 43-4; Njue, Voeten and Remes 2011: 53).[6]

Condoms are further regarded with suspicion by many adolescents, although they are typically subject to multiple sexual health interventions at school and therefore theoretically aware of the protection from HIV that condoms can afford (Nzioka 2001: 109–10; Nzioka 2004: 32). Their suspicions are reinforced by unreliable supplies of counterfeit, faulty or out-of-date condoms, a concern supported by known incidences (BBC 2019; Merab 2018). Worse perhaps is the widespread conspiracy theory that condoms are deliberately infected with HIV as part of a neocolonial plot to use HIV to commit genocide in Africa (McGreal 2007; Sivelä 2012: 51–2). In line with trends elsewhere in the world, in Kenya teenagers are having sex but use condoms only infrequently (UNICEF 2008: 126). Charles Nzioka's research with adolescents aged 15–19 in rural Kenya suggests that for this age group condoms have very mixed meanings; even though they are thought not to work, they are only used by 'bad boys' who have lots of casual sex (Nzioka 2001: 114). Boys may avoid using condoms because norms of heterosexual masculinity have conferred a strange value on (treatable) STDs and fatherhood as proof of sexual experience (Nzioka 2001: 108). Girls who know about and possess condoms could be considered promiscuous by their peers, marking a girl as 'bad' which has different connotations than it does for boys, as girls labelled 'bad' are 'prostitutes' or sugar babies, 'spoiled', 'impure' and potentially HIV-positive (Nzioka 2004: 30–40). The positive benefit that being seen as sexually active apparently has for boys' sense of adulthood and masculinity means it is hardly surprising that the rate of condom use among young people is low, at less than 50 per cent.[7] Regardless of the rates at which condoms are actually used, the perception that condoms are for sexual and social *others* demonstrates that moral narratives of sexual purity have a pedagogical effect.

The YWCA's responses to HIV and AIDS have not been exclusively focused on preventing the sexual transmission of the virus but have extended to care for those who are affected by it, whether they are HIV-positive themselves or their family life has been disrupted by the impact of the virus. The YWCA's response to HIV is connected to and supported by wider institutional processes, as the World YWCA made HIV one of its 'priorities' in 2002 (World YWCA 2002). From 2000 to 2012, YWCA staff received extensive training and attended international HIV and AIDS conferences alongside other African YWCAs, focusing on building skills, sharing knowledge and strengthening possible collaborations among YWCAs. The YWCA supports people who are already HIV-positive or who are coping with the broad impact of HIV and AIDS on themselves and their families, to whom the YWCA referred collectively as 'people living with HIV and AIDS' (PLWHA). It also offered support for carers looking after PLWHA, and for children whose families have been split or dissolved as a result of AIDS illness and deaths, who the YWCA called 'orphaned and vulnerable children' (OVC).[8] In addition, the YWCA supports the provision of 'home-based care' for PLWHA. Hospitals and clinics may be located at a great distance from their homes, and often require the patient to pay for any medical care they receive, so home-based care is a means for a network of family, clergy and medical professionals to meet the needs of PLWHA as an alternative to hospitalization. The YWCA runs workshops to teach about how best to care for people suffering with AIDS, including palliative care, and 'how to care for oneself as a caregiver', and organizes and facilitates support groups to provide a forum for HIV-positive youth and women to discuss their problems and share their stories. By prioritizing this community-based approach to 'care', and a concern for those who perform this labour, the YWCA is engaged in a pragmatic application of an ethics of care. It is connected, I think, to the maternalism that persists within the YWCA's structures. The idea that older women should be advisors to younger women on sexual and reproductive matters is often observed to be pervasive element of African cultural norms, especially pertaining to the various ways in which communities organize the graduation or initiation of adolescents into adulthood (Mapuranga 2016: 59). The confluence of British and African tendencies to construct a social hierarchy of elder women as teachers of younger women has contributed to the maintenance of the internal structure of the YWCA in the present day, which consistently places married middle-aged mothers in positions of decision-making and leadership over younger, single and childless women and youths. As such, the structure of the Association preserves some problematic aspects of the hierarchy that placed colonizer women in a position of maternal seniority over African women.[9]

Many of the women I spoke to at the YWCA described their personal involvement in responding to HIV in their communities, especially among people living in rural areas or in urban informal settlements. Mbari was an engaging and animated interviewee, a veteran of the Kenyan women's movement, a proud mother and grandmother and a long-standing supporter of the YWCA. She interspersed her answers to my questions with descriptions of her varied career in social work, including her time spent studying in the UK. After we had talked for about an hour, I walked with Mbari down the road to her bus stop. She was on her way to visit a young woman who had just discovered that she was HIV-positive, and Mbari had learned that she was contemplating suicide. This information was offered to me lightly, suggesting that it was not the first time that Mbari and the YWCA had intervened to support someone with suicidal ideation brought about by an HIV diagnosis. Despite the medical advances that have been made in recent years, there remains a great deal of stigma and shame surrounding the illness (Kamau 2009: 193–213). A HIV-positive status remains implicated in a deeply damaging and stigmatizing hierarchy that associates being HIV-negative with being pure, clean and moral in ways that intersect with the construction of women's bodies as sites of potential danger and impurity. Mbari's purpose in paying her a visit was to convince her that life was still worth living, and to recruit her into a dedicated support group for women living with HIV: 'I will refer her to our "positive" support group here, and I know she will live. Because unless she sees it, she will not believe; they give life stories' (Mbari, interview, 2012). If all went to plan, Mbari expected that this group would help her to realize that it was still possible to be happy, healthy, maintain relationships, have a family, a job and a full life, while being HIV-positive. I did not meet with Mbari again after that day, so I do not know how that young woman's story ends. But the situation demonstrates that the social stigma attached to HIV is almost as much of a threat to lives as the disease itself. Mbari placed emphasis on the potentially life-saving effects of confronting this young woman with testimonials to contradict doom-laden moral narratives of life with HIV. While the positive support group has clear practical uses, it also serves to facilitate the telling of different stories. This is reflected in the neat reframing of 'HIV-positive' by naming the group 'positive', suggesting optimism and confidence.

Condoms are not only viewed negatively in Kenya. Competing discourses explicitly set up condoms in opposite ways; Christian discourses largely offer a prescriptive, deontological moral perspective within which the use of condoms is a sin. This is reinforced by narratives in which condom use, as emblematic of nonreproductive sex, is morally corrupting to the individual, even posing an existential threat to the family and social reproduction. On the other hand, development appropriates medical discourse to justify the use of condoms as morally good, more often appealing to pragmatic self-interest in avoiding sickness, and utilitarian logics of how to protect the largest possible number of people from HIV. Underneath these discourses promoted and repeated by powerful institutions, urban legends and conspiracy theories sow doubts about the medical and scientific claims made for condoms' effectiveness. That the YWCA has included condoms in its sexual health programmes aimed at young people is significant. In combination with the apparent maternal ethics the YWCA's staff and leaders apply, it demonstrates that some steps are being taken towards breaking down a repronormative, pro-natal construction of sexuality.

Some tensions were felt to emerge between the YWCA's mandate to protect young people from HIV and its maternal responsibility to instil the right sexual ethic, both of which stem from its foregrounding of a Christian organizational identity.

4.4 SRHR, development and feminism

As discussed in Chapter 1, the YWCA declines the label 'feminist'. This is not especially surprising given the animosity towards feminism within many Christian institutions, and the critiques of feminism from the perspective of many postcolonial African critics, scholars and activists. Nevertheless, feminism is relevant when analysing the YWCA's perspective due to the influence various iterations of feminism have had on development discourses of women's rights and gender mainstreaming. The YWCA's programmatic interventions in women's, girls' and youths' sexual and reproductive health represent a modest departure from the trends of international development in two ways. First, as a women's organization that centres the participation of its members in decision-making processes, the YWCA puts Kenyan women in a position to have their input on the content and aims of sexual and reproductive health and rights programmes. Second, in line with what might be expected of a Christian organization, the YWCA sometimes applies 'the principle of purity' (Wandia, interview, 2012) in its interventions, seeking not only to change behaviour but also to encourage specific moral evaluations of behaviour. Some of the issues addressed in these three programmes were considered 'controversial' within the YWCA. The ascription of 'controversial' status, its meaning and its implications for the Association are discussed in greater depth in the next chapter.

The YWCA's adoption of the language of 'SRHR' is a relatively recent development, introduced to the YWCA's work in 2009 at the launch of the SRHR programme.[10] This was inaugurated at a World YWCA-organized African Regional Training Institute in Lagos, Nigeria, on the theme of 'creating safe and secure communities' in response to AIDS and violence against women, as well as in service of SRHR. By February of 2010, applying methods proven to be effective in the YWCA's anti-FGM programmes, the project was underway with peer educators in training at Nairobi Branch. The aim of the SRHR Programme was to 'create safe spaces for young women' aged between 13 and 30 to 'advocate for their SRHR in the context of HIV ... as part of the World YWCA's global strategy' (YWCA 2010: 19–20). These broad aims were supported and justified by citing the International Conference on Population and Development (ICPD) Programme of Action, the Declaration of Commitment on HIV and AIDS and the Millennium Development Goals as sources of guidance. In brief, the programme worked with youth groups, Y-Teen clubs and schools in Siaya, Kisii, Kisumu and Meru. The planned activities for 2011 included the aim to collaborate with other organizations, 'strengthen the capacity of staff and youth leaders' within the YWCA and establish a permanent policy of 'safe spaces' in YWCA branches for young women 'to discuss their SRHR as well as to obtain information and support' (YWCA 2010: 19–20). Focusing on inculcating 'positive behaviour change' such as uptake of VCT services, the YWCA disseminated information and messages around SRHR and HIV through community outreach, workshops and the production and distribution of 'educative materials' and T-shirts.

The YWCA's work on SRHR and related topics is undertaken in two distinct registers. These registers are not compatible with one another and the YWCA makes no attempt to resolve the differences between them. When addressing SRHR in text and in conversation, the YWCA sometimes adopts a more moralizing, Christian tone and at other times adheres more closely to a mainstream 'development' vocabulary. The distinction between these is represented herein by two programme leaflets, the *Advocacy Factsheet for Young Women on Sexual and Reproductive Health and Rights and HIV/AIDS* (hereafter, '*Fact Sheet*') and *My Youth, My Pride*. They address the same basic terrain of youth SRHR, but they are different in tone, content and intended audience. While both were produced by Kenya YWCA, the former was the result of a collaboration with the World YWCA and the latter a collaborative effort with youth YWCA members. The *Fact Sheet* produced as part of the SRHR Programme begins with a brief introduction positioning the World YWCA and Kenya YWCA as 'in the fore front' [sic] of work on issues of women's and girls' SRHR. The tone of the discussion is immediately positive, proclaiming the importance of 'empowering the youth to embrace their sexuality and speak out on their reproductive health needs'. Ideas such as 'empowering' and 'celebrat[ing]' and the exercise of women's human rights are littered throughout the pamphlet. Thus, while not declaring it explicitly, the approach throughout seems to follow a 'sex-positive' logic similar to that suggested by Rachel Spronk (2005), centring pleasure and fun in representations of sex, in contrast to discourses of morality or safety. The overall message conveyed in the leaflet is that information and the 'safe spaces' for discussion provided by the YWCA's programme are critical for young women and girls to 'make informed choices regarding their lives'. The approach it takes is also deeply holistic in its refusal to restrict the programme's scope to ameliorating the circumstances of women's sexual and reproductive lives, but focuses on areas of their lives with sexual and reproductive health and rights that 'extend beyond biology'. As such, the *Fact Sheet* rehabilitates the topic of sexuality in a context where strong taboos and stigma often prevent free discussion. Thus, the YWCA's approach does not straightforwardly perpetuate the legacy of Christian moralizing about youths' and women's sexuality and sexual behaviour. The morals of young people were not the major focus of attention in the SRHR Programme, beyond encouraging openness, self-esteem and confidence.

The *Fact Sheet* explains that the YWCA is concerned to provide young women, in particular, with 'access' to 'information' about sexuality and reproductive health as a partial corrective to the 'coercion and violence' that tend to constrain them otherwise. The leaflet's intended audience is defined as youths who undertake training as peer educators. Peer-to-peer education is a tool often used by the YWCA as a low-cost but potentially highly effective way of reaching adolescents and young people with relevant messages, without the 'strings' that are often perceived to be attached to formal development and social welfare programmes. In the SRHR Programme, the YWCA trained eighty peer educators in its first year, who then facilitated outreach to an estimated total of ten thousand other young people (YWCA 2010: 20). Training peer educators in the SRHR Programme includes equipping them with skills in communication and advocacy as well as relevant information, in this case on the topic of sexual and reproductive health and rights as presented in the *Fact Sheet*. For this reason, among others, the information in the *Fact Sheet* is framed as scientifically true, neutral and objective – as suggested by its title. It therefore lists a number of 'facts and statistics' about youth reproductive health, such as the prevalence of HIV infection, condom use and maternal mortality among Kenyan youths and women.

The tensions between this approach and that taken in *My Youth, My Pride* (c.2009) are significant. The booklet, written with the input of eleven YWCA youth members, addresses an audience of young people with information about HIV prevention and short stories conveying moral messages and prompting discussion through questions. An approach similar to the *Fact Sheet*, which accepts the influence of medical expertise, is mixed with a moralizing tone that strongly discourages sex before marriage, abortion and sex work, while defining sexuality and sexual behaviour in explicitly heteronormative ways. The booklet is fifteen pages long, containing four short stories presented in colourful comic strips, three focusing on young women protagonists and one on a young man. In addition to these stories, it includes an introduction to the YWCA, a list of 'facts' about HIV aimed at debunking popular misconceptions and a glossary of relevant terms. The glossary of terms gives a definition of abortion that mixes medical fact with misinformation. It claims that all abortion risks infection and death, rather than more usefully distinguishing between different methods of medical abortion and their risks, as opposed to non-medical methods. The definition of abortion given further claims that it poses a threat to the success of future pregnancies, before concluding that 'there is a connection between abortion and infanticide … suicide, child abuse, low self-esteem, and even substance abuse'. These claims are common in anti-abortion discourse, although they have been strongly challenged (Cohen 2006). The way these scaremongering claims appear in *My Youth, My Pride* is very similar to those historically made in the Kenyan social ethics curriculum (Mitchell et al. 2006: 517). 'Purity' comes up implicitly in the contrast between 'good' and 'bad' characters in the stories and the consequences of their behaviour. The booklet's title suggests 'pride' as a reward for living up to the demands of purity during one's youth. In my analysis, the content does not avoid the implicit association of the behaviour it condemns with impurity and shame.

Each story follows a young person in a different problem situation, describing their choices and feelings in relation to their relationships, their sex lives and the various consequences of their actions. In the first story, 'When the deal is too good think twice', a young unmarried woman gets a boyfriend, has sex with him and becomes pregnant; but she is warned by an aunty not to abort the pregnancy because 'it would pose great danger'. Subsequently, she discovers that she has contracted HIV and becomes suicidal, only to be guided 'back to her senses' by attending counselling sessions at a VCT centre. At the end of the story the woman discovers her boyfriend has since died and she is left 'to bear the burden of a baby and HIV all alone, wallowing in the miasma of poverty'. While fictional stories can be truthful, claims to truth are also a persuasive technique. As Dina Ligaga's (2020) analysis of moral stories shows, what they communicate with their audiences is not straightforward, because they can be 'read' or heard in many different ways. *My Youth, My Pride* leads beneficiaries of the YWCA's SRHR programmes to certain definite conclusions about the right and wrong responses to risks of peer pressure, alcohol consumption, premarital sex and sex work (referred to in the booklet as 'prostitution'). The inclusion of abortion in the stories about HIV is significant, indicating the many risks of bringing a pregnancy to term and raising children as a HIV-positive woman in Kenya. However, these fictionalized representations of women's experiences are presented in the same way as the inevitability of single motherhood and HIV leading to suffering and poverty. This means that it is possible to read the stories as showing the necessary consequences of premarital sex, rather than some possible consequences.

The next story, 'Subira smiles at last', repeats many of the same plot points while introducing a contrast between the consequences of good and bad choices. Over a four-page cartoon, the reader is introduced to a young woman called Subira, who lives in poverty with her mother. Subira is quickly established as a dutiful, obedient daughter, as she is shown helping her mother. After a conversation with her mother about the dangers of premarital sex, Subira says, 'I promise not to engage in sex until after marriage.' Soon after this, Subira warns her friend Rukia that her boyfriend Matata is untrustworthy, saying, 'He always showers girls with gifts and money only to dump them after having sex with them.' Rukia replies, '*Wacha wivu*' (stop being jealous). Three months later, we are shown that Subira's hard work has resulted in a scholarship to attend the local college to learn dressmaking. Rukia arrives sobbing to tell Subira that Matata has abandoned her, and not only is she HIV-positive but also pregnant. The only explicit reference to Christian faith in *My Youth, My Pride* is made in Subira's story, when she is shown praying with her mother. It seems relevant that *Subira* is a Kiswahili name connoting a sense of 'patience' or waiting, which has strong connotations here of abstinence and/or awaiting a reward for one's good behaviour.

The single story that focuses on a male protagonist is also the only one that is presented with additional commentary. 'Be yourself face the darkness wisely' is a thirteen-panel cartoon depicting Nyangweso, a responsible student who follows two friends to the 'discotheque' on a Friday night. His friends suggest that this will be a great opportunity to meet girls and gain sexual experience. Although Nyangweso dismisses the idea of sex, alluding to HIV as 'the dreaded killer', he goes out with his friends anyway. They pressure him into getting drunk, although Nyangweso's first reaction to the taste of beer is 'yuk'. After their night of drinking, the young men return home. Nyangweso hears a strange noise outside and decides to investigate, at first trying to take a torch so that he can see. His friends ridicule him as a coward, saying he is 'afraid of the dark', and he goes without it. As a result, Nyangweso gets bitten by a snake. This seems like a strange ending for a story that begins with talk of casual sex and shows the young men getting drunk. A short commentary clarifies the narrative's conclusion, saying, 'Maybe Nyangweso could have prevented this by sticking to his idea of a torch', and offers the desired lesson of the story: 'There are vipers waiting for you out there!' While there are many potential readings of this story, it looks critically at the performance of masculinity through bravado, contributing to and/or giving in to peer pressure, alcohol abuse and casual sex. It seems significant that the message apparently aimed at young men does not mention the risks of pregnancy or abortion, focusing instead on HIV, thus centring the risks to the reader himself not to his partner.

There is no explicit Christian reasoning offered in support of the choices suggested through the stories, enabling it to be used as a prompt to reflection and discussion. At the end of each story, a visually distinct section addresses the reader directly, asking them to consider what their decisions might have been in the situation presented and whether the consequences of that choice would have been different than those experienced by the protagonist. Each aspect of the stories is plausible, and their entire sequence of events is likely to have transpired in exactly this way in some cases. However, each story connects one event to the next with a sense of inevitability, a kind of slippery slope that leads seamlessly from a casual premarital sexual encounter to HIV infection, single parenthood and poverty. Thus, they serve as cautionary tales. In foregrounding stories where sex appears as a temptation to be resisted, to the exclusion of more positive stories with plot points centring on commitment, mutual respect or fun, *My Youth, My Pride* describes sexuality only as a threat to young people. The booklet thereby repeats a tendency of Christian and development sexual health education to neglect the fact that people have sex for 'pleasure, intimacy, love, curiosity – and not just coercion, poverty and peer pressure' (Bertrand-Dansereau 2013: 168).

The presentation of short personal stories centred on young protagonists in recognizable scenarios, largely without commentary, allows readers to arrive at their own interpretations. There is a clear difference between the approach taken in *My Youth, My Pride* and the stance towards SRHR expressed in other YWCA materials. The plots and characters conform to the stereotypes circulating throughout moral narratives of proper/deviant womanhood and pure/dangerous sexuality in Kenya. It seems that in order to present themes of HIV, abortion and premarital sex, the YWCA relied on existing and familiar stories even though these pull against its otherwise more reproductive justice-oriented approach. Alongside risk, heterosexuality is presumed throughout all the YWCA's representations of sexual health, making any communication of sex in a positive frame only as positive as can be expected of the exclusion of LBTQI women.

4.6 Summary

With sexuality serving as a battlefield for the oppositional construction of identity and group boundaries, women's sexual lives are always relevant in neocolonial interventions and anti-imperial reactions to them. Late-twentieth-century development industry interventions in women's SRHR have generally plotted a trajectory in continuity with the imperialism of colonial and Christian interventions. Thus, the YWCA's programmes are often positioned in tension between competing explanatory narratives; agency and progress for Kenyan women can either contest the instrumentalization of women's rights and gender discourse by colonizers, churches and development agencies or acquiesce to them. This can be seen in the ways condoms are 'controversial' and attract attention not only from clergy and other Christians taking a moral stance but also from the development industry in response to the epidemic which places the medicalized, problematized African body at the centre of its interventions. The representation of sexual health in YWCA materials is varied precisely because of tensions between different aspects of the YWCA's identity, and the ethical commitments they are taken to involve. In some of the YWCA's SRHR literature, representations of sexual health conform to the hegemonic script of women's human rights and international development approaches. The YWCA movement's Christian identity can accommodate a more 'feminist' approach to sexuality by virtue of the positions, themes and scripts made available and comprehensible within gender work narratives at the overlap of the development industry and the women's movement. However, these positions have been unevenly accepted, with controversial faith issues being identified as such because the YWCA often goes against the 'secular' grain of gender work in development. At other times sexuality is represented in negative and moralistic terms, but the YWCA also regularly goes against the 'staunch' Christian grain of the NCCK and the hegemonic conservative Christianity of Kenya's public sexuality discourse.

The YWCA's work on sexuality and reproduction at times aligns with, and at other times departs from, values widely construed as 'African' and/or 'traditional', as well as those considered to be 'Western', 'secular' or 'feminist'. It is incorrect to assume that because these associations are prevalent, they reflect an essential connection between the given practices or norms and a region, religion or culture. This is evident in the work of the YWCA, since it occupies all these identities and positions simultaneously, or switches between emphasizing one or another in certain circumstances. Due to its simultaneous positioning as a 'Western' religion and its inculturation as an 'African' tradition, Christianity itself flows between these two (indistinct and dubious) categories, allowing the YWCA to negotiate a constellation of more nuanced positions on specific issues rather than accepting one or the other wholesale, in much the same way as postcolonial feminists have negotiated a third space between the competing totalitarianisms of local patriarchal norms and imperial feminisms. For the YWCA in Kenya, a different context prevails, albeit one in which the World YWCA has its own influence. Secular frameworks recur as an absent referent throughout these discourses on women's sexuality. 'Bad' choices in the form of premarital sex, alcohol use, sex work and abortion are typically represented as secular and urban, and having sometimes disastrous consequences. On the other hand, non-Christian values are found to be of use when it comes to positioning sexual health programmes as contributing to women's enjoyment of their rights. The YWCA's simultaneous assertion of both a Christian moralism and a 'secular' rights-based perspective in its sexual health programming places it precisely in the position of having to resolve a very difficult conundrum: to work out its stance in the ongoing competition between overlapping ethical discourses and how to navigate its position in Kenya given the implications of that stance. An everyday narrative understanding of ethics offers a way of thinking about how ethical judgements such as these are embedded in narrative, stories, talk and texts, and are dependent not always on explicit or conscious deliberation but the implicit understanding of how taking up an identity or a position implies certain commitments. Conversely, the assertion of a norm or the promotion of a value implies membership in, or exclusion from, a group or constituency. These tensions in the YWCA's sexual health programmes are resolved through narrative means. 'Controversial faith issues' are at the centre of this nexus of difficult ethical questions.

Part 3

5

Controversial faith issues

As the YWCA became increasingly NGO-ized in the late twentieth century, many of its activities overlapped with those of international and local development agencies, as well as the Kenyan women's movement and churches. As a Christian organization whose programmatic interventions engage it in development, the YWCA navigates a path shared with other faith-based organizations (FBOs), and a public discourse in which Christian voices are prominent. As shown in the previous chapters, commonplace assumptions about Christian sexual ethics, and the long-standing anti-abortion and anti-condom stances of many churches, would seem to present significant challenges to integrating SRHR work with an explicitly Christian organizational identity. The YWCA's activities, policies and programme-related decisions surrounding matters of sexuality and gender necessitated confronting 'controversial faith issues', a phrase that echoed throughout my conversations with my research participants. The 'controversial' nature of these 'issues' surrounding women's and girls' sexual lives and reproductive choices, and the various technologies and legislation associated with them, were addressed using various appeals to the YWCA's Christian identity. The content of the YWCA's approach to controversial faith issues provides a rich example of how persistent and largely implicit questions of how Christians ought to adjudicate in matters of sexual ethics are not necessarily answered with reference to theology or church teachings.

The YWCA's programmes addressing SRHR have the potential to generate controversy because of their implicit or explicit positions in relation to imperialism and coloniality within Christianity and development discourses. My understanding of narrativity in this dynamic suggests looking at how the YWCA passively inherits and explicitly takes scripts and narratives from these influential discourses. 'African', Christian and development industry discourses have inherited a tendency to operate in terms of binary identity categories which implicitly have values attached to them. They seem to be mutually exclusive identities so that placing them together suggests an oxymoron – for example, 'queer Christian' or 'Kenyan feminist'.[1] The oppositional definition of 'African'/'Western' lines up with processes of racialization that define the denizens of these territories as Black and white, respectively, and the evaluation of their apparently singular and clearly bounded cultures as 'traditional'/'modern' or 'underdeveloped'/'developed' or 'uncivilized'/'civilized'. Both development and colonial narratives associate 'modernity' with whiteness, freedom, pleasure and health, while 'tradition' is associated with African-ness, history, constraint and harmful practices (Steady 2005: 315). Therein, 'tradition' can signal a 'heathen' or 'primitive' status (as in the ascription of 'African traditional religion' (ATR) to mark what was not so long ago denigrated as animism, witchcraft, ancestor worship or paganism), while from a 'secular' point of view it can also imply adherence to Christian (or other 'religious') practices (MacGaffey 2012; Mudimbe 1997: 12–21). Furthermore, although Christianity entered colonized eastern Africa as a synonym for, and in a mutually constitutive relationship with, 'civilization', modernity and whiteness, since that time Christianities have pluralized and developed in complex ways.

Christianity was a synonym for 'modernity' in the colonial era because it implied adopting middle-class British cultural norms and practices that were explicitly promoted as progressive. For many in Kenya, Christianity has come to indicate both Africanness and morality, in contrast to the secular West. From development industry perspectives in the late twentieth and early twenty-first centuries, Christianity is more likely to be associated with tradition and resistance to modernity, as it is often deployed in opposition to science, urbanity, consumerism and feminism. Imperialist and colonial narratives are behind many assumptions at work in the development industry, which construct 'African culture' as innately harmful to women and offer Western norms as 'modern' and beneficial to women. The point of rehearsing these alignments and oppositions is not to endorse one or the other but to outline what is at stake for the YWCA in claiming one or more identities under which to operate. Out of this historical context – colonization and Christian women's roles in it, anti-colonial responses and the moral identities established in narratives and histories that recall them – SRHR became a target for intervention within the scope of the development industry. As I have already outlined, institutional and medical forms of health care were a further site for, and a product of, colonial and imperialistic interventions. Uncritical white-feminist and international development approaches to African women's sexual, reproductive and maternal health struggles have deleterious effects. In efforts to control the HIV epidemic and reduce 'population growth', there is a continuing focus on the bodies of women racialized as 'African' as problematically reproductive and sexual (Arnfred 2004; Booth 2004; Pigg and Adams 2005; Tamale 2011; Thomas 2003; Wangari 2002; Wilson 2012).

The postcolonial construction of a 'gender neutral homogeneous "African culture"' (Okech 2019: 6) is a critical response to this discourse that refuses the logic of development interventions from outside. This attempt to construct African cultures as free from gender oppression often essentializes African women as mothers, and potentially delegitimizes African feminist critiques of precolonial cultural practices. Feminists in the 'Third World' have often been discredited by claims that feminism is Western, allowing those hostile to feminists to frame their activism and critiques as evidence of their 'Westernization' and therefore their inauthenticity, as a way of undermining them (Narayan 1997). Struggles to ensure free and easy access to contraception, abortion, pre- and post-natal health care and sex education are often complicated in precisely this way. A rejection of queer sexualities because 'they are not African' is an example of the construction of an 'African' identity through the assertion of a heteropatriarchal family structure, pro-natalism and 'respectable femininities' (Okech 2019: 2). These narratives require their proponents to ignore possibilities for subverting and negotiating sexual and gender norms from within, through the creation of new associations, or recovering old norms and identities. The availability of these narrative tendencies at the level of public discourse in Kenya makes complex ethical positions available (and complex ethical choices necessary) for the YWCA as it sits at the nexus between the churches, the women's movement and development. The question is thus how to improve women's and girls' sexual and reproductive health care and rights, without aligning with or reinforcing neocolonial and imperialist transnational dynamics – a problem faced in postcolonial contexts the world over. African gender theorists and feminist theorists have articulated their responses to this problem by insisting on the existence of options beyond either acquiescing to local patriarchal norms or submitting to white/imperialist/development feminism.

5.1 Defining controversial faith issues

I encountered the phrase 'controversial faith issues' in my first formal interview, with both Wandia and Njeri, conducted in Njeri's office at the YWCA's headquarters. Wandia and Njeri occupied senior positions and both had intimate knowledge of programmes and funding. We discussed the FGM workshop I had attended a few days earlier, and I began to prompt Wandia to talk about the YWCA's Christian identity and the difference it made to the organization or its work, suggesting that she could use the FGM Programme to illustrate this.

> *Eleanor:* From the [FGM] meeting I didn't get any sense that there was a specific kind of Christian influence on the way that these programmes are being run … I don't know if that's a true perception[?] … One of the major questions that I'm interested in, in terms of the YWCA's work, is how the Christianity, or how the 'Christian emphasis', is translated into programmes – if it is, or, when it is. And what difference that makes …
> *Wandia:* Of course, for some programmes it will be just the way any other organisation would do it. But for some, especially with what are controversial faith issues; there, we have to be very clear with how we put it under 'YWCA' … even the way we do our advocacy …
> *Eleanor:* [So, does] it make a difference to come from a Christian organisation with this message, as opposed to a secular one[?] … [Do] you have any comments about the relationship there, between the 'Christianity' and the 'women's' [in 'Young Women's Christian Association']?
> *Wandia:* I think the approach [of the YWCA] is not Christian and has nothing controversial about it, especially for FGM, but for reproductive health programmes … there is a faith issue there. (Wandia, interview, 2012)

In answer to my question about how being a Christian organization makes the YWCA different to other women's organizations, Wandia claimed, and Njeri agreed, that the YWCA's approach to making programmatic interventions was, on the whole, not distinctively Christian. There were two exceptions: first, 'involving churches' was claimed to be a distinctive method, although it was not strongly pronounced in the programmes I surveyed. Wandia further claimed that churches are inclined to welcome and cooperate with the YWCA because it is a Christian organization. Second, there are some sensitive 'issues' that are 'controversial' and therefore require the YWCA to be careful about how they are approached. A few minutes later, Njeri outlined what I came to understand as the paradigmatic account of controversial faith issues.

> When it comes to issues of reproductive health, the issue is of taking our stand, that one has for us to be very clear, when you are talking about issues of abortion, it has to be very clear that we [at the YWCA] do not condone abortion … we do not condone sex amongst teenagers or before marriage … we normally have

to be very careful about how we package our approach so that again it doesn't seem like we are supporting 100% [the] use of condoms. (Njeri, interview, 2012)

Njeri agreed with Wandia that there were certain topics that required special consideration from the YWCA's position as a Christian organization, suggesting a question of organizational identity in terms of differentiating an appropriately 'YWCA' way of approaching these 'issues'. Significantly, this connection between the sensitivity and controversy of some dimensions of the YWCA's SRHR programmes was offered in explanation of the difference having a Christian identity and character makes. The common thread shared by the practices identified by Njeri and Wandia as controversial was the YWCA's confrontation of apparent discrepancies between prevailing Kenyan norms of Christian faith and identity and the needs of young people, particularly young women, especially in consideration of the threat posed by HIV.

Controversial faith issues, in the sense in which it was used by the YWCA in 2012, was a name for a constellation of topics of particular ethical significance from a Christian point of view. The three most controversial faith issues were condoms, abortion and sexuality – specifically, the tolerance or rejection of non-normative sexualities, which came up in conversation as the exclusion of LBTQI women from the Association's work. Many other 'issues' related to sexuality were also problematic, including sex before marriage, sex work and sex education for children and teenagers. These 'issues' were related to sexuality but were invoked less often in my interviews, and were strongly related to those topics that did receive attention as controversial faith issues. For example, sex work and sex before marriage were topics of conversation that could be mentioned as part of programmatic interventions, in peer educator training for instance. However, for any of these to rise to the status of a controversial faith issue it must be defined by three features: first, it is one on which the Association is expected to have a 'Christian' perspective by virtue of its Christian identity; and second, it is directly and routinely confronted in one or more of its programmes. Sex work and FGM both meet these criteria but I do not include them in my discussion of controversial faith issues. Sex work is certainly something that my interviewees considered problematic, but it is an issue that not frequently directly implicated in the YWCA's activities. When it was mentioned, my research participants framed it as a moral problem and expressed no conflict about discouraging young women from engaging in it. The issue of FGM was specifically identified as 'not controversial' by Wandia, despite meeting the first two criteria. It is necessary, therefore, to add a further criterion in order to capture the heart of controversial faith issues, which is that they are cause for serious and ongoing discussion about the appropriate course(s) of action for the YWCA, even raising existential questions about the organization's scope and identity. Neither sex work nor FGM was subject to debate, enjoying unquestioned status as harmful and undesirable practices rejected by the YWCA, and so they were not considered to be controversial faith issues, even if they were acknowledged to be sensitive or provocative matters in general. I will now discuss in turn the three issues that received greatest attention from my research participants in my discussions with them.

5.2 Condoms

Among the primary areas of concern at the YWCA and other Christian organizations engaged in sex education and other SRHR interventions has been the perception of the problem of 'encouraging' and validating sexual intimacy outside the confines of procreative, heterosexual, monogamous marriage. The twin issues of procreative sexuality and heteronormativity make condom use, the most widely promoted way to prevent the sexual transmission of HIV, an area of particular concern for many Christians in Kenya and elsewhere in the world. As discussed briefly in Chapters 3 and 4, many Christian leaders and institutions – most obviously the Vatican – have opposed the use of condoms, on the basis that they 'pervert' the 'purpose' of human sexuality, which is asserted to be procreation – specifically drawing on Augustine's assertion that sex should be for procreation and not pleasure, as articulated in the papal encyclical *Casti Connubii* in 1930 (Pope Pius XI). In Kenya anti-condom sentiment has been expressed, and perpetuated, through public demonstrations such as the burning of condoms (Balchin 2008: 6; Kangara 2007: 6–7). This attitude has remained even in the face of the HIV epidemic, during which time increased scrutiny has been brought to bear on the effects of the churches' sexual ethics (Chitando and Njoroge 2016: 4; Parsitau 2009: 47–8; Van Klinken and Gunda 2012: 118). Less often, the emergence of HIV has led Christian leaders and institutions to revise their previously negative stance on condoms. In the case of the Catholic Archbishop of Mombasa, Boniface Lele, in office from 2005 until 2013, his position on condoms loosened a little to permit their use as a prophylactic for

HIV-discordant married couples (Stroebel and Van Benthem 2012: 2–3). The definition of sexuality according to its potential for reproduction, upon which Catholic and other Christian opposition to condoms rests, is a clear expression of the heteronormativity that is deeply embedded in dominant Christian theological anthropologies. The promotion of condoms as a primary method to prevent HIV transmission further embeds these heteronormative assumptions so that LBTQI women are structurally erased, only included to the extent that they have sex with men.

Condoms were often mentioned by my research participants in response to my prompts about the influence of a Christian institutional identity. Wandia nuanced her earlier assertion that the YWCA conducts itself no differently from other NGOs working on women's rights and gender equality. She described how the YWCA's 'Christian principles' differentiate the organization from others: 'Other youth-serving organisations will just say "Oh the youth, give them condoms!" while for us, we still know that we will end up giving condoms to [some, but] ... we still want to apply the Christian principle of purity, you know, stay pure 'til you're married, delay sexual debut' (Wandia, interview, 2012). Condoms come up here as a challenge to the YWCA's ability to unambiguously promote 'purity', which Wandia defined as abstinence before marriage and monogamy. Purity was largely taken for granted as a standard for youth sexuality, defined by virginity. In a later interview, Njeri claimed that the YWCA's approach to the inclusion of condoms in sexual health programmes 'depends on the person in charge of the programme', emphasizing that the YWCA didn't 'have a stand' and that there was nothing 'stated in our policies per se' to guide decision-making on this controversial issue (Njeri, interview, 2012). However, in practice the YWCA had promoted the use of external ('male') and internal ('female') condoms both for contraception and prophylaxis. This promotion included demonstrating how they should be used, as recorded in photographs of workshops and other events that were later reproduced in the YWCA's annual reports and on its Facebook page. Regardless of the controversial status of condoms, the YWCA did not hide its promotion of them. Evidence from other African contexts demonstrates that many NGOs perceive promoting and distributing condoms to be a risky activity (Horn 2012: 20). Given that other organizations have been 'forc[ed] ... not to engage in activities on issues' that are 'controversial' from Christian perspectives, including abortion and sex work (Ahlberg et al. 2009: 114), the YWCA's persistence appears to be evidence of conviction, and the ability to resist outside influence.

Wandia explained that the twin risks of 'disease' and 'pregnancy' motivated the YWCA to take the approach that 'if you are already [sexually] active, then protect yourself' (Wandia, interview, 2012), a point stressed by almost all my research participants. Framing sex as risk, especially for young women and girls, positions the YWCA firmly in the lineage I have sketched from the colonial era, through development discourse, to popular moral narratives of women's sexuality in the twenty-first century. As a Christian organization, the YWCA's use of this discourse is compounded by an apparent need to conform to particular ethical norms which are understood to be expected by its members and other observers of YWCA activities, like the NCCK. Therefore, condoms present a difficult combination of possibilities for the YWCA depending on the identity and age of its audience. When the audience is young, of school-going age, abstinence takes centre stage. When addressing women in their twenties, the YWCA expects that the majority will already be married. In this case, the YWCA prioritizes its responsibility to protect them from HIV transmission and unwanted pregnancy by equipping them with information about the efficacy of condoms. In both cases, the anticipation that the beneficiaries of its programmes are already sexually active allows the YWCA to set its commitment to sexual 'purity' aside for pragmatic reasons, in certain situations.

> That group is already sexually active, mainly, so the truth is, it is better for us to talk to them about safety and using condoms instead of letting them just have … unprotected sex, which is more risky, you'll get disease, pregnancy … we give all this information and they have to make their [own] decision, so we really don't force [them]. We give the information, then we trust them. Then, some of the centres have condoms for the youth that want [condoms] … we don't come out very strongly that 'YWCA distributes condoms', because we know that these condoms are just for a specific group, and we are not encouraging youth to come to us for condoms. (Wandia, interview, 2012)

The YWCA's attempts to restrict education about condoms to adolescents and young adults who are 'already sexually active' indicate that the Association considers that condoms encourage young people to have sex. In addition to the organizational commitment to promoting 'Christian principles', many of my research participants were professionally committed to the notion that adolescent sexual activity and premarital sex were best avoided. None ever expressed the view that the YWCA should publicly condemn these behaviours, although doing so would be in line with the dominant Kenyan-Christian moral schema.

The requirements of Christianity appear to be difficult to fulfil: both to reject condoms and protect young people from HIV, something that can only be achieved with the promotion of sexual abstinence, motivated by and authorized by the reification of 'purity'. In short, the different moralities and sources of moral authority recognized by the YWCA differ on crucial and 'controversial' points, like the use of condoms, and cause tensions. These tensions are exacerbated because each moral scheme seems to be universal in its claims and scope of application. The YWCA accommodates and resolves the contradictions between these moral worldviews through context-specific ethical reasoning, as summarized by Njeri in relation to condoms:

> We are not encouraging them to use condoms, what we are doing is we are giving them information in order for them to make informed choices ... there was funding ... from the US from PEPFAR [President's Emergency Plan for AIDS Relief] whose main focus [was] on abstinence, and behaviour control. No condoms ... It was quite a debate, because then we were saying, 'So then, what happens to the young people who are already sexually active? ... Would you say that you are not going to reach them, just because you're going to preach [against] condoms?' (Njeri, interview, 2012)

The YWCA makes use of the popular 'ABC' framework of abstinence, behaviour change and condoms, and while promoting abstinence forms part of their strategy, an abstinence-only strategy is considered unrealistic. Here, Njeri suggested that for the YWCA, the protection of the health of young people was a more important, or perhaps better, ethical goal than having them conform to a moral standard of purity or abstinence, even though abstinence was an ideal that could be unproblematically promoted with mainstream Christian moral reasoning. Significantly, Njeri's attitude was infused with an implicit anti-imperial critique, rejecting the US intervention under PEPFAR. This critique was echoed by other research participants. However, for the YWCA, assigning 'controversial' status to condoms has a further narrative function. Talking about it opens opportunities for the YWCA's staff and leaders to (re)tell stories about the YWCA's distinguishing Christian character. This is clear when considering the ways in which the YWCA is able to compare its approach on issues of SRHR to the apparently different approach taken by 'other' organizations, which is to say non-Christian NGOs and development agencies. Controversial faith issues also create opportunities for the YWCA to promote and 'apply' a sexual ethic of 'purity'.

5.3 Abortion

In 2012 the very loud public debate on abortion that preceded the referendum on the proposed constitution in 2010 was still ringing in the ears of many women's organizations. In our discussion of unwanted pregnancy, Wandia demonstrated that even beyond the explicit context of the HIV epidemic, the consequences of some choices are to be weighed against one another. She said that for the YWCA it was 'easier' to 'ask these girls: protect yourselves, don't get pregnant, because of the complications that follow' (Wandia, interview, 2012). In this case, Wandia suggested that the Association's position on condoms was informed by their contraceptive effect, and not only their prophylactic use, to avoid the issue of abortion. The YWCA recognizes that if a young woman gives birth to a child she has not planned for, is not prepared for or does not want, her situation presents much more complex ethical and practical problems. However, the YWCA's position on abortion was less malleable than its position on the use of condoms, seeming not to respond to the difficulties faced by teenage mothers, such as access to prenatal care and continuing their own education, that the YWCA otherwise recognized.

My research participants explained that the YWCA's position on abortion had never been formulated explicitly in terms of policy, theology or ethics, but just as I found on the topic of condoms, they seemed to express a coherent YWCA position anyway. This was characterized by the refusal of a 'pro-choice' label, by stating that abortion is not acceptable, and explaining how the YWCA would support a pregnant teenager. Although my research participants did not explicitly describe a hierarchy among controversial faith issues, abortion was evidently more controversial than condom use: 'As an organisation – [we] believe that the sexual rights – especially for the young [people], they need to know [about their sexual rights]. Where we have a problem is with abortion and the use of condoms ... But abortion it is, for a Christian, we don't, I mean we don't allow it. We – it's not good. For us, it is sin' (Nyaboke, interview, 2012). Nyaboke described abortion as a 'sin', expressing a specifically Christian moral judgement about its status and its effects. At face value, Nyaboke is simply stating the YWCA's rejection of abortion using a recognizably Christian moral vocabulary. However, interpreting this statement in light of Nyaboke's assertion of 'sexual rights' in the preceding sentence, I think that this statement reveals something more interesting. She continued, 'But others will come up and say "If I don't want the baby, what do I do?" – "If it's going to jeopardise the health of the mother, what do you do?" That is, that is a challenge that we have had, and up to now, we don't have a clear answer to that' (Nyaboke, interview, 2012).

In admitting that the YWCA does not have an agreed approach to these exceptional or difficult cases in which abortion may be sought, Nyaboke acknowledged the wide gap between the existence of a moral rule and its application in practice. Similarly, none of my research participants who identified themselves as Catholic expressed a moral rejection of condom use. Wandia explained that the YWCA's opposition to abortion was in part motivated by the perception that abortion is illegal in Kenya, which is the case unless certain exceptional circumstances obtain:

> As YWCA Kenya we would not be expected to support, you know, we would not be able to be pro-choice. ... we would not stand for abortion. ... we are mainly doing awareness, raising awareness ... we mainly do not [provide sexual health] services, we do referrals. So, a girl comes, they are pregnant, we do the counselling ... Maybe the World [YWCA] office would expect me to [ask] the girl, 'What do you want? To carry?' and if she says no, then I should support her to get an abortion. But in Kenya it's illegal, so that already puts the organisation in a difficult position ... supporting a girl to get an abortion is not the right thing to do ... So, it's really a complex issue. (Wandia, interview, 2012)

In Wandia's account, the YWCA is far from expressing total moral condemnation of abortion, but nonetheless operates from a different position from the World YWCA, which she characterized as more straightforwardly 'pro-choice'. As Wandia pointed out, in Kenya the YWCA faces logistical and legislative obstacles to supporting abortion, and not only the ethical status of abortion within Christian discourse.

The circumstances in which the YWCA considers abortion to be a controversial faith issue are significantly different to those surrounding its position on the use of condoms. Condoms, as a relatively discreet and portable item, the use of which does not require medical expertise, are feasibly provided as part of the YWCA's sexual health programmes. Abortion is entirely different. If the YWCA is reluctant to accept abortion as a necessary – if undesirable – part of achieving young women's sexual and reproductive health and rights in the same way it has accepted condom use, it is partly because the Association is well aware of the difficulty of accessing a safe, medical abortion. Even when the restrictive criteria for legality are met, vast numbers of girls and women simply do not have access to medical abortion – lacking the relevant knowledge, opportunity or resources to locate and travel to the clinic and pay for the treatment. Young women especially die in high numbers from the consequences of improperly administered abortions (Ahlberg et al. 2009: 114). It is not something that the YWCA is equipped to provide to its members, so its lack of support is qualitatively different because the question is whether, and how, the YWCA should talk about abortion and make efforts to raise awareness of its availability and limitations. There was considerable concern about where the limits of the YWCA's responsibilities for beneficiaries' medical care lay, and suggestions that those limits would be interpreted broadly.

> So our stand is, we counsel this girl – [if] she is young, of course she really needs a lot of counselling, talking to the parents. Then, ante-natal clinic; it's very important because of issues of maternal mortality, so they have to go to [the] clinic, deliver; then the question: who takes care of the baby? You know, the [birth mother's] parents must be willing to take care of that baby for the girl to go back to school. Otherwise, what happens? Most of them drop out of school. (Wandia, interview, 2012)

Although the YWCA would not support a girl to obtain an abortion, it acknowledges and wrestles with the various material realities associated with encouraging a young, single woman or schoolgirl to have a baby. Regardless of the morality of abortion, the YWCA cannot recommend abortion if it risks serious harm to the girl or young woman. There can be no reproductive justice for the young woman who has irreparably damaged her uterus as a result of inducing an abortion with a sharp object, or died after ingesting a poisonous abortifacient. It is significant that those who seek an abortion in the hypothetical situations given by my research participants were 'girls', not married adults. This is partly explained by the fact that the YWCA is primarily concerned with young women and girls, but the use of this figure to illustrate explanations of the Association's stance on abortion also belies two common assumptions in anti-abortion discourse. First, that older, married women or mothers would not seek an abortion, and second – relatedly – that there are a very limited number of reasons for seeking an abortion: being too young, being single or the pregnancy posing a serious risk to one's health. These assumptions have the effect of occluding the complex realities of unwanted pregnancy among older, married women and those who are already mothers. The implicit story of teenage pregnancy reveals the further influence of the moral narratives of reckless teenagers as those on whose bodies abortion debates are staged, as contrasted to the repronormative figure of the adult woman who is presumed to welcome any and all pregnancies.

The YWCA's concern with abortion initially struck me as an example of what, in Western European and North American contexts, is a stereotypical Christian position on reproductive health and rights. Opposition to abortion has emerged as a group-defining issue for Christian identity, particularly for European Catholics and North American Evangelicals. Kenyan moral and political discussions of abortion at this time were certainly influenced in broader, historical terms by the mainline churches, including the Catholic and Anglican churches, but also by networks of conservative, largely US-based groups (Kaoma 2009, 2012). In *African Christian Ethics*, theologian Samuel Waje Kunhiyop (2008) addresses a vast range of topics, among which an argument against abortion, on the grounds that it 'involves the killing of the unborn baby' (Kunhiyop 2008: 334). The conferring of the status of 'unborn baby' or 'unborn child' is common in anti-abortion arguments, as is Kunhiyop's conclusion that to help prevent abortions Christians should encourage women to bring their pregnancies to term and offer financial and moral support to them throughout the pregnancy and the child's upbringing (Kunhiyop 2008: 342–3). Despite offering what he names an African Christian ethics, Kunhiyop refers to no African theologians or ethicists to lend support to his anti-abortion argument, instead relying on the work of US-based anti-choice scholars and evangelical pastors (Kunhiyop 2008: 330–43). This suggests that Kapya Kaoma's argument about the influence of US evangelical Christianity in Africa needs to also take into account the ways theological education and transnational alliances between institutions inform theology, as well as the political applications of the Christian ethics that arises from these collaborations. However, the YWCA's anti-abortion sentiments were not vitriolic like anti-abortion arguments that rely on terms like 'killing' and represent 'babies' as the central focus of discussion, as Kunhiyop and the NCCK did.

> We [YWCA] don't have a strictly certain Christian way that ... you want to focus things on. Just like the issue of abortion, a number of people in the organisation will say ... '[if it is needed] let it be done, but by a professional.' But then there are those who say 'No, it should not ever happen.' ... [but] personally, I have never really [known] such conflicting voices [to be expressed] clearly within the [YWCA]. (Njeri, interview, 2012)

As is suggested in these statements, no fixed YWCA statement of opposition to abortion exists, in policy documents or elsewhere, and the Association offers no official guidance to its staff and volunteers about the appropriate way to respond in the case of a YWCA member seeking an abortion. Despite the YWCA's affiliation to NCCK, it refused to enter the abortion debate. The prevalent and prominent vocabulary of abortion that positions it as evidence of creeping secularization and immorality did not serve as a primary point of reference for my research participants. Abortion is a controversial faith issue for the YWCA partly because it attracts blanket universal statements and pronouncements on both sides of the public debate surrounding its legitimacy.

The YWCA's opposition to abortion seems more like avoiding expressing any kind of support for it, individually or at the level of national politics and legislation. The consistency with which research participants repeated the point that the YWCA does not have a codified stance on abortion leads me to suspect that this is not a 'lack' at all. Rather, neglecting to set a position in stone is characteristic of the YWCA's approach to controversial faith issues, and one which allows plural Christian positions to exist within the Association. Although my research participants were quick to articulate their own personal anti-abortion attitudes, most took a lot of time and effort reaching for the right language with which to describe the YWCA's position on abortion. It seemed that each member of staff and each leader was expected to have an acceptable moral stance, informed by their commitment to Christianity, and that this was expected to regulate the conduct of the YWCA. This mechanism was illustrated by an anonymous research participant, who suggested that a YWCA leader would not be permitted to take a position in support of abortion.[2]

> [You need] strong Christian values to survive in the culture of YWCA ... [if a leader] saw the YWCA more as a youth organisation than a Christian organisation ... [if] for her it was OK for a thirteen-year-old to abort ... [then] definitely, she is going to end up in problems with the [YWCA] members, the membership will not allow that kind of stand ... The youth and the women [YWCA members], they [would say] 'No, no, no, no ... [she] is not doing what we expect.' The membership ... [has an] expectation, which staff and committee members must make sure that at least they satisfy. (Anonymous, interview, 2012)

Performing an appropriate moral identity as part of an effort to maintain the Christianity of the YWCA emerged as a significant feature of the organization's identity, as discussed at greater length in Chapter 6. Except for Nyaboke, who described abortion as a 'sin', the YWCA did not talk about its opposition to abortion using explicitly 'Christian' moral vocabularies, values or rules. So, the idea that the YWCA's members would reject a leader who articulated support for abortion confirms the extent to which the membership has some control over the ways in which staff and leaders conduct themselves, and also over how and when the organization's Christianity is incorporated into the Association's practices and its identity. Indeed, this story strongly suggests that the YWCA's anti-abortion stance is also a demonstration of the 'right' kind of Christian identity. The hypothetical YWCA leader in this story would be unsuccessful because she did not publicly adhere to the implicit moral schema that was understood by YWCA members and staff to indicate an appropriately 'staunch' Christian faith. That this should be the case also explains why my research participants' discussion of abortion did not invoke any reference to theological or ethical arguments for, or reasoning about, the unacceptability of abortion. It seemed to be taken for granted that abortion should be opposed because the Christian identity of the Association signals adherence to an anti-abortion stance, and conversely that the expression of opposition to abortion demonstrates the Association's Christian identity.

5.4 LBTQI women

In the hierarchy of controversial faith issues, non-normative sexualities and LBTQI women were perhaps the most controversial for the YWCA. In brief, I found that the YWCA's approach to non-normative sexualities was one of avoidance, but 'LGBTs' were occasionally mentioned by my research participants. When they were mentioned, their possible inclusion in the YWCA's programmes was clearly identified as a controversial faith issue. The issue of terminology around sexuality was among the dilemmas I encountered both in the field and in writing about my findings. Wandia uncertainly referred to 'LGBTs' (pronounced as a plural acronym, 'elgeebeetees') while other research participants used the phrase 'gays and lesbians'. Both of these expressions have an objectifying effect by turning adjectives into nouns, and applying them to identify a heterogeneous group in order to exclude them. Using the Anglophone terminology of 'LGBT' or 'queer' to (re)categorize fluid and changeable practices, intimacies, desires and identities of Kenyan women who are excluded by the YWCA is potentially problematic: it does not necessarily reflect the self-understandings of the people it is intended to name (Chitando and Van Klinken 2016: 9). The postcolonial feminist project of 'requeering sexuality' (Kwok 2005: 139–42) suggests avoiding Eurocentric assumptions about sexuality, or even of the primacy of the category of sexuality for organizing desire, behaviour, pleasure and identity. However, these identities have been taken up by activists and academics in African contexts, and in the absence of a better solution, throughout my discussion of the YWCA's attitude I will follow my research participants' terminology of 'LGBTs' (always presenting it in quote marks). When I am not citing the YWCA's discussions, I will opt for the more specific terminology 'LBTQI women' or 'queer Christians'. LBTQI women is apt because the exclusion of people who are not women is taken for granted in the case of the YWCA as a women's organization. Thus, it is the exclusion of women and girls who transgress the norms of cisgender heterosexuality that is at issue in my analysis.

> *Wandia:* It is really [hard] especially when we have to include the transgender, and the lesbians, and what is the other group? I forget.
> *Eleanor:* Bisexual?
> *Wandia:* Yeah, bisexual.
> *Eleanor:* 'LGBT': Lesbian, gay, bisexual, and transgender.
> *Wandia:* Mmm-hmm, elgeebeetees, yeah … There are donors who would be willing to fund some of our work, but just because we do not outrightly support that group, then we miss out on funding. (Wandia, interview, 2012)[3]

The first time LBTQI women were explicitly mentioned by any of my research participants was in response to my question about whether the YWCA would refuse to work with other organizations on principle. As already suggested in the quote, above, the YWCA would not enter a partnership or accept funding from just any organization. Njeri identified a producer of alcoholic drinks as an example of the kind of organization from which the YWCA would not accept funding. This was explained by reference to the way in which alcohol is generally considered a social problem in Kenya, particularly for poorer families where scarce income that might be used to buy food is 'wasted' on alcohol. In development literature, this is often theorized according the problematic notion of 'secondary poverty', which is considered to be gendered, as husbands or male family members 'squander' money on alcohol or gambling, for example, which would otherwise be used to support the family (Wilson 2015: 811). Outside of my specific prompt to consider what organizations the YWCA would work with, Wandia additionally ventured that it would avoid partnerships that would require them to include LBTQI women or issues in their programmes.

> For example, we were doing a proposal to [an NGO] … [but] we checked the internet, it was discovered that they support LGBTs. For them to give you funding, you must be able to include those kind of people in your programmes.

> Now that is controversial ... [for the] YWCA because of faith issues. So then, you leave them out; simply. (Wandia, interview, 2012, my emphasis)

Here, Wandia framed the exclusion of LBTQI women and issues of non-normative sexualities from YWCA programmes with a suggestion that NGOs, potential partners and funding organizations exert pressure on African NGOs and other organizations to accept and promote LGBTQ rights, and the concomitant assertion that this is a form of cultural imperialism (Van Klinken 2014: 272). Wandia's comment that the YWCA 'leave[s] them out' is ambiguous, referring perhaps to both LBTQI women themselves and the queer-affirming or LGBTQ rights organizations that might influence the YWCA's approach. Regardless, LBTQI women and girls are 'left out' by the YWCA's refusal to conform to the demands of certain potential funders and partner organizations. When Wandia went elsewhere, representing the YWCA as a Christian could be a cause of trouble, as many of its partner organizations were willing to adopt a queer-inclusive or queer-affirming perspective from which the YWCA opted out. The YWCA sometimes felt itself to be at odds with organizations it worked alongside in international fora, including the World YWCA which was described as 'liberal'.

> It is difficult for me because I would say I am also a staunch Christian, and ... to be effective in this work I still need to participate in [international meetings with other organisations cooperating on sexual health programmes], yet I cannot agree one hundred percent with the [other organisations]. Yeah, so it is really [difficult] – especially when we have to include [LBTQI women]. (Wandia, interview, 2012)

Wandia focused on the difficulty she personally experienced when participating in these meetings as a representative of the YWCA and a 'staunch' Christian. The connection between her own faith and her role within the YWCA was felt to be a source of strength in Kenya, because she and other staff are held to account by the Association's members. This apparently obvious connection between a Christian identity and a tacit, unquestioned, heteronormative ethical stance is a narrative achievement. The value of adopting this identity and the associated requirement to passively exclude LBTQI women had material consequences for the YWCA.

> There's a lot of money supporting SRHR programmes but we do not get [it] because of our faith. You know, there are donors who will not give to faith-based organisations because they want you to be able to reach any group, including a

group that is not within what YWCA can reach ... [an NGO] we tried, [we] even did a proposal to them, but these people will not move our agenda. (Wandia, interview, 2012)

Wandia framed this refusal as a positive example of the YWCA's commitment to Christianity; the organization would not be persuaded to change its stance on sexuality in order to receive funding. This refusal can be represented as proof of the YWCA's staunch Christianity in contexts where non-normative sexualities are commonly assumed to be unchristian.

The claim that the YWCA lacks the capacity to and/or is just unsuitable to 'reach' sexual minorities is appealed to in order to explain the YWCA's lack of attention to this constituency. Wandia expanded on this point to claim that the YWCA does not deliberately include LBTQI women as part of its current projects because LBTQI women were 'a group that is not within what YWCA can reach'. This reasoning positions the question of the ability of the YWCA to include LBTQI women as logically prior to any ethical considerations of whether they should include them. The YWCA's inability to include LBTQI women serves as justification for its refusal to do so. However, if the ethical or theological grounds on which the exclusion of LBTQI women stood were considered strong enough on its own, then perhaps there would be no need to add this further layer of justification. Wandia further explained that 'we do not necessarily support those values', meaning challenging heteronormativity, and 'we are not willing to support that minority', referring to 'LGBTs' (Wandia, interview, 2012). This was a relatively mild statement of indifference to the marginalization and oppression of sexual minorities in Kenya, as compared to the often crowing and moralizing tone of public Christian homophobia. Wandia's tone of voice and body language during this exchange suggested to me that this was an uncomfortable topic for her to discuss, and beyond her area of expertise, but she evidently felt that what she was telling me was a simple matter of fact. It apparently was not felt to require an explanation to establish why including LBTQI women would not be a priority for a Christian women's organization; it was obvious.

The exclusion of LGBTQ persons is supported and encouraged by the explicit heterosexism of Christian institutions. These trends serve to discourage queer Christians from 'coming out' to their churches, and their apparent absence from Christian spaces reinforces common assumptions that 'Christian' and 'LGBT' are mutually exclusive categories. Clearly, however, this is not the case and there are many queer Christians who are active members of churches, including as clergy (van Klinken 2019). The YWCA's avoidance of the topic is only slightly different to the official position of the Anglican Communion. Given the British and Anglican roots of the YWCA, it is interesting to consider the value the Anglican Communion has placed on 'unity' in the long-standing debate about homosexuality (Rubenstein 2004: 344–5). In the Anglican Church's position, established at Lambeth Conferences in 1998 and 2008, the unity of the church is given equal treatment or even priority over the inclusion of LGBTQ Anglicans on an equal basis with straight Anglicans.

It is accurate to assert, as Wandia did, that LBTQI women are 'left out', as opposed to being deliberately targeted for exclusion with formal barriers that prevent their use of YWCA accommodation or participation in programmes. The YWCA neither aims any of its programmes at LBTQI women nor puts any energy into excluding them from its programmatic interventions in SRHR, HIV, FGM or other connected issues. The exclusion of women who deviate from the cisgender, heterosexual norm is achieved through more subtle and informal means. In fact, the only times I heard the YWCA mention LBTQI women were in my interviews. This fact does not excuse the damage that the YWCA may do to the sexual and psychological health of LBTQI girls and women by working with a heteronormative understanding of SRHR. In my assessment, LBTQI women would not be prevented from participating in many of the YWCA's programmes because participation is often quite informal, especially in the case of workshops. Nonetheless, LBTQI women, if and where they are present within the YWCA, are not well-served by the heteronormative assumptions embedded in its SRHR programmes, which focus largely on contraception and male-female HIV transmission. Above all, what is revealed by the YWCA's categorization of non-normative sexualities as 'controversial' is that the conceptual framework with which it approaches sexual health programmes remains entirely centred on the normative figure of the cisgender, heterosexual mother and the cisgender, heterosexual girl who will become a mother. This heteronormativity is also thoroughly embedded in the assumptions of development industry interventions. A gender binary, repronormativity, and the small monogamous nuclear family are all explicitly promoted as goods, goals or ideals by mainstream SRHR development narratives and practices (Cornwall and Jolly 2009). In this vein, it is striking to observe how little has changed compared to the promotion of domesticity and British gender norms by missionaries and colonial women's groups.

Other interviewees did not engage in as much discussion of LBTQI women as Wandia, perhaps because of their relative lack of involvement in areas of YWCA work that would require them to engage with this controversial faith issue. Responding to a question about the Christian basis for the YWCA's work, Joyce suggested that not only the inclusion or exclusion of LBTQI women but all controversial faith issues might stem from taking on a 'human rights agenda':

> During the 1960s, 1970s, early 1980s, most of our programmes were basically welfare, so there was no conflict with our Christian basis – not that there is a conflict now – but there was that controversy once we got to gender and development, and we started looking at issues of human rights … The question for the Y[WCA], for example, since we have a human rights programmes [is], would we be advocating for the rights of commercial sex workers? Would we be out there advocating for the rights of gays and lesbians? (Joyce, interview, 2012)

The idea that human rights could pose a 'controversy' for faithful Christians parallels a long-standing opposition to international agreements, like the Universal Declaration of Human Rights (UDHR), from the perspectives of formerly colonized nations. The UDHR, especially, has been contested on the grounds that it reflects Eurocentric assumptions. In comparison to the well-established discourse that positions human rights as instruments of imperialism, Christians have had a mixed reaction to human rights despite their arguably theological origins (Chitando and Njoroge 2016: 3; Mwaura 2012: 37–9; Nichols 2009: 655). In the confrontation between human rights and Christian organizations in development projects, both the imperialism and the secularism of human rights can be problematic. For the YWCA, as suggested in Joyce's comment, above, human rights legislation posed a problem in that relying on the values laid out in human rights instruments, like CEDAW for instance, was thought to imply supporting sex workers' rights and gay rights. My research participants stopped short of providing a definitive answer or solution to this 'conflict', and framed their discussions in ways that allow them not to have the 'right answer'. The questions and challenges that the Association faced in relation to human rights and controversial faith issues were considered as no less than serious and worthy of deliberation.

On the basis of these observations about the YWCA's exclusion of LBTQI women, I am critical and sceptical of the YWCA's ability to speak as a women's organization that is, most of the time, aligned with an African feminist politics. My unease is not only a result of my experience of conducting research with an organization that turned out to be antagonistic to bisexual women like me; nor is it grounded in a sense of Western sexually liberated superiority. Throughout Christian history the various 'intersection[s] of homophobia, ethnocentrism, and other religious practices' have aligned to represent religious difference in the figure of what Kwok Pui-lan calls the 'sexual Other' (Kwok 2005: 140–2). In dominant Christian narratives, the 'Other' is consistently positioned as queer or sexually deviant in contrast to Christian normalcy. This can be seen in representations of colonized peoples in the Old Testament; for example, Rahab is a 'prostitute' because as such she invites, facilitates and justifies the 'domestication of the promised land' (Dube 2000: 70–80, citing Josh. 2–6). The more recent scopophilic racialization of Black African women facilitated their objectification, vividly illustrated in the enslavement of Sara Baartman and the desecration of her body after her death, based on her status as the ur-representation of Black female sexuality (Qureshi 2004: 233–4).

Going further than this, the postcolonial feminist project of 'requeering' sexuality suggests avoiding Eurocentric assumptions about the separability of gender from sexuality, or even of the primacy of sexuality as an identity (Kwok 2005: 139–42). This is not to suggest that African same-sex desire/behaviour is apolitical and closeted, in contrast to an implied public, political identity of Western queers (Dhawan 2013: 201). This much is illustrated by my own refusal/failure to make my sexual identity known to my YWCA interlocutors. Rather, 're-queering' sexuality suggests that the sexual norms of African contexts may have been 'queerer' before mission and colonization so that the appropriate way to frame the present project of mobilizing for queer liberation in Africa may take its lead from a return to (some) precolonial values and practices. The male–male 'corporeal intimacies' of a Bugandan monarch, Mwanga II, serve to complicate and refute assumptions of a uniform precolonial eastern African heterosexual desire, identity and intimacy (Rao 2014: 2–4). The non-heterosexuality of Mwanga and others in his court does not, however, justify an interpretation of these people and practices as 'queer', with critical analyses pointing to other possible readings of sexual intimacy in relation to ritual, power and non-binary constructions of gender, and misinterpretations of these by white European missionaries (Njambi 2020; Rao 2014). Nonetheless, assertions of African essential heterosexuality are the explicit support for popular claims that 'homosexuality is unAfrican', claims which have come to reinforce Christian heteronormativity (Mwikya 2014).

5.5 Summary

Abortion, condoms and sexuality, as the paradigm and scope of controversial faith issues, were a significant feature of the YWCA's everyday ethics in

2012. They allowed multiple, somewhat contradictory positions to be held simultaneously by the organization as a whole and by its constituent parts – its staff, members and leaders. Identifying and naming controversial faith issues also served as an instance of discontinuity or trouble that offered the YWCA and its spokespersons the opportunity to reiterate the YWCA's Christian identity. This was partly achieved through the retelling of its ontological narratives, connecting its conduct to its identity, and *vice versa*, but it was also addressed through practices of 'Christian emphasis'. Christian emphasis is the name given to a range of practices that are considered to maintain the YWCA's Christian character. My research participants listed worship, prayer and Bible study as instances of Christian emphasis. These were not positioned as the practices that substantiate its claim to 'be' a Christian organization but as ways in which the YWCA could make Christianity more central and prominent in its everyday operations. These are overseen by branch-level Christian Emphasis Committees and directed by the National Christian Emphasis Committee, representatives of which attend National Board meetings. These committees were responsible for organizing prayers and praise songs at meetings and other YWCA events, organizing the YWCA's participation in the 'Week of Prayer and Fellowship' in unison with other YWCAs and YMCAs around the world and coordinating committed members to provide pastoral support to members in need, such as after bereavement or in other difficult circumstances. Christian emphasis, which refers to both the formal work of the Christian Emphasis Committees and the practices themselves, emerged in my field research in parallel to controversial faith issues. As I have already suggested, this is not a coincidence. Rather, Christian emphasis is a key part of the YWCA's response to controversial faith issues, and a prerequisite of their existence. The Christian Emphasis Committee had a great deal of impact on the way in which the YWCA's identity is understood, managed and represented. I discuss Christian emphasis in full in Chapter 6, following an outline of the YWCA's three major versions of its identity narratives and their inheritance of Vera Harley's account in *Rickshaws to Jets*. For now, I focus on how Christian emphasis connects to and ameliorates the tensions that arise from controversial faith issues.

My research participants suggested that the YWCA's nuanced and largely non-prescriptive approach to controversial faith issues might not be good enough. The 'needs of the present', namely the emergence of controversial faith issues, meant that it was useful to construct Christianity as 'what has been lost' in order for it to be recovered and emphasized (King 2000: 28–9). In a circular manner, controversial faith issues are also a part of Christian emphasis to the extent that they present YWCA staff with a chance to flex their moral identity by expressing an appropriately Christian point of view. Controversial faith issues were dealt with first through identifying, naming and discussing them as controversial. The three 'issues' discussed in this chapter are affected differently by this treatment; naming condoms as controversial allows them to remain a part of the YWCA's sexual health programmes while giving individual YWCA members and staff the opportunity to demonstrate and voice their scepticism or disapproval. By labelling abortion as controversial, the YWCA performs its Christian identity while grappling with the serious implications of teenage and single motherhood. As a perhaps unintended consequence of this, the YWCA has begun to open up a discursive space in which abortion can be discussed, even if it is in the end dismissed as a viable option for young women in Kenya. Finally, the YWCA considered the possibility of including LBTQI women to be too controversial to consider. It acts on the assumption that its members do not wish to 'support' LBTQI women, but in conducting itself this way the YWCA subjects itself to scrutiny or even censure by prospective donors and partner organizations who are not faith-based, are feminist or approach non-normative sexualities as a human rights issue. The informal ascription of 'controversial' status to these 'issues' further allows the YWCA to not codify its values in policy documents. As a consequence, the YWCA is less able to enforce one version of Christian sexual ethics. Relying on the aforementioned presumption that Christians share a self-evidently Christian ethical perspective, the YWCA is able to cite its ecumenical character as a way of explaining its fluid and accommodating approach to condoms, abortion and sexuality.

This approach to controversial faith issues leaves the YWCA with the perception that it is necessary to 'emphasize' its Christian identity. The position of Christian emphasis at the YWCA seems to suggest that any friction caused by controversial faith issues is caused not only, or not primarily, by the Association's ecumenical basis but also by the tension between its identity as a women's organization and its Christian identity. The centrality of Christian identity for the Association's ethics and moral values is clearly not expressed in the application of authoritative Christian teachings or principles. Rather the evidence of controversial faith issues suggests that the YWCA negotiates a Christian sexual ethic at the nexus between institutional identity stories and moral narrative reasoning. The values, principles and attitudes that motivate the YWCA's programmes and decisions are not best understood as the straightforward application of beliefs or obedience to doctrine, or as failures to live up to the demands of these. In its gender work, the YWCA operates largely with values that align with the orthodox positions of a gender and development perspective within the context of the development industry. Controversial faith issues are the exceptions to this general tendency, taking on heightened significance as boundary-defining issues of its Christian identity. Nevertheless, the language my interlocutors used to discuss sexuality was markedly different from the moralizing or absolute terms typically employed by NCCK spokespersons and sensationalist moral narratives in popular media. Attention to the context of the YWCA's activities explains why these three 'controversies' have been answered in different ways. The HIV epidemic has increased the audibility of Kenyan women's demands with respect to gender and sexuality, and allowed Christian women to address sexuality more openly. So, discussions of condoms have become acceptable within that overriding context, but there has not been an equivalent contextual change that would encourage a similar shift in attitudes in favour of abortion, or LGBTQ rights. It seems that the YWCA finds abortion just controversial enough to remain equivocal in its judgement, compared to its more complete refusal to engage with sexual minorities. The YWCA's interventions in sexual health and reproductive rights thus reflect the wider context that provides it with the narrative materials out of which it crafts its identity.

6

'We are Christians'

The substance of my argument in this chapter is that 'controversial faith issues' generate the need for the YWCA to 'emphasize' its Christianity, and that this is achieved sometimes by telling a version of the organization's ontological narrative, and at other times by citing Christian emphasis. The theoretical connections between identity, ethics and narrative suggest how stories of the YWCA's past can be used to make this 'emphasis', and to repair the strategically identified breaks in continuity between its Christian identity and its programmatic interventions in SRHR. The tensions introduced into the Association's work by controversial faith issues are resolved through retelling certain institutional stories. I asked my research participants what difference it made that the YWCA is a Christian organization, and why the YWCA made the programmatic interventions it did. My research participants told me that the YWCA acts because 'we are Christians', sometimes using these words, as did Wandia, Nyaboke and Njeri, and at other times narrating this claim at great length. I focus on three versions of this identity story, all of which are expressions of what I call the YWCA's 'ontological narrative', in which Christianity makes the necessary connection between the Association's identity and its activities. I show how this narrative came into circulation and how its effects have changed over time, including legitimizing its sexual health programmes in a heteronormative, pro-natal context riven with suspicions of imperial and colonial feminisms. I argue that ontological narratives also speak to a deep-seated connection between identity and ethics, because they provide an ethical foundation for conduct by way of a circular logic: 'We are Christians because we do x' and 'We do x because we are Christians'.

I came to understand this answer as a part of the identity-constituting narrative practices that I describe at greater length in this chapter. This reference to Christianity as the reason for conduct is significant, I argue, because it offers a way to narratively resolve moral questions. A story requires the right occasion to be told, and often an apparent problem – such as controversial faith issues – is both required as the occasion to tell the appropriate story and resolved by telling of that story. So, the identification of controversial faith issues creates opportunities for the YWCA to emphasize its Christian identity, by positioning them as a challenge to its status as a Christian organization. Thus, I describe these processes of narrative ethical reasoning, and the connections between ethics and identity in narrative, to clarify this function of controversial faith issues.

The YWCA's identity as a Christian organization has featured in much of the discussion thus far, but I have not shown how this comes to be known and how it is (re)constructed in everyday YWCA practices. The Christian identity of the YWCA depends on two dimensions: first, the Christian identities and commitments of its constitutive elements: its committees, staff, leaders and members. The Christian faith and practice of these constitutive elements is consolidated in the YWCA's institutional practices of 'Christian emphasis', which emerged as the primary way through which the YWCA explicitly, deliberately sought to ensure it had an appropriately Christian character. Second, the YWCA's identity as Christian depends on the narrative constitution of organizational identity through three distinct themes that circulate in accounts of what the YWCA is, or 'who we are'. These narratives draw on different sources of support for the YWCA's Christianity. These are the YWCA's Christian origins, its ecumenism and the 'staunch' Christianity of its members. Each of these three themes was summarized in the statement that 'we are Christians', which was often repeated by my research participants. This claim turns on a revealing grammar linking the personal Christian faith and practice of the speaker with the Association's Christian identity.

6.1 The YWCA's ontological narrative

My narrative analysis reveals that the YWCA's ontological narrative appears in summary form throughout its publicity materials. In classifying this narrative as 'ontological', I am pointing out that this story establishes the relationship between the YWCA's existence and its conduct (Somers 1994: 617). An ontological narrative can be told about another in the second or third person, but the most common ontological narrative is a self-narrative, often telling one's life story. Telling ontological narratives of organizations and institutions occupies an overlap between self-narrative (in the first person) and other-oriented (in the third person) narrative practices. For members of an organization who are able to speak on its behalf, using 'we', the narrative is not completely identical with one's autobiography. It nevertheless requires some personal identification between speaker and subject, and is thus 'autobiographical', even though it is not an autobiography. The narrative is not only spoken by people associated with the YWCA on its behalf; at certain times the YWCA seems to speak for itself. For example, in a general publicity leaflet the YWCA gives an overview of its current programmes, and supplies practical information such as branch locations and contact details. The ontological narrative is presented in summary form under the heading 'Background Information'. Interestingly, this instance of the narrative is told in the third person to perform a degree of objectivity by introducing distance between the author and the subject of the narrative.

> The Young Women's Christian Association is one of the oldest women's organization [sic] in Kenya, having been founded in 1912. From its inception, its mission has been to bring girls and women together in an effort to respond to socio-economic, political and cultural issues affecting them. (YWCA n.d.)

This summary of the ontological narrative glosses over any changes over time, and does not give specific details of the YWCA's past activities. Instead the ontological narrative gives an account of the *kind* of organization the YWCA is. It was repeated to me by my research participants in conversations and interviews, connecting the organizational Christian identity to Christian origins. It relies for its meaning on a fuller, longer version of the story, which has taken shape gradually as a result of many retellings over time, as well as through explicit editing and attention to its messages. Institutional narratives are generally the cumulative result of many authors and speakers and, in this case, it is possible to trace the story through various iterations over time. Approaching identity as narratively constructed suggests that processes of writing and retelling histories and other accounts of organizations' conduct, and change or continuity over time, always have effects and implications beyond the immediate context in which these stories are told. Of particular significance in this regard are accounts of pivotal moments in the life of an organization. As a case in point: the YWCA's ontological narrative relies on Vera Harley's intervention in the 1950s, and the subsequent development of the YWCA as a multiracial organization, but does not mention it. A noisy silence surrounds the YWCA's historical racism in retellings of the YWCA's identity as *religiously* Christian, as opposed to a former identity as *culturally* Christian – an identity read as 'white' or 'European' during the colonial period (Linde 2009: 196). In this context, a noisy silence is a gap or an absence, unacknowledged in the text but central to its structure.

Identifying this gap suggests thinking about the emergence of this version of events and its purpose, to understand why such a gap exists. This involves asking basic questions of critical textual analysis, including whose voices have been preserved, and whose left out; where and when the text was produced, and how it has since been amended. In the discursive field contoured by the colonization of Kenya, 'Christian' was a word that signified moral, respectable whiteness at least as much as, if not more than, it signified a religious faith. In returning to this line of reasoning here, I wish to draw attention to the fact that the historical narrative appealed to by my research participants is selective in its recruitment of material from the Association's past. The selection of useful themes is dependent on the purposes for which the narrative is intended. In the case of the story I analyse and (re)tell here, the YWCA's former exclusive whiteness is a focal point because of my own interests and my methodological commitment to postcolonial feminist analysis.

As a primary source for the YWCA's ontological narrative, the history told in *Rickshaws to Jets* has a great deal of influence on how the organization talks about itself. The process by which the YWCA shifted to include Black Kenyan women as members and eventually to employ them in leadership and managerial positions is significant in this regard because Harley incorporates it in her narrative through her recollections of her own involvement, among which was a conscious effort to craft a shared Christian identity. Introducing the start of this process, Harley notes that in a 1958 committee meeting 'it had been said that "as a Christian movement we cannot but be multi-racial here"' (Harley 1995: 73). By using the passive voice, Harley suggests that it does not matter who said this, reinforcing the explicit claim that Christianity implies being 'multiracial' as obvious and inarguable. As will become clear through my analysis, this is a central part of how the discourse of 'multiracialism' functioned at the YWCA. I have already noted that 'multiracial' politics was a colonial strategy that did not imply any substantial changes to colonial structures of governance or the unequal distribution of power in white hands. At the YWCA and elsewhere, becoming 'multiracial' meant removing some of the barriers that excluded Black Africans from entering and mixing in formerly white spaces and institutions, but it did not imply making substantial changes to the internal structures of those institutions.

While acknowledging the contributions of other YWCA staff and leaders, Vera Harley basically positions herself as the one who decided to end white leadership of the YWCA in 1963. She recalls that 'with independence coming to Kenya in December ... the time had come for an African woman' to replace her as the NGS (Harley 1995: 130). It is not clear, from Harley's account, why Margaret Mugo was considered for this role, or how she was known to anyone at the YWCA – Harley states only that she was not a YWCA member.[1] Furthermore, Harley does not mention pressure from Black Kenyan YWCA members to reform the YWCA, nor their interest or involvement in choosing someone to fill the role. In short, Harley made no attempt to incorporate African YWCA members' own experiences of this period into her account, even when they are the focus of the narrative. It was evidently important that the YWCA was seen to be ending its racist exclusions, but Harley does not reflect on the ways the performance of multiracialism represented continuity with, and not a break from, the Association's colonial past. Harley addressed the YWCA for the last time at the National Convention in Mombasa, in January 1965. In *Rickshaws to Jets*, she reproduces the text of her speech as follows:

> Vera asked [the assembled delegates] to think back to the time when they first joined the Association and suggested they tried to remember why they had joined. As everyone knew, there were now several organisations for women and girls in Kenya, but none of the others was multi-racial, ecumenically Christian, but with membership open to women and girls of all creeds. It was therefore an all-embracing movement. Vera reminded Full Members that they had dedicated themselves to the service of others and said that there could be no limit to the quality of that service ... Other organisations carried out programmes similar to that of the YWCA and it was up to the Full Members to ensure that the Association's standards were as high or even higher than any other. There must be no envy or jealousy, but co-operation and loyalty. Reminding them of the YWCA motto, ['By love, serve one another'] she urged them to live by it. (Harley 1995: 144–5)

Similarly to the ontological narrative, above, Harley constructs her authorial voice as more authoritative and neutral by using the third person to talk about herself. With this speech, Harley completed the symbolic transfer of power to Black Kenyan women that she had begun by stepping down six months earlier. While Harley had demonstrated a commitment to relinquishing white control of the YWCA, and allowing Black Kenyan women to take charge of the YWCA for themselves, the same cannot be presumed to be true of the rest of the Association's white members. Harley reports that the period of overlap between her tenure as NGS and Mrs Mugo's was at the insistence of the latter, and formed part of her training for the job (Harley 1995: 139). However, it is possible that Harley's prolonged farewell to the YWCA was necessitated in part by the continued resistance of white members to Mrs Mugo's leadership and to the concept of integration, amidst the widespread waning of institutionalized white privilege in independent Kenya. This interpretation would make sense of the fact that Harley needed to use her final official act as NGS to unite the YWCA's members. To this end, she issued not particularly subtle warnings against 'envy' and urging 'co-operation' [sic], which seem to have been directed primarily at the Association's Black Kenyan members because there remained significant material inequalities between them and the shrinking contingent of white YWCA members.

Harley's narrative intervention in the identity of the YWCA had far-reaching effects. To 'include' Black Kenyan women as members evidently challenged the YWCA's identity, necessitating the promotion of an 'all-embracing' Christianity as Harley attempted in her speech. Harley invoked the idea that Christianity implied Black Kenyan women's access to and leadership of the YWCA. The change from exclusive whiteness to inclusive Christianity was not achieved by setting out an argument explaining why racial discrimination is wrong and all people are equal, although a convincing case could have been made, perhaps including references to theological principles. The new meaning of the Association's Christianity as a shared faith identity eclipsed the YWCA's previous self-understanding as a home away from home for British women. The ethical or political reasoning behind this connection of Christianity and inclusion was not made explicit. Instead it was through telling a different story about what the YWCA is and does, implicitly appealing to a sense of self-evident Christian ethics and/or conduct, that the YWCA was finally able to integrate Black Kenyan women as full and equal members with white women. This suggests once again that at the level of quotidian ethical discourse, explicit reasoning is less effective, less important, than a convincing story. In the YWCA's case, contextual factors specific to 1960s Kenya meant that a Christian organizational identity was able to facilitate and make sense of 'multiracialism'. Having made this narrative intervention in 1965, Harley then reinforced her version of events by publishing it as part of *Rickshaws to Jets* in 1995. As I have already suggested, *Rickshaws to Jets* then became a significant part of the YWCA's corpus of narrative resources from which it could draw in subsequent retellings of the its ontological narrative. This is clearest in printed, textual versions of the story, such as when Dr Abok described the 'diverse' membership of the YWCA as central to its mission in *Winds of Hope* (2004). In her retelling of the YWCA's ontological narrative, Dr Abok did not mention the YWCA's racist exclusion of African women from 1912 to 1955. Dr Abok begins her account of the YWCA's history with a retelling of some of the key elements of Harley's version of the ontological narrative:

> [Kenya YWCA] traces its origin from the World YWCA, which was formed in 1855 in London ... Founded in 1912, the YWCA of Kenya is a membership, non-profit ecumenical interfaith women's organization. It has the task of bringing women and girls from various ethnic groups, different denominations and diverse social backgrounds together in an effort to promote their status. (Abok 2004: 89)

Here, the story Dr Abok tells glosses over the details of how and when the YWCA took upon itself this task of 'bringing together' diverse women. The minor factual error Dr Abok made when she associated the 1855 date with the inception of the World YWCA (which actually was formed later, in 1894), rather than the original English YWCA, reveals an interesting point. Consistent with all other examples of this narrative, it establishes that the YWCA in Kenya has its roots in a much older movement that began in Victorian England. This small mistake further reveals that the accurate dates do not need to be memorized in order for the story to be told in this way, nor for it to achieve the desired effect of authorizing the YWCA based on longevity and continuity over time.

Approaching the silence in this version of the narrative shows that Dr Abok's account of the YWCA's history has emerged out of Harley's previous narrative construction. It made sense for Dr Abok to represent the YWCA as a Christian organization because that has been its prevailing identity characteristic since 1965. Noting the imbrication of personal identity in the narration of a collective identity as a 'we', it is interesting to note that collective and personal identity is explicitly linked in the preface to *Winds of Hope*, by Musimbi Kanyoro, who writes, 'Mwajuma [Abok] *lives out her social action* through the YWCA' (Abok 2004: ix, my emphasis). There are personal and professional reasons Dr Abok may be inclined to believe the best possible version of the YWCA's history, a history in which her presence and participation can be understood as meaningful and significant. As such, the repetition of the noisy silence on the YWCA's colonial history can be read as an example of the mutually reinforcing relationship between personal moral identity and YWCA Christian identity. Harley's major contribution to changing the racial dynamics of the YWCA was the reformulation of its identity, by uniting the Association's membership under the shared identity of Christian faith. As I have already argued, this unification was not a matter of articulating an existing understanding of shared Christian identity. Rather, it required a persuasive story that made new sense for its audience of white Christian women in order to create a new shared identity.[2] Thus Dr Abok's account is evidence of the success of Harley's narrative intervention in the Association's identity and an example of narrative induction at work (Higgs 2016). Furthermore, Dr Abok herself reinforced this version of the ontological narrative when she applied it to the next period of YWCA history in her own book, which was similarly present and available at the YWCA's headquarters (Abok 2004).[3]

The ongoing effects of this historical change in the YWCA's identity include the availability of the ontological narrative as a resource on which YWCA staff and members were able to draw as a means of reinforcing, or emphasizing, the Association's Christianity. Narratives emphasizing the YWCA's Christian identity circulated through the Association because it was useful, serving a particular purpose each time a YWCA leader, volunteer or member retold it. By the same token, it is evidently not considered useful or relevant to narrate the YWCA's identity as changeable, or its origins as colonial as well as Christian. Harley's narrative intervention emphasizes a different element of the historical record, allowing the ontological narrative to be a more useful story about the Association as a group of like-minded Christian women. Women who have been through a process of narrative induction speak the story of the YWCA with the same emphasis on Christian origins, inherited through Harley and Abok and probably hundreds of unnamed co-authors over the century. During my field research, different versions of the YWCA's ontological narrative, centring on origins, ecumenism and staunchness, were told in response to diverse cues. These cues included the qualities required for leadership, the motivation behind YWCA programmes, not being feminists, distinguishing the unique contribution of the YWCA, dealing with controversial faith issues and others. What makes these occasions pertinent is that they seemed to be offered at times when a citation of theology, or a different, public Christian narrative, could have achieved the same effect of establishing the YWCA's Christian identity, and connecting it to its conduct (and *vice versa*). The fact that this was not the case suggests that part of the narrative induction process at the YWCA is learning to tell its ontological narrative on these kinds of occasions. By learning what stories about the YWCA can be told in what situations, new recruits demonstrate their integration in, and commitment to, the Association. At the same time, this process is what constituted their belonging, as they develop the ability to speak on behalf of the YWCA in the first-person plural 'we'. The three predominant versions of the narrative – origins, ecumenism and staunchness – all display the use of generic techniques of organizational identity-building: appeals to origins, establishing continuity over time and suggesting the distinctiveness of its perspective compared to other organizations (Van Tonder and Lessing 2003).

6.2 Origins: 'We have always been Christians'

Appealing to origins is an effective way of establishing identity because it authorizes itself by claiming to be factual and historical; it implies longevity and creates the impression of stability over time (Linde 2009: 3–9). Thus, it is not surprising that the most often-repeated version of the identity narrative at the YWCA is the narrative of the Association's origins as a Christian organization. Origin stories, especially those that rise to the status of myth, sort the messy jumble of the past into a clean and distinct trajectory that moves neatly from a clear beginning to the present moment. In the case of an institution, particularly if its date of inception was within the last couple of centuries, its origins can be supported by citing documentary evidence. Institutional 'origins' stories can thus seem to be more straightforwardly 'true' than those mythic narratives that give origins to nations or religious groups in the very distant past. However, the example of the YWCA shows that this can be an unhelpful assumption, as origins can be presented in misleading ways, including in ways that contradict the historical record. Christian origins and heritage were frequently cited to establish Christianity as the defining characteristic of the YWCA in the present by telling the story of its Christian origins. These origins are often established by referring directly to the foundation of the YWCA as an expression of the sincere Christian faith of Emma Robarts and Lady Kinnaird: 'These two ladies who started the YWCA, they were prayerful, doing Bible studies, and that was the vision of these women when they started the YWCA so we should continue … since it was based on faith, then it should continue in faith' (Wandia, interview, 2012). As such, the YWCA's historical narratives contain an influential model on which leaders can pattern their own engagement with the Association: as an expression of their own Christian faith. This connects with the theme of 'staunch' Christianity, to which I turn shortly. Edith further explained the Association's Christian character by referring to the origins of the YWCA, and by reframing them as part of the contemporary YWCA's effort to emphasize Christianity through the formal work of a committee formed for this purpose, to which I return at the end of this chapter.

> *Eleanor:* I'm wondering, was the Christian Emphasis Committee something that's always been part of the YWCA, and if not, when did it come in?
> *Edith:* If you look back to the beginnings of the YWCA in Kenya, in 1912 the big focus was Bible study ... women met to study the Bible, to encourage one another...to sing hymns. It might not have been called 'Christian emphasis' then but for me, I look at it as Christian emphasis...And, for a long time Bible study, singing, Bible sharing, strengthening one another, it has been part and parcel of everything that we do in the YWCA. (Edith, interview, 2012)

Using the simple past and present tenses ('was based on', 'we do'), Wandia and Edith both expressed the YWCA's Christian identity as a factual, permanent state. Setting aside the reference to Christian emphasis for now, Edith's reiteration of Christian origins draws on the same resources as Wandia's; prayer and Bible study are cited as evidence of a foundation Christian identity, and positioned as a continuous 'part and parcel' of the YWCA's identity. In this version of the narrative, prayer and Bible study are offered as unambiguous evidence of Christian faith. Welfare projects or development interventions were not claimed as characteristically Christian activities, although they could be, for example using the language of the social gospel. Thus, the YWCA appears to sense that Christian institutions can become 'secularized' by engaging in gender work and/or development.

While conversational references to YWCA origins are usually general ('we have a Christian basis') not specific, the underlying influence of institutional history gives anyone who has been narratively 'inducted' into the YWCA two options from which to choose a founding moment of Christian identity when telling the origins story: the original YWCA in Britain in 1855 or the 1912 YWCA in colonial Nairobi; both ignore the 'multiracial' moment in 1955. The origins story is a collective memory in narrative form. It archives one aspect of the organization's past and allows it to be learned and 'remembered' by people who were not present for the events it describes. By contrast, the narratives of ecumenism and staunchness that I analyse below are focused on recent and ongoing history, events in the lifetimes and the personal experiences of the ones telling them. The origins narrative constructs a shared understanding of the place Christianity has in the YWCA movement, but it also offers a 'schematic' or template for the narration of other aspects of the YWCA's past (Wertsch 2008:120–4). The origins story gives an account of the YWCA's history, but its primary purpose is not to inform its audience about the sequence of significant events in the past. Rather, it is told in order to emphasize the organization's Christian identity in the present. This is effective even when this intention is made explicit, as in Edith's version cited above. The way in which the origins story is used to emphasize Christianity demonstrates that it is an ontological narrative, as it connects 'who we were' in the past to 'what we do' in the present. The origins story is significant component of the informal process of narrative induction because it also shows the recruit's comprehension of, and agreement with, the tacit connections between Christian identity and conduct. By telling the origins story in answer to the 'correct' cues, they reinforce the 'truth' of the idea that the YWCA's programmes are self-evidently the Christian thing to do, even if this connection is contradicted by or juxtaposed to the discourse of controversial faith issues.

6.3 Ecumenism: 'We are all Christians'

Establishing a clear, singular point of origin helps to promote an understanding of a shared Christian identity as similarly obvious and internally coherent. Of course, the invocation of a unified Christian identity is not unique to the YWCA. However, the specific nature of the shared Christian identity that emerges from listening more closely to my research participants' words is complex. It suggests a careful balance between denominational differences, revealing in fact a divided Christian identity that is maintained in the midst of some significant tensions. Since any impression of a singular Christianity is illusory, the fact that the YWCA feels the need to address tensions and differences in its navigation of interdenominational cooperation is not evidence of a problem specific to the YWCA. The narratives through which the YWCA constructs its public identity gloss over, rather than enumerate, the diversity of various Christian ethical and theological positions.

When ecumenism was specifically mentioned, it was more often than not as a result of my prompts. At the National level, the cooperation of women from many denominations seems to have posed challenges in relation to controversial faith issues, but there were other times when different practices have caused minor problems. The most common is the experience of members of the Seventh Day Adventist (SDA) church, who keep the Sabbath on Saturday rather than Sunday. YWCA members and branch representatives who are part of the SDA church are faced with the choice of participating in National meetings and events which are often organized on Saturdays or following the distinctive practice of their denomination. Nyaboke, who had held various positions in the

YWCA for many years, described how upon discovering the YWCA held regular meetings on Saturdays, she decided to prioritize her participation at the meetings:

> I am from the SDA denomination, but when I came [to YWCA] I discovered that the schedule of meetings are on Saturdays ... I said 'I will not change [the day of the meetings] because I know I'm in the minority' ... I think we need to tolerate each other when we have those differences, and we [within the YWCA] are getting on well. (Nyaboke, interview, 2012)

Nyaboke was clearly willing to make exceptions to her usual practice in order to participate more fully at the YWCA. On some issues, like this one, those staff and members who are in the minority are largely expected to accede to the majority point of view. This majoritarian approach is, in part, a consequence of the YWCA's quasi-democratic structures and processes that establish a consensus based on the invited participation and representation of all eligible members. A similar sense of togetherness and disagreement is at work in the YWCA. Njeri pointed out precisely the sense compromise in her discussion of the challenges posed by ecumenism:

> We are mixed, there are those very staunch Christians, you know the Pentecostals, Evangelicals ... whose stand on some issues will be quite strong ... I give the example of say family planning. This is one of the earliest programmes that the YWCA became involved in: family planning, and how they were going to teach women on how to plan for their families, and use of contraceptives, and all that. But then within the YWCA there's also Catholics ... So the Catholics will say, 'Ah-ah, no. Why are we teaching about family planning?' ... [Being an ecumenical organisation] means we have to accept each other's views. If maybe there's a place where you feel strongly you cannot participate, then fine. (Njeri, interview, 2012)

The picture of interdenominational cooperation that emerges from Njeri's description is one in which the (potentially) opposing perspectives of some of its staff and members are tempered by the necessity of coming to a consensus and acting in concert with others. Although the point about ecumenical cooperation across difference is apt, the few Catholic YWCA members I spoke to made it clear that they did not agree with the Vatican's teachings, so there may be a perception of denominational differences where there are none. As discussed in Chapter 5, my interviewees emphasized that there have been 'no arguments' about the Association's stance on condoms. The overall inclusion of condoms in the YWCA's sexual health programmes seems to indicate that the YWCA has defined its ecumenical Christianity as a space where those who oppose the use of condoms are required to tolerate the (albeit uneven) incorporation of condoms into the vision of SRHR that the YWCA promotes. Njeri's definition of ecumenism as the toleration of difference is one that was repeated by other research participants, but it is striking that tolerance seems to be the position taken by the majority while those in the minority compromise or opt out. The YWCA's ecumenism thus seems not so much a middle ground between the perspectives of denominations but the pragmatic application of Christian unity to issues that provoke disagreement. Whether or not any of the YWCA's staff and volunteers actually disagree with, for example, the inclusion of condoms in the Association's sexual health programmes is not clear. My research participants all expressed the same cautious support for condoms for certain groups, but mostly also acknowledged the presence of Catholics within the Association who were presumed to be opposed to the use of condoms.

6.4 Piousness: 'We are staunch Christians'

Staunchness, which means something akin to 'piousness', is part of the Kenyan repertoire of Christian narratives (e.g. Gez 2018: 1–6; Parsitau 2012: 5). The YWCA's use of the expression 'staunch Christian' stuck out to me, because it is not popularly used in British vernacular. It was a frequent point of reference for the YWCA when describing 'who we are'. The identification of 'very staunch Christians' in relation to ecumenical cooperation draws on a stereotype; they are said to be strict and devout, and to adhere firmly to their faith. This could be a good thing, or not, depending on who or what was being described. Staunchness and piety seemed to suggest a kind of respectability politics for Wandia. It was associated with refusal to include or support LBTQI women, and to not be 'liberal', as well as 'not be[ing] out there on the street, shouting' or being 'too radical' (Wandia, interview, 2012). What was clear in all instances of emphasizing Christian identity was the connection between personal conviction or faith and participation at the YWCA. This was institutionalized by scheduled worship sessions as focal points for collective performance of Christian identity at the opening and closing of almost all YWCA events, from staff meetings at the headquarters to youth groups in the branches. Many of my research participants considered this inclusion of worship in the YWCA's work to be among its distinguishing features. Wandia gave me a more explicit description of the relationship between Christian values and the YWCA's activities. She said,

> The fact that it's a Christian organisation, I think that also makes YWCA unique ... yes, women's organisations are doing very good work, but I think for the YWCA, it's unique, because of its Christian principles, and Christian foundation, that makes it really a place where you want to belong to, a place where you want to practice your Christian teachings and principles, and to make them a reality in terms of transforming the lives of women and young women. (Wandia, interview, 2012)

By locating the difference between secular women's groups and the YWCA in the latter's identity as a Christian organization, Wandia explained that the collective and institutional recognition and encouragement of Christian values was part of the attraction for many YWCA women. In another conversation, Wandia had described her participation in regional and international SRHR meetings as troubling. She expressed a sense of marginalization because of the way she felt the YWCA's Christian ethos – and her own – required her to stand, for example, against abortion.

Personal and group Christian identities are strongly connected, and a sense of belonging to and representing a group is heightened when the relationship is formal, such as in this case. As demonstrated in my discussion of the YWCA's ecumenism, there is no singular Christianity from which this identity flows. Identifying staunch Christianity allows for distinctions to be made between types of Christians without threatening the interdenominational unity the YWCA constructs. At other times in our conversations, my research participants implied that having staunch Christian faith was a prerequisite for taking on certain responsibilities within the YWCA. Potential staff members, and especially leaders, were expected to have 'nurtured' their faith, and be 'mature Christians [who] can be trusted to represent YWCA everywhere without having the "C" being challenged' (Winnie, interview, 2012). Here, Winnie cited the recurring motif of 'the "C" in the "Y"', to which I return below, illustrating the intertextual connections between different strands of the YWCA's identity narrative.

Staunchness thereby functioned both as a self-ascribed position, usually a way of emphasizing commitment and seriousness in one's faith, and a way to compare oneself or the YWCA to other Christians on a spectrum: 'not so strong', 'staunch' and 'very staunch'. As an example of 'staunch' as a positive descriptor, consider this statement from Mbari: 'I'm a really staunch Catholic – staunch *Christian* I should say ... [and] I used contraceptives' (Mbari, interview, 2012). Mbari emphasized her Catholic identity but quickly corrected herself, suggesting that she sought to prioritize (in this instance) her personal faith over her belonging to the Catholic

Church. In this instance, Christian identity performed much the same function on the personal level for Mbari as it did at other times for the YWCA at the institutional level. It establishes the speaker's Christian identity and invites the audience to understand their conduct in relation to that identity; even seemingly contradictory behaviour is represented as ethically acceptable. It is Mbari's own staunchness, and not Catholic doctrine, against which her conduct ought to be evaluated. It is a moral identity that is reinforced by YWCA membership, and appealed to strategically, but which is liable to misfire or to be misinterpreted in some circumstances.

While Wandia and Mbari used staunchness to describe themselves positively, other research participants expressed a concern that the staunchness of leaders and representatives within the YWCA might be counterproductive. The public Christian identity of the YWCA was considered to discourage young people from becoming members: 'I think a lot of people ... [think the YWCA is] a closed organisation ... when they get to know what we do [at the YWCA] and who the members are, they get so surprised – "Oh my goodness! But I thought [the YWCA is] for the real staunch Christians!"' (Njeri, interview, 2012). The continual and deliberate reinforcement of the YWCA's Christian identity was not questioned, even when it could have a detrimental effect on the recruitment of new members. Nevertheless, for Njeri and others it stood in tension with an awareness of how representing the YWCA as staunchly Christian sometimes made a negative impression, depending on the audience. Evidently, the YWCA was not so concerned about the potentially off-putting effect of emphasizing Christianity that it abandoned the project. Rather it was considered an obstacle that required careful attention to allow potential new recruits to see the YWCA as a good fit for them, which was in turn important because of the economic necessity of increasing revenue from membership fees. Later, echoing her earlier comments about interdenominational cooperation, Njeri suggested that the staunchness of some YWCA staff and members complicated the Christian identity of the YWCA, because 'there are those very staunch Christians ... whose stand on some issues will be quite strong compared to ... [others] whose stand might not be so strict' (Njeri, interview, 2012). Here, the reference to 'some issues' was a gesture towards controversial faith issues, and soon thereafter Njeri turned her attention directly to family planning and abortion as examples. Despite Njeri's observation that some YWCA members were 'more staunch' than others, neither she nor my research participants thought this posed a particular problem for ecumenical unity. Indeed, all agreed with Njeri that women join the YWCA in the knowledge that it is an ecumenical organization, and that the type and extent of a member's participation was dependent on her personal conviction. Of course, this appeal to personal conviction can cause problems for members who are in the minority on some faith issues, as I described above, which is why the narrative of ecumenical unity is so prominent.

My research participants insisted on two contradictory points; the YWCA would not make interventions that were the same as 'any other organisation' and instead would have to 'present a Christian perspective'. Nonetheless, 'for some programmes' the YWCA acts 'just the way any other organisation'. Above all, the ability to attract and earn the loyalty of women who make up its membership base, volunteers, representatives, staff and leaders relied to a large extent on the pleasures and rewards of acting out of a shared, interdenominational, staunchly Christian identity. However, this Christian identity and the implications it seemed to have for the YWCA's activities was typically described in terms of the ways the YWCA had failed to meet its demands.

6.5 Christian emphasis

Identity narratives are also explanatory narratives of behaviour. The YWCA's use of its ontological narrative illustrated this, as my research participants told stories about what the YWCA does in order to represent their personal and collective identity as Christian, and *vice versa*; they told me about their personal Christian faith and moral identity as part of explanations of the YWCA's conduct. The effect of narrating the YWCA's identity as Christian is to resolve tensions around controversial faith issues, and the Christian emphasis narrative was the most prominent and distinct aspect of these practices as I encountered them in 2012. The YWCA dismissed its approach to controversial faith issues as not 'good enough' – specifically, that it might fail to be 'Christian enough' – thus necessitating Christian emphasis and 'reaffirming its commitment [to Christianity] through Christian Emphasis Programmes' (Abok 2004: 93). The practices that are launched under this label are accompanied by two narratives that explain the need for Christian emphasis: first, the YWCA's forgetting and failing and second a narrative of secularization, which often makes use of the trope of 'the "C" in the "Y"'.

The first theme of the Christian emphasis narrative is of the YWCA as an organization that has forgotten, or failed to live up to, its Christian origins. This was initially curious to me, since the primary focus of the YWCA's ontological narrative is to construct and reiterate its identity as Christian. The project of

Christian emphasis rests on presenting these origins as having been overlooked. Edith explained that the development of the YWCA involved a shift in focus away from its Bible-centred beginnings.

> I must admit, that ... as we focused more ... on economic empowerment for girls and women, I think we were so much focused and concerned with ... empowering women to take control of their lives, to be economically more independent, that we kind of forgot – we forgot the concentration on Christian[ity] ... really, we were just left with the mission, the logo and making sure that each time we start a meeting we dedicate it to God, we have devotion, we pray, we sing, and I don't quite remember when we said, 'Wait a minute, aren't we moving away from the centre, too much from the centre?' ... it is not enough that every Monday we start with prayer, and we start all the meetings with prayer. We want everybody who comes to the YWCA to be spiritually fed, [so] that by the time they leave at least they have [gained] something. (Edith, interview, 2012)

This is a rich and complex statement that reflects the struggles of a committed staff member with the implications of her position and her responsibilities, and her concerns for the future of the Association. As a long-standing member of staff, Edith had played an active role in the reorientation of many of the YWCA's activities, including being around during the 1980s and 1990s during which time the organization moved towards formal development interventions. When considering the role of the appeal to Christian origins in narrations of the YWCA's identity, the crucial aspect of Edith's comments is the understanding of Christianity implicit in her assessment that prayer is 'not enough'. Given the considerable focus on including worship in the YWCA's activities and presenting it as constitutive to the YWCA's Christian identity, I conclude: the inclusion of worship and prayer is felt to be necessary but not sufficient for the YWCA to claim a Christian identity. At the same time, Edith makes a distinction between the 'empowering' projects of the YWCA and its Christian identity, further complicating the link between 'being' and 'doing'. When she recalls the reflexive critique that the YWCA might be 'moving too much from the centre', Edith reaffirms that Christianity is the centre of the YWCA, even while suggesting that specific efforts are required to properly act on this reality. Economic empowerment programmes are not especially problematic, but here stand in for all the YWCA's more technocratic, donor-driven, formal programmatic interventions which have become the focus of the YWCA's activities since the late twentieth century. Changing the activities of the YWCA introduced a sense of contradiction between what the YWCA did and how the YWCA understood its identity. Once the contrast between these became too great, a narrative resolution was sought. So, appeals to origins are central in narrations of the Association's Christian identity as a foundation for its activities in the present day, but they also offer a set of criteria against which to judge whether it attains the standards of conduct implied by Christianity.

The sense of failing to achieve or maintain a sufficiently Christian standard was shared by other research participants. Whenever the discussion moved in the direction of critiquing, doubting or complicating the Christian identity of the YWCA, my research participants overwhelmingly tended to go on to (re)place emphasis on the ways in which YWCA also performs its Christian identity through integrating worship and prayer into its operations. Further, most research participants would then describe the steps that the organization has taken to retrieve its Christianity through the Christian Emphasis Committee.

> I suppose by the time a Christian Emphasis Committee is formed, that means there's a need to strengthen that Christian aspect … if it's on issues of reproductive health, it's the Christian Emphasis Committee that should actually guide the YWCA Board in terms of policy, that 'As a Christian Committee, this is what we feel the stand of YWCA should be on this issue' … because before, it was just … the Monday prayers, help organise when we have the World YMCA-YWCA Week of Prayer – then it's quiet. (Lavender, interview, 2012)

Such comments form an important part of the YWCA's Christian identity narrative, wherein somehow the organization has failed to live up to its ideal of integrating Christianity into everything that it does. The frequency with which I encountered this element of the YWCA's identity story indicated that it was an important vessel for carrying a collective memory about the Christian origins of the Association. The idea that the YWCA was not adequately representing itself in the public sphere was addressed both as part of the 'staunchness' theme in ontological narrative, as a problem of being perceived as 'too' Christian, and also in the theme of failure. As Wandia put it, 'My friends who hear that I work for YWCA … quite a number have told me that we need to come out strongly as a Christian organisation. It's not like we are doing anything bad, but we need to voice our "C" a bit more than we have been doing' (Wandia, interview, 2012). The perceived need to publicly represent the YWCA as Christian is an expression of the impetus towards Christian emphasis in outward-facing mode, making use of a common YWCA discourse of 'the "C" in the "Y"' which, in addition to themes of failure and forgetting, was connected to the second theme; secularization. This strand of the Christian emphasis narrative implicitly offers secularization as an explanation for the YWCA's changes over time. Reading Christian emphasis narratives at face value would tend to accept the secularization thesis as an explanation for dwindling religiosity and neglect the active use of narratives to construct identity. I do not interpret the narrative in this way. Secularization was embedded in my research participants' accounts of the YWCA's Christian identity, and in this context means both the influence of non-Christian (even anti-Christian) influences from outside the YWCA and tendencies within the YWCA to drift 'away from the centre', as Edith put it. Both dimensions of secularization are attributed to certain programmatic interventions, particularly those related to controversial faith issues, development, human rights and HIV and AIDS. In a circular manner, secularization could be considered both the impetus behind such programmes and the result of them.

The expression 'the "C" in the "Y"' has been widely used to frame questions about the place of Christianity within the YWCA movement. This is a well-established way of talking about YWCA identity that I have heard the YWCA use elsewhere (Seymour-Jones 1994: 224). The expression makes a play on the YWCA's name, highlighting the 'C', which stands for Christianity. The Association's name is an aspect of its identity I have not yet explicitly addressed; and my research participants did not comment on the YWCA's name in their narrations of its identity *except* when referring to 'the "C" in the "Y"'. The use of the YWCA name and logo is permitted only if the Association meets certain criteria set out by the World YWCA in its 'conditions of affiliation' and becomes a paying member association of the World YWCA. These criteria include being a membership organization and being led by women; but being a Christian organization is not explicitly mentioned. Njeri was quick to tell me that the YWCA of England and Wales had recently decided to drop the YWCA name, telling me that 'the World YWCA constitution is very clear, that the name stands [for] Young Women's *Christian* Association ... but even then, they have problems with Platform 51 ... it is actually a YWCA that has changed its name' (Njeri, interview, 2012). After it renamed itself Platform 51 in 2010, it ceased to be a FBO, reasoning that a Christian organization was no longer relevant to young women in Britain and citing the difficulty of attracting funding.[4] This recent history gave heightened significance to the YWCA's practices of Christian emphasis, as they demonstrated the YWCA's resistance to 'secularization'. This has instrumental value particularly in evangelical and conservative Christian discourse, within which conforming to the norms of 'secular' society is considered falling short of appropriate Christian conduct, or behaving like those who are not Christian. At the YWCA in Kenya, 'the

"C" in the "Y"' discourse has continued to have meaning in the project of Christian emphasis: 'We started running Christian programmes that would enhance the work of YWCA putting a lot of emphasis on "C"; which stands for Christian, which makes us unique as women, and gives us our identity as Christian women' (Winnie, interview, 2012). This is significant, as I have already suggested, because it is not inevitable; the YWCA has other identities to which it could appeal or that could be selected for emphasis. Its proximity to the women's movement and to international development means that the 'W' could be singled out as the central characteristic of the YWCA, in order to position it as a women's organization above all else. The fact that this is not the case is partly explained by the way in which historical articulations of YWCA identity have centred Christianity, particularly in paradigmatic accounts such as Vera Harley's, as I outlined above.

Doubts about the YWCA's ability to live up to its Christian name have been constant features of the YWCA's internal discussions about its purpose and activities. In 1917, the idea that the YWCA could not attract enough young women to its Bible study classes, for example, was concerning not only because it suggested a trend away from active Christian faith. It was concerning because of the implications it seemed to have for the longevity of the YWCA itself, and the implications this lack of interest could be inferred to have in the narratives that constructed Christianity as synonymous with white womanhood and moral identity. However, as noted already, at this time in the YWCA's history, the colonial context permitted whiteness to subsume other meanings of 'Christianity'. (Further, the combined influence of the social gospel and the cult of domesticity framed the YWCA's imperial maternalism *as* Christian.) This situation prompted introspection about whether to remain a Christian organization at all, a question that would recur decades later as the discourse of 'the "C" in the "Y"'. These concerns were not limited to the YWCA in Kenya but arose and reverberated throughout the movement. At a World Council in 1920, the World YWCA decided to remain explicitly Christian, while including Catholic and Orthodox women who had previously been ineligible for membership. This decision prompted the YWCAs of South Africa and Ireland to leave the YWCA movement in protest, since they were both invested in specifically Protestant evangelical Christianity and opposed to Catholicism.

In Kenya, the conversation around membership eligibility took on a different cadence, focusing on racist exclusions. It is likely that this was largely the result of the wider colonial anxiety about maintaining exclusively white spaces, due to the comparatively low numbers of settlers. Harley's reframing of YWCA identity did not resolve the question of the place Christianity should have in the movement. During the 1960s there seem to have been suggestions that the YWCA should cease to be a Christian organization, in order to allow non-Christian women to be full members with the right to vote for YWCA leaders and representatives. In 1969 this idea was rejected by Mrs Mugo, in her role as NGS, when she told the Programmes Committee that 'without the "Christian" the organisation would lose its identity'. One of the outcomes of this commitment to Christianity was the boundary-making effects it had; excluding Christians from full YWCA membership ruled out the possibility of interracial and interreligious cooperation that might have otherwise been presented. In the mid-1970s, a group of Kenyan Indian women in Eldoret wrote to the headquarters requesting that a branch of the YWCA be opened for the benefit of a large number of middle-class women in their community. However, while records report that they were 'quite willing to join hands with the Christian ladies of Eldoret', this branch did not materialize. That these women were not Christians evidently prevented the YWCA from considering them a valid constituency from which to draw members. Once again, the YWCA's Christian identity resulted in practices of exclusion along the lines of race. At around the same time, the YWCA refused to allow men to join as members, but this refusal and its focus on women did not become a repeated trope in its ontological narrative.

The narrative of failure implies a degradation of Christianity over time, as the YWCA is considered to have moved from authentically Christian origins, to unsatisfactory performance of Christian identity, to an attempted revival of Christianity in the present. Usually, the trope of 'the "C" in the "Y"' is mentioned as an example of resisting the temptation to do what is popular or modern, rather than what is characteristic of the YWCA or what is Christian – an instance when the YWCA could have chosen to renounce its Christian identity and extract its faith basis, but in fact remained staunch. Much is asserted by the telling of this version of the YWCA's history. Even in this narrative, the shift towards a 'multiracial' Christian unity in the early 1960s is not mentioned, and instead the Christian core of YWCA identity is attributed to the exclusive, white colonial YWCA – despite the fact the story of how the YWCA became multiracial *could* be narratively incorporated into Christian emphasis practices. It could serve as a narrative of redemption, by position the YWCA as 'sinful' or deviating from the standards implied by Christianity before a 'road to Damascus moment'. A past 'worldly' or selfish life can be used to narrate one's experience being 'saved' by establishing a contrast with a reformed character and behaviour, demonstrating its life-changing effects (Gez 2018: 263–303).

The Christian Emphasis Committee plays an active role in the narrative as a site of conscious identity construction and ethical debate, as the focus of more renewed efforts to secure the Association's Christian identity. In 2011, the National Board decided that the Christian Emphasis Committee would be given greater decision-making powers and challenged to develop policies to deal with controversial faith issues, particularly abortion. This was a potential area of contribution that was considered by my research participants to be important for the future of the organization as a Christian organization. Edith described what she considered the YWCA's past failure to address itself in a meaningful way to the demands of its context, but considered the Christian Emphasis Committee to be the avenue through which this could be addressed in future.

> Unfortunately, I wouldn't pinpoint a particular project that has been influenced by the Christian Emphasis Committee directly, but based on the mandate of the Committee, and related to the projects that we do, we have talked about reproductive health, we could even talk about FGM, you could bring in HIV and AIDS [and] see how ... the theological reflections, the Biblical reflections, through the Christian Emphasis Committee, would impact on those three, for example. (Edith, interview, 2012)

Perhaps understandably, other members of staff were keen to stress the success of the Christian Emphasis Committee and present it in a positive light. My research participant who had greatest involvement in the Christian Emphasis Committee, Winnie, gave the impression that the Christian Emphasis Committee was successful and had a great deal of impact on the Association as a whole: 'Every programme of YWCA has learned to integrate its activities with Christian faith, so that there is no demarcation [distinction] between our work and our Christian faith: it becomes an automatic witness in what we are doing as women within the Y[WCA]' (Winnie, interview, 2012). Recalling these different accounts highlights the fact that the Christian Emphasis Committee can be called upon to perform different narrative functions, and that it is used in different narratives by different staff in different situations. For instance, the Christian Emphasis Committee provided my research participants the opportunity to themselves emphasize the Christianity of the Association by identifying an element of the organization's structure which was dedicated to integrating Christianity into its quotidian activities as well as marking special occasions with worship. The Christian Emphasis Committee therefore had a great deal of impact on the way in which the YWCA's Christian identity is represented.

6.6 Summary

In this chapter I have shown that the YWCA understands itself primarily according to a threefold narrative of its Christian foundations and the purported influence of Christian principles on its work. This narrative answers ethical questions – both implicit doubts arising organically in the everyday life of the YWCA and more explicit questions posed in the course of my research. The YWCA's ethical reasoning does not straightforwardly represent the simple application of a self-evident Christian ethics. Rather, its SRHR programmes present opportunities to emphasize the organization's Christian identity. The context in which the YWCA exists provides a matrix of narratives out of which it draws resources for the retelling of its own stories, as well as presenting occasions for the strategic 'emphasis' of its Christian identity, including narratives that circulate within the YWCA movement. Explaining the relationship between organizational identity and conduct in this way allowed the YWCA to pre-empt and incorporate staff and members' reactions to, and evaluations of, the YWCA's conduct, successes or failures into its self-representation as Christian. This is the case because what the YWCA does relies on the cooperation, participation and acquiescence of these constituent parts of itself. The YWCA's identity is constructed not only narratively but also relationally; while identity is narratively constituted, some changes in identity and behaviour can be explained by the 'shifting relationships' between the YWCA, and the narratives used to constitute its Christian identity, and its audiences (Somers 1994: 627). Both the reiteration of identity narratives and the evaluation of YWCA programmatic interventions (and internal efforts like Christian emphasis) are central dimensions of the narration of the YWCA's narrative identity. It is due to the collaborative participation of many people over a long period in this narrative effort that the YWCA's collective memories are preserved and known.

The YWCA's programmatic interventions in SRHR hardly make an appearance in the identity narratives I have discussed herein. They are the background against which a narrative of Christian identity is necessary and meaningful. The YWCA's programmatic interventions, and its overall proximity to women's movements and development agencies, instead create occasions of doubt, tension and controversy that give rise to a need to emphasize Christian identity. Out of the apparent tension between the organization's Christian identity and its activities, a narrative has emerged that represents the YWCA as failing to live up to its own Christian standards. A crucial element of this narrative is that in recognition of the struggle to conduct itself as Christian, the YWCA has taken steps to address tension it perceives between the story it tells about itself and its activities. These narratives communicate multiple messages to their audiences, including (but not limited to) these four primary focal points. First, they demonstrate that the Christian aspect of its identity is the organization's focus, over and above its gender work. Second, they present an answer to the problematic question of applying Christian sexual ethics by positioning the YWCA's activities as Christian by definition. Third, they claim that its staff are Christian enough to ensure the moral integrity of the organization and its work. Fourth, they suggest that even if the Association's SRHR programmes do threaten to undermine the YWCA's Christian basis, there are numerous ways in which it reinforces its Christianity.

7

Everyday Christian ethics

The YWCA's narrative construction of a Christian identity, as I have shown, establishes a direction for its activities and a frame in which they can be interpreted as Christian. The theoretical concern of this chapter is to elaborate the concept of 'everyday Christian ethics', explaining how the YWCA's identity narratives shape its ethics, and outlining the value of 'life' I see operationalized in the YWCA's practices. My notion of everyday Christian ethics incorporates narrativity and the significance of identity in ways that explain the impasse that seems to come up when disagreements arise over the content and direction of Christian ethical thought and conduct. In the first part of this chapter, I discuss of the YWCA's vision statement, which cites the popular Christian value of 'fulfilled lives', in order to draw together my observations about the ethical values that seem to be assumed and applied in the YWCA's programmatic interventions and its representations of these in its narrative practices. I consider this an expression of a multivalent ethics of life at the YWCA – 'multivalent' because 'life' has multiple overlapping meanings and an expansive range of applications, both within the YWCA and outside it. I elaborate on the meaning of fulfilled lives, including some theological uses of the theme, and offer a consideration of the political and ethical positions it has been used, or could be used, to support. In the second part of this chapter, I outline my notion of everyday Christian ethics. The study of Christian ethics can be pursued through an ethnographic focus on institutions and/in people's everyday lives rather than starting with assumptions about Christian beliefs. In making this suggestion, I draw on the evidence provided by my research with the YWCA and the theoretical contributions of 'ordinary' theology and ethics. 'Ordinary theology' asserts that Christians who are not academically trained theologians engage in theology in a quotidian and ubiquitous manner, and it is possible to approach thinking about Christian practice and belief through this route (Astley 2002). Members of the Circle of Concerned African Women Theologians (hereafter, 'the Circle') have long insisted that the location of theology is not only at the pulpit or in the seminary but also in the reflections of African women at the grassroots, as they work, parent, worship and otherwise live in community with others (Kanyoro 2001: 51; Njoroge 1997: 78). Finally, the focus of the chapter returns to the relations between sexuality, 'controversial faith issues' and Christian identity at the YWCA in Kenya as mediated through the narrative construction of identity.

There is no single, unchanging Christianity to which the YWCA or any other Christian person or group can simply refer, nor is there a coherent 'Christian identity' to which they can simply conform. Rather, Christianity is 'unstable, uncertain, and plural' (Anidjar 2015: 40). Consciously and unconsciously, people mean very different things when they say that they 'are' Christian, because the concept of 'Christianity' connotes and contains reference to long and diverse histories of practice, conflict and theological reflection (Klassen 2013: 344–6). There are multiple Christianities – evident in the existence of many Christian denominations and the diverse applications to which these institutional reifications of Christianity have been put. Further, Christianities have been made to fit around different sets of cultural norms, as in the reinterpretation and 'inculturation' of Christianities by African clergy, communities and scholars in the twentieth century (Hinga 2017: 62–8). Each iteration of Christianity draws on a complex network of narratives that allow the multiple, overlapping construction of many Christianities as moral identities, collective identities and gendered and racialized identities. Christians are constituted as such partly by claiming and being able to narrate a Christian identity, as I have outlined in terms of the YWCA's narrative practices. But they are also Christians by virtue of being part of a community of Christians, although it may bear as many differences as similarities to other Christian communities (Chryssides and Gregg 2019: 11–14; MacGuire 2008). YWCA staff and members' shared exposure to a broad collection of Christian stories in their participation in churches and other Christian communities furnishes the Association with a common knowledge base. Some of these narratives directly support certain of the YWCA's narrative practices, such as the ability to call oneself 'staunch', while others feed themes and citations into other narratives, such as the vision statement, discussed below.

Many other kinds of narrative circulate in Christian communities, including but not limited to stories of miraculous healing, punishment for sin, reward for patience or obedience, and prayers answered. These stories offer interpretations of everyday life, promoting certain explanations, such as the capacity of god to intervene in the lives of Christians, while discouraging others, as for example in the contestation of the beginning of life at conception (in relation to abortion).

However, other kinds of tacitly accepted Christian common sense have emerged more recently. Missionary legacies, African Christianities and global evangelical connections represent three broad sources for narratives of everyday Christian ethical reasoning on sexuality and gender in Kenya, each of which relates to narratives and themes I have established already in the history of the YWCA from 1912 to 2012. The legacies of colonization and mission include the ways in which Victorian British missionaries and settlers infused their cultural and social norms into the Christianity they imparted – 'the lessons of coloniality' in Oyèrónkẹ Oyěwùmí's words (Oyěwùmí, personal communication, 2015). Common-sense ideas about Christian womanhood reflect colonial uses of missionary Christianity and the uptake of these by peoples in colonized eastern Africa for a variety of personal and political reasons. The embeddedness of British and Victorian gender ideology in missionary Christianity, a variety of Eurocentrism, reflects the context specificity of theology.

All theological reflections are made with particular aims in mind, for particular audiences, and from specific positions. Postcolonial African Christianities are context-specific theologies that are transparent about their aims, positions and audiences. I include here AICs, efforts towards the inculturation and Africanization of Christian practices in 'mainline' churches and more scholarly iterations of Black, African and liberation theologies. These all resist the definition of Christianity according to British and European norms. In Kenya, Christian converts took the various resources offered to them by missionary churches and repurposed them as illustrated by the female circumcision crisis. The common thread among this diverse range of African Christianities is the distinction between the elements of Christianity that hold meaning and are useful to Africans in situations of colonization, imperialism, exploitation, and impoverishment, while refusing those that did not make sense or that were harmful. These African reclamations of Christianity constitute a denial of the missionary claim that 'African' and 'Christian' are necessarily in opposition (Okech 2019: 33). A discourse of 'African' and 'un-African' has emerged to help excavate European interpretations of Christianity from values and practices that are relevant in postcolonial African contexts, but also to claim an authoritative basis for rejecting non-normative sexualities and abortion, or defending polygamy and 'female circumcision'.

Global evangelical connections have emerged from recent attempts to forge alliances, mainly between US-based evangelical groups and African churches (Kaoma 2009, 2012). These relationships are filtered through the Africanization of Christianity mentioned above, but reflect the new oppositions and connections between churches, states and other transnational actors in the context of a globalized media and economy. North American evangelical ideologies reflect US geopolitical interests and activate a variety of Christian narratives related to fellowship, salvation and the meaning of the 'great commission' (Mt. 28.16-20, NIV). Anglophone Africa appears in this worldview as a largely undifferentiated space in which Northern-based organizations can act with relative freedom. Evangelical FBOs in charity, humanitarian aid and the development industry also seem to be part of this nexus of interests (Hearn 2002; Hofer 2003). Tapping into these dynamics on the personal level, white-saviour projects of mission and 'voluntourism' in Africa allow Global North Christians to construct a righteous and compassionate moral identity.

These general tendencies converge and crystallize in highly specific ways in the Kenyan context. Awino Okech (2019) describes the way Christian common sense has informed developmental and 'modern' interpretations of Luo 'widow inheritance' practices. The colonial construction of Christianity as modern allows Luo Christians, who are explicitly positioned in this discourse as 'saved' or 'born-again', to reject widow inheritance as sinful and archaic. The partnership of a widow with her brother-in-law after her husband's death is considered sinful because it contradicts Christian promotion of love marriage and monogamy, and frustrates the purpose of sex by putting it to use outside monogamous procreation. This perception of Luo sexual practices informed some of my research participants' expectations of what could be achieved in relation to SRHR in those communities. For example, Wandia described her understanding of sex in Nyanza, where the population is mainly Luo, as too 'casual':

> In Nyanza ... they use sex as a ritual ... during harvesting, during major celebrations, sex is part of what – everybody who can have sex should do as part of the celebration ... How can you just make it that casual? It cannot be that casual. But if you have been bought up in such a society, you'll think that is the norm ... So, we have many, many girls – young girls with babies ... who should still be depending on their parents. Now they have this dependent. (Wandia, interview, 2012)

The YWCA actively takes from multiple scripts in its negotiation of sexual ethics, incorporating Christian moral narratives of good womanhood, alongside a 'developmental' approach identifying the influences of social norms and introducing an analysis of the social and economic systems in which young mothers operate. In the latter, Luo widow inheritance is interpreted as subordinating the desire of the widow to the continuation of a 'traditional' practice. It thereby comes up against 'modern' ideas of freedom and autonomy that are promoted as part of gender-mainstreaming discourses. These critiques are compounded further by the context of HIV, which categorizes all sexual activity as potentially risky and therefore reframes the practice in terms of an increased risk (Okech 2019: 32–40). The clear lineages of colonial, white women's interventions and missionary Christianity in these understandings of widow inheritance are illustrative of the ways everyday ethics are informed by historical context. The YWCA's reflections about Christian morality and controversial faith issues reveal the mutual narrative constitution of its Christian identity and its ethical perspective within the narrative matrix of Christianity and development. The YWCA's ontological narrative of Christian identity achieved the necessary alignment of 'being' Christian with activities, namely its interventions in SRHR. For the YWCA, publicly claiming a Christian identity is a means of legitimizing its activities and granting itself authority in the context of deep suspicions about feminism and sexuality. However, it also speaks to a much more deep-seated connection between identity and everyday ethics.

7.1 Living fulfilled lives

The YWCA communicates its purpose and identity through its statements of 'mission' and 'vision' which feature prominently on publicity materials. Mission statements and similar texts are key tools for the construction of institutional identity in organizations, serving to identify and highlight key characteristics (Van Tonder and Lessing 2003: 25). Since its inception in 1855, the YWCA has made use of this kind of institution-building technique to create and communicate its purpose. The World YWCA similarly uses these organizational techniques to establish a reason for its existence and present this as connected to its activities. In 2012 the World YWCA's vision statement was accompanied by a statement of 'purpose': 'Our Vision: A fully inclusive world where justice, peace, health, human dignity, freedom and care for the environment are promoted and sustained by women's leadership[.] Our Purpose: To develop leadership and collective power of women and girls around the world to achieve justice, peace, health, human dignity, freedom and a sustainable environment for all' (World YWCA 2012).[1] Compared to the Paris Basis and aims of the YWCA in the nineteenth century, discussed in Chapter 2, the World YWCA's identity appears to have altered substantially. The World YWCA has set aside Christian motives in these statements, and left them to be inferred by the reader, while it expresses its purpose without using references to scripture or really any Christian vocabulary at all. For the YWCA in Kenya, its mission and vision statements are part of Christian emphasis. The mission statement is also a significant example of the Association's narrative use of its Christian identity. In 2012 it read, 'Based on its belief in Jesus Christ, the YWCA, a non-profit volunteer membership organisation, exists to develop the leadership and collective power of women and girls to achieve social and economic empowerment, human rights, health, security, dignity, freedom, justice, and peace for all humanity' (YWCA 2011). In the space of one long sentence, the mission statement claims a Christian foundation, and connects these to a list of ambitious goals. In a similar manner to the abbreviated ontological narrative used in leaflets, discussed in Chapter 6, the mission statement claims a Christian basis but does not make clear how the activities pursued under its auspices are connected to it. The vision statement in use in 2012 was: 'A society where girls and women live fulfilled lives'. For those who recognize its use of Christian vocabulary, this sentence offers a distinctively Christian expression of and approach towards working 'on women's issues', as Njeri put it. Edith explicitly mentioned this, suggesting that it marks the significance of 'spirituality' and shows that it is woven into the fabric of the Association: 'The YWCA['s vision is that it] exists to improve the socio-economic status of women, to enable them to live fulfilled lives. And "fulfilled lives" at the end, is from the book of John [in the New Testament] … spirituality cuts across the whole fabric of YWCA activities' (Edith, interview, 2012). Edith made a point of referring me to it, pointing out that it includes a Bible reference in its use of the phrase 'live fulfilled lives'. Thus, presenting the vision and mission in conjunction, the YWCA situates itself within other narratives with which Christians are already familiar.

It is the vision statement that is of greater interest to me because the mission statement was not discussed by my research participants, and also because it suggests a guiding principle for the YWCA's work, citing a passage from the New Testament, Jn 10.10. The King James Version (KJV) gives the passage as follows: 'The thief cometh not, but for to steal, and to kill, and to destroy: I am come that they might have life, and that they might have it more abundantly' (Jn 10.10). It refers to a metaphor for the salvific intervention of Jesus in the story of a shepherd protecting his flock in the face of existential danger; it asserts that in this way, Christians are enabled to live fulfilled or abundant lives. The 'fulfilled' life in translation in Jn 10.10 is derived from the Greek adverb transliterated as *perissos*, which is commonly rendered in English as 'abundantly'. 'Abundance' suggests great quantity, and throughout the KJV abundance typically describes attributes of god, such as abundant mercy (1 Pet. 13, KJV). Otherwise it often accompanies an injunction to make one's behaviour or devotion to god all-encompassing and unending, as in 'abundant love' (2 Cor. 2.4, KJV) or 'abundant thanksgiving' (2 Cor. 9.12, KJV). In relation to life it seems to indicate plenitude, hence the popular use of 'abundance' to indicate a very contemporary kind of material wealth, or prosperity (Gez 2018: 119–22). In the YWCA's vision statement, the citation of Jn 10.10 follows translations which opt for the language of 'fullness' or 'life to the full'. While the phrase 'abundant life' is most common in African theological and moral scholarship, the language of 'fulfilment' is found in more recent translations of the New Testament including the New International Version (NIV). In the NIV, the passage is rendered thus: 'The thief comes only to steal and kill and destroy; I have come that they may have life, and have it to the full' (Jn 10.10, NIV). Having life 'to the full' gives the sense of a 'full measure' (Jn 17.13, NIV), the flourishing, completeness and satisfaction of each life. Two notable exceptions to the predominant translation of abundance or fulfilment stand out as particularly emphasizing the materialist perspective implied by 'abundance'. The New Living Translation (NLT) gives 'my purpose is to give them a rich and satisfying life' (NLT, Jn 10.10), while the Wycliffe Bible (WYC) gives 'I came, that they have life, and have [it] more plenteously' (Jn 10.10, WYC). In these translations the difference between abundance or plenteousness of life and the fulfilment or satisfaction of life becomes clear; the sense of flourishing in both 'fulfilment' and 'abundance' is excessive, overflowing. The fulfilled life is one in which every need is met, including (as Christians would have it) the spiritual need to know god and to be 'saved'.

The imperial uses to which the New Testament as a whole was put by colonizers in Africa serves as a crucial backdrop to contemporary readings of scripture. Musa Dube's critical postcolonial feminist readings of Bible texts show how power relations modelled on biblical descriptions of god and the Israelites were used to justify colonization, and fundamentally informed the construction of colonial hierarchies of race and civilization (Dube 2000: 57; 2002: 60). According to her analysis, the gospel of John represents 'a site of struggle for power', setting Jesus' life in a sweeping historical narrative which alternately emphasizes Jesus' power and powerlessness (Dube and Staley 2002: 10). Even the life-giving creative and salvific power attributed to Jesus could be used to reinforce colonial power relations. Missionaries 'bringing Jesus' to colonized peoples could present salvation as connected with, even dependent upon, submission to colonization. The co-constitution of white and Christian identity in the processes of colonization positioned organizations like the YWCA as saviours, too, as I suggested earlier in terms of 'imperial maternalism'. However, Jn 10.10 can represent something other than imperial power.

The YWCA's citation of Jn 10.10 in its vision signals an implicit judgement about women's lives; they are not *yet* fulfilled. This has theological implications, as perhaps women require the salvation offered by Jesus, but it also has a political orientation towards this-worldly implications of 'fulfilment' for women, discussed below. By phrasing the vision statement as 'live fulfilled lives', as opposed to using the translation 'life abundant' or even 'to have life', the YWCA clarifies that this principle is being applied to life in the ordinary sense, not to life after death. In my reading of the vision, this grammar suggests that it is the value of 'life', rather than fulfilment, that is of central significance; 'fulfilled' is the adjective applied to the plural noun, 'lives'. By using 'live' as a verb, the vision also gestures towards women's agency as a dimension of fulfilment; the message communicated is that living fulfilled lives is something women and girls should be able to *do*, and that the YWCA will pursue that goal. 'Life' is a multivalent value in this context. As I show, below, it points towards values of pro-natalism and maternalism, care ethics, resistant and liberating political theologies, and it could offer support for either an individualistic or a communitarian ethics. 'Fulfilled lives' allows for a broad range of interpretations. It permits the exercise of contextual decision-making and individual conscience, and presents opportunities for Christian women's moral agency outside the patriarchal structures of the churches.

7.2 A multivalent Christian ethics of life

The value of abundant or fulfilled life is strikingly prominent in African theologies. Abundant life has been interpreted to represent the necessary physical and spiritual support for progress towards better living conditions or well-being. The Circle has emphasized abundant life as the achievement of justice, health and atonement towards which African women personally and collectively struggle (Chitando and Njoroge 2016; Kanyoro 1999: 56; Oduyoye 2001: 83–6). Circle theologians have described the multiple structures of oppression in the everyday lives of African women, including patriarchies and imperialisms, that stand in the way of fulfilment (Getui and Theuri 2002: 1; Kanyoro 1999: 59 n.6; Njoroge 1997: 77–83). Jesus' promise of abundant life symbolizes the conquering of death and embeds theology in the materiality of lives, mitigating against a dualistic or ascetic denigration of the body that would privilege the life hereafter over life here and now (Daly 1994: 295–314). Abundant life is thus sometimes incorporated into African and liberation theologies to undergird a concern for the poor and resistance against death via poverty, imperialism and injustice (Ganusah 2014: 217; Vuola 2002: 64, 198). 'Life', in this schema, is more than mere biological existence, but the meaningful and specifically human experience in/of the material world, or 'creation', as good. As suggested above, the value of life remains open to a wide range of interpretations. Its primary meaning in the YWCA's case is, as outlined above, in furnishing the YWCA with a goal towards which it aims. As Winnie told me, 'We have only one earthly life – and I think we want to live it to the maximum – so you want to embrace a religion that does not oppress you, a religion that does not deny your burdens' (Winnie, 2012, interview). While life can offer a frame through which to reinterpret Christianity in service of women's empowerment, peace and social justice (to echo the YWCA's thematic areas of focus), it can equally be mobilized to condemn abortion, contraception and LGBTQ sexualities. Herein, I address the two primary senses in which 'life' had meaning for the YWCA in its activities; first, it seems to mitigate against abortion due to its pro-natalist inflection; and second, it offers support for the related values of maternalism and repronormativity.

As demonstrated in the Kenyan context during the drafting and debating of the new constitution between 2008 and 2010, many churches and spokespersons for Christianity have appealed to the value of 'life' in anti-abortion arguments. A 'pro-life' vocabulary was not quite in evidence in these debates, but the same sense of positioning abortion as death was certainly achieved. The value of life, in this sense, seems to imply the celebration of all human life, but it is telling that this has resulted in the strengthening of anti-contraception and anti-abortion politics. Part of the difficulty in negotiating the distinction between meaningful lives worth defending and life in a purely literal sense is that some African feminist or womanist politics are also strongly pro-natal – reflected in the occasional preference for the name 'motherist' (as discussed by Getman and Nadar 2013). Some well-known figures in the field – like Gwendolyn Mikell, who has claimed with approval that 'no self-respecting African woman fails to bear children' (1997: 9) – have reinforced the connection between conceiving and giving birth, on one hand, with motherhood as a status and role granting social and political power to women, on the other. As I discuss in greater detail, below, this connection is not necessary in order to value mothers and the labour of mothering. In a very different vein, Oyèrónkẹ́ Oyěwùmí describes the metaphysical and ontological status, in Yoruba culture, of children as eternally bound to their mothers and *vice versa*, from before conception until after death (2016: 61–3). If becoming a mother is approached in this way, then it may be difficult to theoretically accommodate or socially accept the technologies that enable women and girls to refuse it.

If 'life' is of ultimate value and furnishes pro-natal perspectives in the way I am suggesting, then it follows that abortion would be suspect on the grounds that it diminishes and destroys life. Dominant narratives of 'African' and 'Christian' identity, and the commitments these identities imply, are mutually reinforcing on this point. For some theologians, abundant life connects pre-Christian African traditions with biblical values in such a way as to facilitate the Africanization of Christianity. Life is not merely biological processes but specific social practices; the maintenance, extension and creation of the relationships that sustain these practices are reframed as a central moral obligation. Nyambura Njoroge cites the value of life reflected in African cultural norms as a responsibility to instantiate 'right relations' among individuals and groups (Njoroge 2000: 111–14). The value of life in abundance is in this way claimed to have already been part of African sociocultural norms prior to the arrival of missionary Christianity. The significance of unchosen interpersonal ties and obligations is another potential avenue through which the notion of abundant life can lend support to strongly pro-natal attitudes.

Conversely, a moral schema which permits abortion would not be considered to treat life with due concern – as in various critiques of secularism and imperialism that consider contraception 'anti-life' or associate it with death (Vuola 2002: 219–20). Abundant life is often taken in the sense of procreation, as an obligation to increase life, to 'be fruitful and multiply' (Gen. 9.1, KJV). However, I am suggesting that 'life' in the sense the YWCA uses it does not mean sheer biological existence, but the quality of a person's journey from birth to death. 'Life' expressed in terms of a continuity from those yet to be born, to the ancestors, and across a wide extended family, is very different to the dominant Western orientation towards mortality.[2] The *fulfilment* of life in this sense refocuses the discussion on a wide web of interrelations that links the pregnant person and their community in relationships of responsibility for, and accountability to, 'others beyond the present' (Rivera 2007: 99). This could be read in ways that support or reject abortion, although since I am pro-choice I am able to see how this interpretation could accommodate abortion. Abortion could be justified in terms of responding to future generations by ensuring that they enter the world at such time as they can be cared for, and achieve the fulfilment of their own lives. The YWCA's affirmation of the value of fulfilled lives values women's bodies and opinions, and in theory permits women to exercise not only bodily autonomy but also moral agency. However, the heteronormativity and repronormativity of much of the YWCA's work on SRHR limits the scope of the value of fulfilled lives. Its position on abortion, sketched in terms of the figure of the pregnant teenage girl, demonstrates a mixture of these perspectives.

The YWCA often applies a maternal ethic that prioritizes care and communal responses to social problems. Caring was evident in a variety of forms, for instance, Mbari's direct intervention in the life of a young HIV-positive woman, the institutional provision of care for OVCs, a concern with the well-being of carers for PLWHA, the humanitarian response to the post-election violence in 2008 and the mandate of the Christian Emphasis Committee to provide pastoral support to YWCA members. When discussing condoms in relation to the HIV epidemic, the YWCA emphasized the importance of protecting young people. A sense of intergenerational difference inflected the responses of many of my research participants in discussions of young peoples' sexual behaviour. While the values of 'purity' may well be at the heart of the YWCA's sexual ethic, my research participants nonetheless realized they could not hope to change the (sexual) behaviour of all the young beneficiaries of the YWCA's SRHR programmes. Dorcas stressed the threat of HIV by likening the YWCA's role in its provision of sex education with her relationship to her own children.

> There are these ways to prevent getting infected with HIV and AIDS. I wouldn't like [my children to be having sex], but it's good that they know that these measures exist. And most parents are like me ... most members of YWCA are like me, so that's what most mothers or most fathers would feel. (Dorcas, interview, 2012)

Dorcas appealed to parenthood, particularly motherhood, as a source of wisdom borne of experience, and reasoned that the YWCA's perspective on SRHR interventions with teenagers was based on a common position as parents, sharing the same concerns and bearing the same responsibilities in relation not only to their own children but also to the next generations. This ethic maps directly onto the hierarchy of the YWCA in which a generational split between older YWCA leaders and the younger programme beneficiaries is enabled by structural maternalism. The institutionalization of an age-based hierarchy in the form of maternalism may serve the YWCA's interests by making it compatible with African tendencies to confer age-related power and status on elders in general, and women in particular. Through the ageing process, older women may be positioned as mothers or grandmothers through seniority in terms of age, rather than their childbearing capacity or biography (Steady 2005: 319).

The YWCA's programmatic interventions in SRHR have reinforced rather than challenged heterosexism and the predominant connection of women with motherhood in a normative patriarchal family structure. LBTQI women were excluded from consideration and conceptually positioned as beyond the 'reach' of the YWCA. The theoretical and everyday promotion of motherhood, pro-natalism, is repronormative. The YWCA works from the repronormative assumption that women can, will and perhaps should produce children, and the assumption that women as mothers will perform the labour of raising them. The repronormative implications of 'life' are complicated by lack of reliable access to SRHR information and services, maternal health care and medical care. By encoding repronormativity and pro-natalism in its SRHR interventions, the YWCA acquiesces to the marginalization of women who are unable, disinterested or unwilling to have children, and asserts straightforward biological differences between female and male bodies. This can have significant implications for trans and/or intersex people, such as who can be recognized as a parent, who is allowed to raise children and in what conditions.

However, the risks inherent to affirming such a multivalent value as 'life' may be the greatest strength of the YWCA's approach. The inarguable relevance and potency of maternal identities and practices for many African Christians suggests it may be a useful, powerful ethical metaphor (Hinga 2017: xix n22; see also Higgs 2019). It could promote voluntary parenthood and reproductive justice, in the sense suggested by Sistersong (2015), as a dimension of fulfilment. Christian women in Kenya have been known to emphasize mothering as a practice that informs their ability to lead, in Christian contexts and in their everyday lives, broadening mothering beyond the confines of biological relatedness (Ngunjiri 2010: 115). The principle of abundant life is capable of valuing LGBTQ and other 'non-reproductive' sexualities, and alternative family formations. A pro-natal and maternal orientation of abundant life does not necessarily have to be interpreted according to an essentialist and confining heteronormative framework (Dube 2007: 358; Getman and Nadar 2013: 66–70). In 2012, the YWCA was concerned with LBTQI women only in so far as they constituted an outside group and therefore implicated in its boundary work. Whether this stance changes will ultimately be subject to the collective decision-making of its members in whose name the YWCA acts. Further, the organization as a whole has demonstrated the capacity to withstand relatively radical changes to its identity, the turbulence being absorbed and transformed through incorporation in collectively authored narratives, as it did when it shed its racially exclusive whiteness and became 'multiracial' in the late colonial period. There is thus reason to think that the YWCA could reorient its efforts towards a more inclusive definition of 'fulfilled lives', but any changes are more than likely to reflect the prevailing ethical and moral narratives circulating through Christian communities in Kenya. Given the evidence of recent history as I have presented it in this book, it is doubtful that this interpretation can challenge hegemonic patriarchal Christianities in Kenya.

7.3 Approaches to Christian ethics

As Rachel Muers and Michael Barton (2013) have pointed out, 'The study of [Christian] ethics is often assumed to be … the study of what "Christianity" says ought to be done' (Barton and Muers 2013: 169). However, the academic field of Christian ethics is problematic, asserting unity over a heterogeneous field that offers contradictory conclusions (MacIntyre 1974: 111). There are nonetheless certain shared tendencies which constitute the meaning of 'Christianities' as a family of ethical perspectives, traditions, theologies and institutions, which share much while differing on many points. Arguably, moral philosophy in the West owes an unacknowledged debt to the long history of Christian thought about morality on which it is largely based. An illustrative example is the lineage Alasdair MacIntrye traced from Aristotelian virtue ethics, through Aquinas's reformulation and Catholicization of these, to contemporary beliefs about equality (MacIntyre 1974: 118). Despite the evident interplay of non-Christian influences like Plato and Aristotle with Christian theology, articulations of Christian ethics nevertheless assert their uniquely Christian character just as routinely as 'secular' Western ethics ignores or downplays its Christian inheritance. Far from being a total, Christian moral theologies often admit their partial and processual nature. The category of *adiaphora*, or issues about which Christians are not obliged to act in any particular way, is derived from the New Testament; for instance, 1 Cor. 7.18 is often cited as evidence that the circumcision of boys is an *adiaphoron* (Haselbarth 1976: 23).[3] A related problem arises for Christians when they are confronted with ethical questions that arise and/or have been answered somewhat outside of Christianity, such as the status of condoms in relation to the HIV epidemic. Since this virus emerged many years after the Bible's authors died, it is not a topic on which they expressed an opinion, and therefore it is necessary for Christians to decide whether non-Christian ethics overrides Christian ethical principles (Outka 2005: 199–200).

The YWCA's controversial faith issues are arguably more controversial where there are greater resources in tradition, doctrine and scripture upon which to ground ethical judgement – in other words when they are not *adiaphora*. However, I am more interested in the implications this distinction between Christian and non-Christian ethics has in relation to narrative identity constitution. According to Gene Outka (2005), Christians have recourse to at least three orthodox responses to such ethical dilemmas: the first and simplest is to reject any ethical principles that arise and are justified independently of Christianity. The second response is to accept the ethical principle if it *can* be justified using Christian reasoning. The third is to freely accept any such non-Christian ethical principle on the grounds that Christian ethics 'is never at odds with what [non-Christian] rational persons apprehend morally' (Outka 2005: 200). However, this third response does not really depart from the first. It is based on the assumption that Christians have a privileged perspective from which to adjudicate what is moral. Thus, any ethical stance that is deemed incompatible with Christianity is, basically, considered to be the result of not being Christian. If this account of Christian ethical reasoning on new or 'secular' problems is complete, it implies that the only solution is to claim a Christian identity because it simply would not be possible to argue with Christian ethics as a non-Christian. This explains part of the puzzle of the relationship between Christian identity and ethics, a theme to which I return shortly.

Despite the evident diversity of Christian ethics in theory and practice, there is a tendency to generalize about the ethical perspective held by Christian individuals, communities and institutions. Such generalizations sometimes serve to underline critiques of Christianity from 'outside'. One such example particularly pertinent to the focus of this book is the tendency to make feminist critiques of Christianity which begin from the assertion that it is necessarily and by definition misogynistic (Jantzen 1998: 7; Vuola 2002: 107–8). Evidently, misogynistic attitudes are both explicitly held and passively perpetuated by clergy and Christian institutions, theologies and social norms, but the existence of counterexamples – such as the YWCA – serves to illustrate that the content of a Christian perspective is not necessarily determined in advance. Churches and their spokespersons also frequently make and employ generalizations about Christian ethics. There are, however, clearly differences in the content of such declarations between denominations and institutions. While one perspective may be shared by a group of Christian churches, for example those grouped together in the NCCK, the underlying epistemological assumptions that guide the articulations of institutional Christian positions tend to exclude the possibility of valid disagreements between ethically competent equals. As I described in Chapter 2, the NCCK's appeal to represent the Christian voice of Kenyans in the constitutional debates was based on a similar assertion of unified Christian identity, and expressed the belief that alternative positions were not just mistaken but also sinful (e.g. the claim that people who voted for the constitution 'will surely die'). References to a unified Christian identity are often a rhetorical device for asserting the authority and legitimacy of whatever interpretation is being offered at the time. This type of dynamic was identified by my research participants on the level of the individual, who is able to assert Christian identity as a means of shielding their actions from scrutiny:

> [In Kenya] we have that attitude that that person [who is] a Christian cannot do [something wrong]; and yet [we know that] not all who say, 'Lord, Lord', belong to Him. So it sometimes becomes difficult to identify, who is this person with those Christian values? And [if he] actually practices those values in the office? Some of us will just say 'yes, we are Christians', and yet we are just covering ourselves. (Nyaboke, interview, 2012)

Similar generalizations are often made with the intention of assigning Christian identity to those who share a certain ethical perspective. In these cases, too, declarations of ethics – 'moralizing' – are performative rather than revealing a necessary feature of Christian ethics. Thus, the assertion and rejection of identities is a central feature, and often an intended result, of expressing Christian ethical positions. The reverse also seems to be the case: it is clear from recent events and the testimonies of my research participants that it is near impossible, in Kenya, to maintain an identity as a Christian and be openly 'pro-choice' on the question of abortion (Osur 2011). As such, the function of identity and sexual ethics requires further examination in order to answer the pressing question of why 'the religious Other and the sexual Other mutually constitute each other' (Kwok 2005: 139). Given the ways in which Kenyan Christian leaders and institutions have treated wider topics of sexual ethics as a means of policing group membership, there is ample reason to suspect that the 'religious Other' in Kenya could be constituted by their stance on controversial faith issues.

Ordinary ethics and ordinary theological ethics differ from approaches to the study of Christian ethics in the overlapping fields of moral philosophy, the study of religions and theology. Both 'ordinary ethics' and 'ordinary theological ethics' broaden the focus of moral and ethical thought from academic theory to social life, but ultimately neither moves the frame of reference far enough to seamlessly apply to the YWCA's everyday ethical and narrative practices. Nevertheless, I find much of value in each of them. I consider, first, the field of ordinary ethics that emerged out of anthropology and, second, the notion of ordinary theological ethics, and expand upon these to outline everyday Christian ethics as a more apt description of the YWCA's approach.

7.4 Towards everyday Christian ethics

Considering ethics as 'ordinary' is to recognize the ubiquity of ethics in judgement and action, and to reinstate it as accessible by anyone, not only moral philosophers. Almost all people are regularly engaged in processes of thinking about what is good, and refining their moral judgments, even if those thought processes may be unmarked as 'ethics' and perhaps less complex than what counts as moral philosophy. Ethical conduct – talk and action – is inherent to social life: 'relatively tacit, grounded in agreement [and] in practice … and happening without drawing attention to itself' (Lambek 2010: 2). Building on observations from anthropology, ordinary ethics suggests that ethics is exercised in judgement, expressed in uncomplicated, commonplace language, does not rely on the existence of a universal (such as god) and requires no special training. The 'ordinariness' of ethics describes its form and its relationship to social, communal practices, and the contents and effects of ethical speech and action (Fassin 2012: 3). In other words, ethics is a property of human behaviour and not of academic enquiry. Scholarship in and of ordinary ethics emphasizes that our ethical deliberations are often mistaken, and the conclusions we draw from them can be harmful. This insight shades Veena Das's explorations of ordinary ethics, as she observes that 'so many ethical pronouncements that are made in the public domain seem to be either hollow or plain dissimulations' (Das 2015: 55). The rhetorical strategy of declaring oneself as morally good, often employed by politicians and clergy, would be considered ethical (they are engaging in ethics) but in any subsequent analysis the content of the declaration is not separable from its effects. Arguments about the effects of such public pronouncements are about how people exercise power in speech, not about the field of ethics per se. The ethical and the normative are disentangled for the purposes of analysis but recognized to be intimately conjoined in social life. I agree that ethics is expressed in 'life taken as a whole rather than … [at] dramatic moments of breakdown or ethical dilemmas as the occasions for ethical reflection' (Das 2015: 56). However, trouble and controversy provide opportunities for moral stories to be told, as a way to 'make sense' out of 'trouble' (Daiute 2011: 329).

Ordinary ethics, as I have described it here, is to be critiqued for the philosophical and theoretical terrain on which it draws to conceptualize ethics and study morality. While scholars of ordinary ethics do not engage in prescriptive moral philosophical argument, they do assert a degree of continuity between the ordinary ethics of non-specialists and the work of philosophers and theologians wherein ethics can be 'enunciated more explicitly' (Lambek 2010: 63). This seems largely to be identified in relation to the two dominant European traditions in moral philosophy and their uptake in the 'ethical turn': the lineage from Aristotle to Michel Foucault, or the influence of Immanuel Kant, as for example in the work of Emile Durkheim (Fassin 2012: 9). Often, the vocabulary with which ordinary ethicists describe their findings seems unquestionably derived from Kant, suggesting that ordinary ethics tends to inscribe the theoretical inheritance and unmarked assumptions of Eurocentric, northern scholarship onto its objects of analysis (Zigon 2014: 750). Theorizing ordinary ethics using only these philosophical resources limits the varieties of ethical expression and practice which can be used to identify and analyse. This is an outcome I explicitly wish to avoid. Critical postcolonial feminist and decolonial scholarship strongly suggests that the lives of women in postcolonial Kenya might not be describable using the terms of the European philosophical canon. I therefore attempt, below, to answer this question based on scholarship and insights that sit outside the above-mentioned theoretical terrain, namely the output of the Circle. Furthermore, I offer further material towards the critique that ordinary ethics neglects religion; Christianity 'is not necessarily the opposite of the ordinary and everyday' (Robbins 2016: 769).

In popular discourse, 'theology' is often used as an example of irrelevant academic and religious self-indulgence, confined to debating the number of angels who can dance on the head of a pin. This perception is certainly partly true. The practices characteristic of academic theology – like many other disciplines including philosophy, anthropology and literature – reflect the assumption that it will be practiced by elite men, in circumstances of affluence and security, but this is not the whole picture. In practice, theology is an expansive category that includes Vatican encyclicals, the vocational training of priests, Sunday school activities and more scholarly pursuits in many subfields including hermeneutics, Mariology and missiology. In theory, theology is a name for any reasoning, speculation or storytelling about god/s – *theo* meaning god and *logy* talk or study. Its purposes can equally be varied, but it centrally involves an effort to understand the world in the light of a personal faith and/or experiences of belonging to a community of practitioners. I do not seek to defend the worst excesses of Christian theology, as it has wielded significant colonial power (Dube 2000; Kwok 2005; Rivera 2007) and informed many damaging assumptions about 'religion' (Asad 1993). Nor am I interested in *doing* theology; rather, I want to include the contributions of theologians in my analysis to expand the theoretical terrain from which everyday ethics can draw.

Ordinary theological ethics offers an alternative to a popularly assumed Christian morality of a deontological, patriarchal model of ethics as fixed, known through instruction and authorized by a church acting on god's command. It focuses instead on people ('ordinary Christians') who do not have 'explicit training in theology and ethics', whose ethical 'action and reflection often places them in an uneasy relationship with the church' and whose ethics take shape in 'communities [that] are not part of recognized church structures' (Barton and Muers 2013: 170). Ordinary theological ethical reasoning involves, first, Christians engaging in innovative, if unorthodox, ethical reasoning 'striving for an embodied praxis' and, second, coming to 'recognize ... disconnects between faith as they have been taught it ... and the lived practice of their faith community'. They do not refer to official theology to repair these fractures. Third, context and community provides Christians with 'the material for the reasoning through which ... [an ethical] conclusion' is reached. Finally, the aforementioned 'disconnects' can result in Christians who differ from the norm 'increasingly identifying with, and being formed by and into, the communities these [extra-ecclesial organisations] constitute' (Barton and Muers 2013: 2013: 172–5). I have found that the YWCA, as a lay women's movement grappling with controversial faith issues, facilitates and encourages these kinds of everyday ethical reasoning. It illustrates each of these dimensions of 'ordinary theological ethics'. The dissatisfaction that my research participants sometimes expressed with the absence or marginalization of women's voices in other Christian institutions particularly allows the development of personal identification with the YWCA – to encourage staff and members to speak on its behalf by saying 'we'. It is interesting that the YWCA did not display the same level of 'conscious and complex engagement with scripture and tradition' as the Christian vegetarians in the UK on whom Rachel Muers and Michael Barton's theorization is based (Barton and Muers 2013: 170). Rather, the YWCA made use of the potential problems caused by controversial faith issues in its narrative practices of Christian emphasis, as described in Chapter 6. While Barton and Muers spoke with Christians who reflected on their *personal* vegetarian ethics from within and on behalf of their denomination-specific theological commitments, I spoke to representatives of an *organization* who reflected on ethical conduct across interdenominational differences.

I distinguish my approach from 'ordinary ethics' because I am not situated within the debates over morality in the discipline of anthropology out of which ordinary ethics emerged. I begin with a different set of theoretical and disciplinary influences, so I use the term 'everyday Christian ethics', which I flesh out with reference to the YWCA. I refer to everyday, instead of 'ordinary', Christian or theological ethics in order to emphasize the difference made by focusing on the narrative practices of an ecumenical institution, rather than on focusing on personal ethics. 'Everyday ethics' is a term that has long been used in medical ethics scholarship to describe the dilemmas faced by medical professionals, and their responses to them, in institutional clinical settings (Kane and Caplan 1990; Zizzo, Bell and Racine 2016). In a similar way to ordinary ethics, it foregrounds ethical questions as they are encountered by people engaged in applying ethics in practice, and it continues to rely on the same unmarked theoretical lineages as ordinary ethics. My (re)formulation of everyday Christian ethics combines insights from ordinary theological ethics and the output of the Circle. Even though I am not a theologian, I find the work of the Circle very useful for understanding some of the connections between gender, Christianities and postcolonial African realities. In thinking about the YWCA's everyday Christian ethics, I draw on the work of the Circle not as spokespersons for African Christian women, although their expertise and insights are based partly on that positionality. Rather, the Circle has produced a body of scholarship that has considered women and gender in African contexts from an explicitly Christian point of view, analysing precisely the terrain in which the YWCA has operated.[4] Thus, I approach the output of the Circle as the most relevant critique of androcentric and racist tendencies in Christianities, both in terms of practice and in terms of theoretical and theological scholarship. The work of Circle theologians on Christian ethics is additionally significant because it contests hegemonic patriarchal interpretations of Christianity in academic theology and in institutional practice, and insists that African women are producers of theological knowledge whether they are in the academy or not.

Recognizing the power of narrative to persuade, inspire, comfort and teach (as well as connect people to a shared identity), one of the most striking features of the approach taken by many Circle members is their use of narrative, with the personal and collective life stories of African women often suggested as a basis for a contextual theology. Musimbi Kanyoro recalls that early in its history, the Circle was inspired by the observation that Jesus' encounters with women were 'always followed by a command that involved speech' (1992: 24). As Esther Mombo has pointed out, women's informal storytelling within communities and families is an important mode of religious communication in contexts with a history of oral traditions, as is the case in much of Africa (2003: 97). Creative storytelling practices can serve to reclaim myths and proverbs about women and their experiences, status and roles from postcolonial nationalist projects that (re)invent and perpetuate gender inequalities (Ayanga 1996: 19–20). Circle theologians have thus long been engaged in reclaiming and retelling a range of biblical stories. Reflecting the sociocultural reality in many present-day African contexts, Circle theologians seek to recover the significance of many female Old Testament figures and their stories. Musimbi Kanyoro suggests that African women theologians find ways to 'rescue' Old Testament women such as Orpah, the daughter-in-law of Ruth who goes back to her natal family after her husband dies. The stories of these marginal characters are reimagined to provide 'models of blessing' for women who are presented with similar choices in the present day (1995: 22). Nyambura Njoroge reads the story of Hannah, who despairs at her inability to have children, as directly speaking to the contemporary experiences of childless or infertile African women (1996: 21–6, citing 1 Sam. 1–2.21). Through retelling and reimagining biblical stories in such a way that they speak to African women, Circle theologians reflect the realities of African women's lives (Getui 1998: 52–9; Njoroge 2000: 126–8). Musa Dube takes a similar approach to the character of Rahab, a Canaanite woman who represents the subjugation of Canaan and the interests of the colonizing Israelites; her person and her voice are appropriated and used against her (Dube 2000: 70–80). The Bible employs rhetoric that legitimizes invading and colonizing 'other' lands, including by representing those nations in the figure of a woman who can be incorporated by marriage, or rape, into the nation of the colonizer (Dube 2000: 57).

Thus, in Circle theologies, everyday practices of telling stories are affirmed as valid ways of doing theology, and moreover African women's life stories themselves are often considered be tools for social transformation, with an implicit orientation towards ethical evaluation (Ayanga 2016: 3–4). Narrativity suggests an epistemology based not on the written word but on listening to the spoken word (Oduyoye 2000: 147–9). Emphasizing the Bible as a source of ethics above all other dimensions of Christian practice is colonial, to the degree that it prioritizes literacy and formal European pedagogical approaches over aurality/orality and other modes of learning. A metaphor of speaking and listening is repeated often in Oduyoye's work and it has permeated Circle theologies as a whole. The value of dialogic, intersubjective reciprocity points to the importance of making space for the other to speak, in a relational and interpersonal ethics of dialogue. This orientation is accommodative of the model of mutual narrative identity constitution outlined in Chapter 1. As Musa Dube writes, for many African women including preachers and pastors, even reading the Bible is secondary to hearing and telling theologically meaningful stories, alongside personal experience of salvation and participation in worship (Dube 2000: 42, 192–4). While ethics is largely tacit and circulates through social life without naming itself as such, evidently there are numerous examples of people and institutions explicitly articulating ethical rules and values – a phenomenon encountered regularly in the study of religions. It is here that the connection between narrative and ethics contributes to explaining the quotidian nature of ethical deliberation; when we learn and talk about ethics we use a range of narrative methods, or in other words, we tell stories.

What I am outlining under the title of everyday Christian ethics is a description of the YWCA's practices that takes the postcolonial feminist theological critique of the Circle as the theoretical terrain from which to establish definitions of Christianity, theology and ethics. The YWCA's everyday Christian ethics is narrative because it depends on a sense of 'who we are', a narratively constituted organizational identity – the ability to say 'we are Christians'. The YWCA's Christian identity is, in turn, co-constituted in narratives of moral identity on the part of its members, in its ontological narrative expressed in various ways and in its narratives of Christian emphasis that respond to the trouble created by controversial faith issues. All of these narratives are influenced by the repertoire of YWCA stories, and the matrix of dominant public narratives that it has inherited from its context, in which the development industry, feminisms, Christianities and 'Africanness' have all focused questions of gender and sexuality on African women's bodies. Narratively constituted identities are both limited and enabled by what has gone before, by what positions are available for the organization to take up while remaining legible in its context. The YWCA's everyday Christian ethics is narrative also because it employs and responds to various moral narratives. Moral narratives do at least two things: they provoke empathetic or affective responses to the consequences of actions which encourage judgements of right and wrong, perhaps in addition to explicit judgements in the narrative, as in *My Youth, My Pride*. They additionally form part of the way in which gender and sexuality are performatively co-created in narratives of appropriate, good, femininity and masculinity, of womanhood properly performed and of bad women who neglect to act in the ways the norm prescribes.

The processes that constitute everyday Christian ethics are iterative, and can take place over a long period of time, relying on narratives that are identified with no single author other than the institution itself. The ubiquitous narratives that inform the dominant conceptual frameworks of the traditions that constitute Christianity, both in the everyday sense and in formal theology and ecclesial contexts, provide a wide corpus of stories that exert their own influence on narrative practices of Christian identity constitution, as well as constraining the commitments with which that identity can be associated. However, identities, narratives and commitments can and do change, deliberately and accidentally. For instance, revisions of an organizational identity narrative can have unexpected effects, as in the case of Vera Harley's intervention in the YWCA's Christian identity in 1965 and 1995. These narrative shifts always make use of that which has gone before, such as the appropriation of a metaphor, (e.g. 'life') or the revaluation of a stereotype (e.g. the 'staunch' Christian).

The contribution of the moral identities of YWCA members and staff to everyday Christian ethics is significant; they are constituted in interaction with organizational identity narratives, but they are likely to be held before joining the YWCA and form a part of the motivation to do so. Certainly, my research participants presented a unanimous picture of the YWCA as a place in which their personal faith aligned with their professional work. There are personal benefits that result from adhering to a Christian identity, and sanctions incurred from deviating from it. Moral narratives of respectable femininity associate a range of behaviours as beyond the acceptable limits of Christian womanhood. The YWCA rewards its staff and members by presenting opportunities to achieve recognition as 'staunch' Christians by adhering to the lessons taught by these moral narratives (or, appearing to do so). By emphasizing the YWCA's Christian identity, its members and staff avoid the possible negative stereotype of 'feminists', and benefit from the reinforcement of the maternal status through which women's exercise of power is more socially acceptable.

Everyday Christian ethics is 'everyday', in the sense of its ordinariness, because it is based on and informed by experience and practice, not primarily by the official positions of churches. I affirm that the YWCA's everyday ethics is Christian because, as established by the contributions of the Circle, African Christian women's practices can be taken as definitive of Christianity, even if they remain marginal to academic theology. I recognize the everyday deliberations and behaviours of Christians as expressions of theology and ethics, because it is this conduct upon which Christians draw when telling their life stories. So, I accept the self-definition of the YWCA as Christian, through the narrative constitution of a Christian organizational identity. I acknowledge that the YWCA could be mistaken about its ethics, such as when it claims it does things 'no differently' to other women's organizations, and that its ethics could be harmful to women, as I think it is on questions of sexuality and abortion. In practice, I infer a multivalent ethics of life as a common thread running through the YWCA's programmatic interventions in SRHR. The availability and ubiquity of the value of 'life' lends itself to everyday ethics by connecting the YWCA to a matrix of Christian narratives from liberation theologies to conservative nationalism. To approach a African Christian women's organization like the YWCA using a framework of everyday Christian ethics permits the effects of context, and its potential for nuance and change, to be recognized rather than dismissing the organization as a mouthpiece for the patriarchal and misogynistic ethics of the churches.

7.5 Summary

I have shown how when the YWCA talks about Christian ethics, it does not specify theological, biblical or other principles or teachings as a basis or source of authority. Instead it relies on a shared, narratively constituted Christian identity and a set of values associated with that identity, which remain largely unarticulated. This is made possible by the YWCA's shared knowledge of narratives that inform and shape Christian communities' expectations of ethical conduct. I have suggested that the vocabularies, plots and ideas that inform narratives of a YWCA Christian identity come not only from the YWCA's own history but also from a long line of colonial and imperial interventions in African women's lives, from colonization to development interventions, and discourses and representations arising from these. This suggests listening to and reading the narratives in circulation within a Christian institution or organization, and its context, as a means of finding out about Christian ethics. The stories that circulate are important: it is not that doctrine or official theologies are irrelevant, but that they are not at the forefront of everyday ethical deliberations. Moreover, when Christian women's conduct differs from Christian teaching or mainstream expectations, this is not necessarily evidence of misunderstanding, failure or resistance. The marginal influence of the doctrinal pronouncements of Christian institutions in the YWCA's overall stance on controversial faith issues demonstrates that Christian ethics is more complex than the official positions of clergy and churches. Even when it is explicitly theological, ethics is not necessarily about adherence to doctrine in the everyday and collective decisions and practices of Christian women. The Christian ethics of the YWCA depends to a great extent on the meanings attached to its identity in hegemonic Kenyan Christian discourse, and such constructions depend on their context within a matrix of other narratives from which they draw and into which they feed. One of these narrative elements is 'abundant life', which has been absorbed by mainstream Christian culture in Kenya as it has elsewhere in Africa.

The YWCA is not a Christian community in the same sense as a church congregation, but it is a membership organization constituted by women who are active, 'staunch' Christians, and who are also members of other Christian communities. The range of acceptable Christian conduct that informs the tacit understanding on which the YWCA's ethics is based seems to be learned partly through what is shared by women from diverse Christian backgrounds. The pedagogical function of models and examples of Christian identity and conduct, including those that act as moral narratives, furnish a tacitly accepted, common-sense knowledge of how the YWCA should conduct itself as a Christian organization in twentieth-century Kenya. A more nuanced understanding of the activities of Christian organizations in African contexts requires paying attention to the wider landscape of moral narratives and the power relations implicated in making programmatic interventions in relation to gender and SRHR. Therefore, while the YWCA's ethical perspective may not be especially distinctive, it recognizes and facilitates women's moral agency and has the potential to be deployed for social transformation towards reproductive justice. The ontological narrative operative in Christian emphasis does not describe the YWCA's changing ethical stance and how it informed the various programmatic interventions it staged. What it shows is the ability of a story to generate and reiterate a collective identity in ways that makes room or new meanings under the name 'Christian'. These meanings have nonetheless been highly dependent on what the surrounding context could accommodate. It is likely that patriarchal, homophobic, transphobic and misogynistic political and moral narratives and clerical pronouncements will remain a dominant aspect of Christian discourse, in Kenya and around the world. But the YWCA's history shows that such influences can be negotiated. As the colonial association of Christianity with whiteness gave way to the possibility of seeing Christianity as a faith-based identity, the YWCA was enabled to become 'multiracial'. Thus, there is reason to hope that a similar narrative process could expand the range of positions viable for the YWCA to pursue under the name 'Christian'.

Postscript

In 2012 the YWCA in Kenya barely resembled the organization it was in 1912. However, the white British women who founded the YWCA in Nairobi laid the foundations for its later success by importing a world view marked by imperial maternalism and coloniality, and by establishing an institutional structure that would withstand a century of change. By narratively constituting and reconstituting its identity as Christian, the YWCA's concerns could shift in line with its perception of the interests and needs of its members. The YWCA's proximity to rural and impoverished communities allowed it in the 1970s to expand its community-based welfare projects into programmatic interventions supported by partner and donor institutions in the development industry. It has continued to encourage young women to identify with, and act on the basis of, their Christian faith – but it has found its own Christian identity to be in constant need of 'emphasis'. Identifying certain matters of sex and sexuality as 'controversial faith issues' has allowed the YWCA to work on SRHR while maintaining a Christian identity, and moreover, to use the tension generated by confronting controversial issues as an opportunity to reassert its Christian identity. By narratively emphasizing a Christian identity through strategic appeals to the YWCA's origins, ecumenical unity and staunch piety, the YWCA has used stories of 'who we are' as a shared perspective from which to engage in everyday ethical discussion, to position itself in relation to other organizations, and to establish itself as legitimate and authoritative.

In the years since I completed my field research in Nairobi, the YWCA has implemented some of the changes that my research participants alluded to in our conversations. Its website attests to many of these changes, including a new vision statement, and some restructuring of the National Board and other constitutive governing and decision-making bodies. However, it remains committed to the same broad programme of social change in pursuit of gender equality, as a Christian women's organization and part of the World YWCA movement. It is still the largest YWCA in Africa, by membership, and the fourth largest in the world (World YWCA 2019). The World YWCA remains a powerful transnational Christian women's organization, unique in its longevity and its strong internal process and structures for participation and representation. Its significance on the global stage is the result of its longevity; its first meeting was held a quarter of a century earlier than the first meeting of the League of Nations in 1920 (Duguid 1955: 173). Since then, the World YWCA has gained a place in international women's rights and development initiatives, working alongside UN bodies as well as Christian institutions, including the World Council of Churches. The World YWCA gives Christian women, especially those from the Global South, the space and institutional backing to advocate for themselves within the existing global structures of governance and power, in ways that 'secular' groups have not. This dynamic seems to be mirrored within Kenya, as the YWCA's membership of NCCK positions it to make small interventions in the patriarchal social influence and political power of the churches. My analysis has shown that while YWCA offers a version of Christianity that is defined in service of girls and women, it has not contested the heteronormativity of dominant Christian discourses. The increasing audibility of the testimonies and life stories of LGBTQ Kenyan Christians may enable the YWCA to change this.

An itinerary for future scholarship

'Everyday Christian ethics', as I have deployed it herein, describes the YWCA's conduct as I observed it in 2012. A narrative methodology for studying Christian ethics might also be applicable in other contexts, in service of developing a feminist theory of everyday Christian ethics. My focus on the YWCA means that the approach I have developed is particularly applicable to congregations, Christian institutions and (semi-)formalized laypeople's groups. Everyday ethics can be found in social practices between people, rather than in ideas abstracted from their material contexts; and I have found ethics especially in collaborative and dialogic engagements with identity narratives. As such, I propose a tripartite approach in which scholarship on everyday Christian ethics, at least in groups similar to those mentioned here, moves between mapping the narrative context, establishing what moral and institutional identities are supported in/by those narratives, and applications of these. Historical and contemporary narratives that shape the group's context can be traced to establish who says, or has said, what about whom, and in response to what kinds of prompts to remember and retell the story. These include – but are not limited to – explicitly 'Christian' narratives of all kinds – origins stories for particular denominations or organizations, as well as biblical narratives and others, which can be analysed to expose the power relations and structures that are maintained and/or challenged in/by them. Analysis of these narratives with an eye to, for instance, norms and values, gaps and silences or appeals to origins will produce a picture of what personal moral identities and organizational identities they constitute, and in turn what ethical commitments they are able to motivate and sustain.

My research has depended on the availability of texts in which to identify narratives for analysis, including talk and deliberation in everyday conversations, as well as publications, archives, documents and ephemera, with a special focus on life histories and auto/biographies, including those of the organization itself. Reading and hearing stories of 'who we are' at the YWCA, and noting on what occasions these were told, has allowed me to see what exclusions were maintained or inclusions achieved by narratively constituting an identity and its boundaries. In the study of other groups and organizations, too, I would expect the influence of the matrix of public narratives to be strongly connected to the tacitly accepted range of responsibilities, commitments and attachments of that identity. What can be done or said in the name of the group or identity in question depends on the ways in which that identity is constituted and understood in its context. For example, the moral identity of a white priest in the Catholic church in Ireland will be different from that of a Presbyterian laywoman in Kenya, and the factors determining these differences will be highly changeable over time, specific to their localities and be enmeshed in discourses and histories that are not necessarily or exclusively 'Christian'. The range of responsibilities, commitments and attachments these identities support will be evident in the uses to which these narratives are put in everyday institutional life. Ethical themes and practices are found in everyday situations, not necessarily in moments of tension or trouble. The scholar may have to interpret the presence and meaning of ethical values and principles in the conduct of the group, including in moments when 'ethics' is not the explicit subject of discussion. However, as I have found at the YWCA, organizations account for their conduct in 'autobiographical' ontological narratives that explicitly connect their identity to conduct and conduct to identity. In such cases the moral identity under (re)construction is clear, but its wider implications and applications may be unpredictable and varied.

Notes

Introduction

1. To preserve their anonymity, I use pseudonyms for all research participants and avoid specifying their job titles.
2. The strategic planning meeting was part of a process of restructuring the YWCA as, for example, it was considered that the National Board was too large. As a result of this process various changes were made; so my account of the YWCA does not represent the structure or governance of the organization since 2012.
3. Throughout this book I use the terms 'West', 'Global North' or 'Western'/'Northern' – and their counterparts 'Third World' and 'Global South' – for the sake of convenience. I do not wish to suggest that these categories refer to distinct and stable geographical regions (see, e.g., Jackson et al. 2016). Rather, these ways of thinking of the world are the contingent results of historical and contemporary power relations, as mobilized and reconfirmed in 'the production of the "Third World Woman" … [in] (western) feminist texts' (Mohanty 1988: 61).

1 Identity and ethics in narrative

1. I refer to speech and action as 'ethical' if it pertains to judgements about right, wrong, good, bad and how to live. In contrast to the way the word 'ethical' is often used in popular discourse, 'ethical' does not mean 'good' but 'in the domain of ethics'. Its opposite is not 'unethical', as in bad, but 'outside the scope of ethics, or which is amoral'.
2. This logic has gone by other names, including to 'colour-blindness', 'non-racialism' and 'diversity' (see Ahmed 2012; Clark Mane 2012).
3. For example, the idea that the 'boy-child' is now disadvantaged compared to the 'girl-child' as a result of decades of interventions that have sought to counteract sexist discrimination against girls. This is sometimes presented as an example of feminism 'going too far'. I have heard this perspective articulated in terms of, first, a sense that NGOs and development agencies operate unchecked behind the shield of 'gender', second pointing out an apparent obsession with gender to the exclusion of other angles of analysis and third the awareness that 'gender' should not be a synonym for 'women and girls', but that it in fact often functions this way.

4. For instance, Sara Ahmed (2014) gives an account of a Grimms' fairy tale as an example of 'poisonous pedagogy', a story that can be heard as a command, backed with a violent threat, by the child who listens to it.
5. One example is an advocacy project 'No White Saviors', by the Ugandan organization Kusimama Africa, which points out, explains and discourages white saviourism particularly as perpetrated by northern organizations and white voluntourists in African contexts.
6. Its full name is the Sistersong Women of Color Reproductive Justice Collective.

2 Imperial maternalism, 1855–1965

1. Missionary work was not limited to British missions, but included Dutch, German and North American Protestant missions, as well as French and Italian Catholic missions. The emergence of large Quaker (Society of Friends) and later Seventh Day Adventist (SDA) communities in Kenya is testament also to the presence of other missionary activity.
2. Use of the term 'mutilation' to name these diverse practices is the result of white feminist interventions, attempting to eradicate the practices from outside (Njambi 2004: 285–6).
3. I distinguish 'de-colonization' with a hyphen to denote the top-down process engineered by the British colonial authorities, as opposed to 'decolonization' as a radical deconstruction of colonial power relations, involving but not limited to the return of colonized land and expropriated resources to indigenous, formerly colonized peoples.
4. In Kiswahili, *Maendeleo ya Wanawake* means for 'progress for women' or 'development for women'.
5. The whiteness of Europeans in colonial Kenya was complicated by the presence of 'borderline' whites, including Greek, Jewish and Afrikaner settlers.
6. The position of NGS is a salaried member of staff, effectively the highest managerial position in the YWCA. Thus, although Mrs Kiano had been the first Black woman to hold a leadership position in the YWCA, the fact that she was a US citizen and served in a voluntary capacity means Mrs Mugo's appointment as NGS was a significant step.

3 From welfare to development, 1965–2000

1. 'Africa' in general and often particular countries have functioned as points of comparison against which Western 'progress' can be measured. For example, the

Centre for Reproductive Rights compared the maternal mortality rate in Mississippi with that of Kenya, where it is lower, in order to illustrate the effects of racism on the reproductive lives of Black women in the United States (CRR 2014: 13). Here, Kenya functions as a synechdochic representation of 'Africa', as a place where the rate of maternal mortality is *expected* to be higher than that in the United States. Maternal deaths in Kenya are framed by the narrative of Western progress/African inferiority.
2. Here, I follow the periodization of YWCA history suggested by Alice Mwajuma Abok, PhD, in her book *Winds of Hope* (2004). Dr Abok served as NGS (1996–2011) and also sat on the World YWCA executive board.
3. 'Mainline' churches are those brought by missionaries, including the Anglican, Methodist and Presbyterian churches, as opposed to those referred to as African Instituted Churches (AICs) that were established by African Christians, and other independent churches, like Pentecostal churches, that are not part of a denomination.
4. My research participants confirmed that the YWCA sees itself as 'the women of the NCCK', of which the YWCA is an associate member.
5. This expansion work was funded by a grant of $150,000 from the YW/YMCA of Sweden. Bilateral funding from other YWCAs, especially Sweden and Norway, is a major source of material support for the YWCA's programmes in Kenya.
6. 'Millennial' is generally understood as the generation born between 1982 and 1996.

4 African, Christian, feminist? 2000–12

1. A few prominent members of the clergy broke ranks and publicly came out in favour of the changes implied by the proposed constitution, including former Archbishop of the Anglican Church of Kenya, David Gitari (Kapinde 2016: 195–200).
2. The American Centre for Law and Justice (ACLJ) is a Christian Right organization engaged in campaigning and litigation across a range of causes – many of them anti-abortion, anti-gay and in support of 'family values … the sanctity of human life, and the two parent, marriage-bound family' (Kaoma 2012: 9).
3. However, it is important to note that none of these supports the continuation of 'FGM' practices; their critique is of representations of FGM and its consequences.
4. The YWCA has received funding and support for its HIV and AIDS programmes 2000–12 from a wide range of Kenyan and international donors and partner organizations including state funding from the National AIDS Control Council (NACC) and District AIDS Control Councils (DACC). International donors have included Church World Service (CWS), Interchurch Organisation for Development Cooperation (ICCO), International Centre for Reproductive Health (ICRH), UNIFEM, USAID, World YWCA and the YW/YMCA of Sweden.

5. These dimensions of the HIV epidemic are not fully visible in the following discussion because the YWCA has not attended to intravenous drug use or medical malpractice. The YWCA's interventions mention these facts about HIV transmission, but they focus on prevention and care.
6. Men's prejudice against condom use is reported elsewhere in the world, but in African contexts this tendency is read in light of the colonial pathologization and objectification of African bodies.
7. Estimates suggest that around 10 per cent of 15–19-year-old girls used a condom 'at their last sexual encounter' (Nzioka 2004: 40). Other estimates of condom use among young people in Kenya are slightly higher; UNICEF statistics show 25 per cent of girls and women and 47 per cent of boys and men aged 15–24 'used [a] condom at last high-risk sex' in 2005–6 (UNICEF 2008: 127).
8. 'Orphaned and vulnerable children' is a category including children who have been taken in by already-impoverished family members after the death of their parents, those whose parent is unable to care for them adequately due to their AIDS and children who live under the care of their eldest sibling.
9. This is a tendency of which the YWCA is well aware. It explicitly encourages young women to take up positions in all its decision-making bodies, with a World YWCA instituted quota for 25 per cent of representatives to be younger than 30 (World YWCA 2007).
10. The SRHR project was planned in conjunction with the World YWCA with funding from the David and Lucile Packard Foundation, a US-based grant-making foundation, alongside SRHR programmes in seven other YWCAs in Africa (World YWCA 2011: 5).

5 Controversial faith issues

1. For example, if Kenyan identity is understood to imply Christianity, and Christianity is understood to affirm only heterosexual desire and practice, then asserting a Kenyan LQBTQ identity might be unintelligible. LQBTQ Kenyans are thus able to be dismissed as either 'not really Kenyan' or 'not really LQBTQ'. Other versions of this syllogistic logic can be sketched to identify the mechanism for the popular opposition of feminism and Christianity or the foreignness of 'homosexuality' or feminism to 'Africa'. Teresia Hinga's *African, Christian, Feminist* (2017) and Adriaan Van Klinken's *Kenyan, Christian, Queer* (2019) are examples of this observation turned around, with the construction of identities apparently impossible in the Kenyan context foregrounded as authentic and meaningful.
2. At the request of the research participant, I have edited this quoted material (from a verbatim record) to further remove any identifying information.

3. I was particularly uncomfortable in this interaction, because I had to prompt Wandia to remember the term 'bisexual', which is how I describe myself. I did not 'come out' to my research participants.

6 'We are Christians'

1. I have found no other details of Mrs Mugo's biography, and institutional records covering the years prior to 1968 were not available to me, so it is not possible to triangulate the details of her appointment or gain a better understanding of her qualifications for the role. This gap further emphasizes the differential authority granted to white and Black voices and the significance of their lives in the writing of history.
2. It is perhaps worth noting that there was an undertone of 'shared womanhood' that helped Harley in this endeavour, but was not the banner chosen under which to forge a unified YWCA identity. This seems to show, yet again, that there can be no assumption of a shared identity as 'women' across differences of race.
3. In fact, I was told about *Winds of Hope* and purchased my copy at the headquarters, suggesting that although it has not reached the same status as *Rickshaws to Jets*, it is used in a similar way as a shared point of reference.
4. It was known until 2013 as Platform 51, but has subsequently been renamed again as the Young Women's Trust (YWT) and no longer retains any affiliation to the World YWCA movement (Birkwood 2014). YWT is to be distinguished from the YWCA of Great Britain, which remains part of the World YWCA movement.

7 Everyday Christian ethics

1. In 2012, the World YWCA was using vision and mission statements similar in tone and length to those used by Kenya YWCA. In 2020, the concept of a 'vision' statement was included in a glossary of key YWCA terminology, defined as 'the answer or mental picture that comes up when asked "what do we want to achieve, in the long run?" It provides guidance and inspiration to the movement' (World YWCA 2020: 10).
2. As characterized by Grace Jantzen (1998) in contrast to her notion of 'natality'.
3. *Adiaphoron* in the singular, a Greek word literally translated as 'indifferent things'. In Western moral philosophy the word has come to denote that which is amoral – neither moral nor immoral.

4. There are also material connections between the YWCA and the Circle. Prominent Kenyan theologian and Circle member Musimbi Kanyoro was World YWCA General Secretary from 1998 to 2007. South African activist Brigalia Bam was a member of staff at Durban YWCA, and at the World YWCA in the 1980s (Seymour-Jones 1994: 160, 502), and among the founding members of the Circle in 1988 (Kanyoro 2006: 22). Mary Getui, a Kenyan Circle member and academic, had served as the chairperson of the YWCA's national Christian Emphasis Committee. Other staff and leaders at the YWCA indicated that they had occasionally participated in the Circle's activities (Joyce, interview, 2012).

References

Abok, Mwajuma Alice (2004), *Winds of Hope*, Nairobi: Starman.
Achebe, Chinua (2010), 'An Image of Africa: Racism in Conrad's Heart of Darkness', in Vincent B. Leitch (ed.), *The Norton Anthology of Theory and Criticism*, 1783–94, New York: W.W. Norton.
Ahlberg, Beth Maina, Anne Kamau, Faith Maina and Asli Kulane (2009), 'Multiple Discourses on Sexuality: Implications for Translating Sexual Wellness Concept into Action Strategies in a Kenyan Context', *African Sociological Review*, 13 (1): 105–23.
Ahmed, Sara (2012), *On Being Included: Racism and Diversity in Institutional Life*, Durham, NC: Duke University Press.
Ahmed, Sara (2014), *Wilful Subjects*, Durham, NC: Duke University Press.
Akin-Aina, Sinmi (2011), 'Beyond an Epistemology of Bread, Butter, Culture and Power: Mapping the African Feminist Movement', *Nokoko*, 2: 65–89.
Anderson, David (2005), *Histories of the Hanged*, London: Weidenfield and Nicolson.
Anidjar, Gil (2015), 'Christianity, Christianities, Christian', *Journal of Religious and Political Practice*, 1 (1): 39–46.
Aniekwu, Nkolika I. (2006), 'Converging Constructions: A Historical Perspective on Sexuality and Feminism in Post-Colonial Africa', *African Sociological Review*, 10 (1): 143–60.
Anyangu-Amu, Susan (2010), 'Kenya: Victory for Anti-Abortion Lobby', *AllAfrica*, 2 February. Available online: http://www.ipsnews.net/2010/02/kenya-victory-for-anti-abortion-lobby/ (accessed 20 September 2020).
Appiah, Kwame A. (2005), *The Ethics of Identity*, Princeton, NJ: Princeton University Press.
Arnfred, Signe (2004), '"African Sexuality"/Sexuality in Africa: Tales and Silences', in Signe Arnfred (ed.), *Re-Thinking Sexualities in Africa*, 59–76, Uppsala: Nordiska Africainstitutet.
Asad, Talal (1993), *Genealogies of Religion: Discipline and Reasons of Power in Christianity and Islam*, Baltimore, MD: Johns Hopkins University Press.
Astley, Jeff (2002), *Ordinary Theology: Looking, Listening and Learning in Theology*, Aldershot: Ashgate.
Atkins, Kim (2008), *Narrative Identity and Moral Identity: A Practical Perspective*, London: Routledge.
Aubrey, Lisa (1997), *The Politics of Development Cooperation: NGOs, Gender and Partnership in Kenya*, London: Routledge.

AWID (Association for Women's Rights in Development) (2004), 'Facts and Issues. Intersectionality: A Tool for Gender and Economic Justice', *Women's Rights and Economic Change*, 9: 1–8.

Ayanga, Hazel (1996), 'Violence against Women in African Oral Literature as Portrayed in Proverbs', in Grace Wamue and Mary Getui (eds), *Violence against Women: Reflections by Kenyan Women Theologians*, 13–20, Nairobi: Acton.

Ayanga, Hazel (2016), 'Voice of the Voiceless: The Legacy of the Circle of Concerned African Women Theologians', *Verbum et Ecclesia*, 37 (2): a1580.

Bagnol, Brigitte, and Esmerelda Mariano (2011), 'Politics of Naming Sexual Practices', in Sylvia Tamale (ed.), *African Sexualities: A Reader*, 271–87, Dakar: Pambazuka Press.

Baitu, Juvenalis (2008), 'The Church as an Actor of Civil Society in Responding to HIV/AIDS in AMECEA Region', in Marco Moerschbacher, Joseph Kato and Pius Rutechura (eds), *A Holistic Approach to HIV and AIDS in Africa*, 90–105, Nairobi: Paulines.

Bakari, Mohamed (2013), 'A Place at the Table: The Political Integration of Muslims in Kenya, 1963–2007', *Islamic Africa*, 4 (1): 15–48.

Balchin, Cassandra (2008), *Religious Fundamentalisms on the Rise: A Case for Action*, Toronto: AWID.

Bannerji, Himani (1998), 'Politics and the Writing of History', in Ruth Roach Pierson and Napur Chaudhuri (eds), *Nation, Empire, Colony: Historicizing Gender and Race*, 287–301, Bloomington: Indiana University Press.

Barasa, Lucas, Oliver Musembi, Rose Kamanga, Winnie Molly Owuor and George Munene (2012), 'Clerics Ask Mutula to Quit in Skirt Row', *The Daily Nation*, August 7. Available online: https://nation.africa/kenya/news/clerics-ask-mutula-to-quit-in-skirt-row–821120 (accessed 20 September 2020).

Barrett, David B., George K. Mambo, Janice McLaughlin and Malcolm J. McVeigh, eds. (1973), *Kenya Churches Handbook: The Development of Kenyan Christianity 1498–1973*, Kisumu: Evangel.

Barton, Michael, and Rachel Muers (2013), 'A Study in Ordinary Theological Ethics: Thinking about Eating', in Leslie Francis and Jeff Astley (eds), *Exploring Ordinary Theology: Everyday Christian Believing and the Church*, 169–77, Farnham: Ashgate.

BBC (2019), 'A Million Faulty Condoms Recalled in Uganda', https://www.bbc.co.uk/news/world-africa-50472710 (accessed 21 September 2020)

Benhabib, Seyla (1992), *Situating the Self: Gender, Community, and Postmodernism in Contemporary Ethics*, New York: Routledge.

Bernal, Victoria, and Inderpal Grewal, eds. (2014), *Theorizing NGOs: States, Feminisms, and Neoliberalism*, 1–19, Durham, NC: Duke University Press.

Bertrand-Dansereau, Anaïs (2013), 'Sex is a Gift from God: Paralysis and Potential in Sex Education in Malawi', in Susie Jolly, Andrea Cornwall and Kate Hawkins (eds), *Women, Sexuality and the Political Power of Pleasure*, 161–83, London: Zed Books.

Birkwood, Susannah (2014), 'Case Study: The Young Women's Trust Emerges from Two Rebrands', *Third Sector*, October 16. Available online: http://www.thirdsector.

co.uk/case-study-young-womens-trust-emerges-two-rebrands/communications/article/1313364 (accessed 28 March 2017).

Blacker, John (2007), 'The Demography of Mau Mau: Fertility and Mortality in Kenya in the 1950s: A Demographer's Viewpoint', *African Affairs*, 106 (423): 205–27.

Booth, Karen (2004), *Local Women, Global Science: Fighting AIDS in Kenya*, Indianapolis: Indiana University Press.

Bose, Christine (2012), 'Intersectionality and Global Gender Inequality', *Gender and Society*, 26 (1): 67–72.

Boulanger, Sara (2008), 'A Puppet on a String: The Manipulation and Nationalization of the Female Body in the "Female Circumcision Crisis" of Colonial Kenya', *Wagadu: A Journal of Transnational Women's and Gender Studies*, 6: 61–74.

Bradley, Janet E., Joseph Dwyer and Karen J. Levin (2001), 'Norplant® Expansion in Kenya', *African Journal of Reproductive Health*, 5 (3): 89–98.

Brauer, Jerald C., ed. (1971), *The Westminster Dictionary of Church History*, Philadelphia, PA: Westminster.

Brouwers, Rita, and Achola O. Pala (2004), *The Role of Women's Organisations in Civil Society Building in Kenya: Country Report Kenya for CFA Programme Evaluation*, Kenya Country Report for CFA Programme Evaluation EOS Consult.

Butler, Judith (2001), 'Giving an Account of Oneself', *Diacritics*, 31 (4): 22–40.

Carbonnier, Gilles (2013), 'Religion and Development: Reconsidering Secularism as the Norm', *International Development Policy*, 4 (1): 1–5.

Cavarero, Adriana (2000), *Relating Narratives: Storytelling and Selfhood*, London: Routledge.

Chanika, Emmie, John L. Lwanda, and Adamson S. Muula (2013), 'Gender, Gays and Gain: The Sexualised Politics of Donor Aid in Malawi', *Africa Spectrum*, 48 (1): 89–105.

Chant, Sylvia (2010), 'Gendered Poverty across Space and Time: Introduction and Overview', in Sylvia Chant (ed.), *International Handbook of Gender and Poverty: Concepts, Research, Policy*, 1–26, Cheltenham: Edward Elgar.

Chitando, Ezra, and Adriaan Van Klinken (2016), *Public Religion and the Politics of Homosexuality in Africa*, London: Routledge.

Chitando, Ezra, and Njyambura Njoroge, eds. (2016), *Abundant Life: The Churches and Sexuality*, Geneva: World Council of Churches.

Chryssides, George D., and Stephen E. Gregg (2019), 'Vernacular Christianity', in George D. Chryssides and Stephen E. Gregg (eds), *The Bloomsbury Handbook to Studying Christians*, 5–16, London: Bloomsbury.

Clark Mane, Rebecca L. (2012), 'Transmuting Grammars of Whiteness in Third-Wave Feminism: Interrogating Postrace Histories, Postmodern Abstraction, and the Proliferation of Difference in Third-Wave Texts', *Signs: Journal of Women in Culture and Society*, 38 (1): 71–98.

Cohen, Susan A. (2006), 'Abortion and Mental Health: Myths and Realities', *Guttmacher Policy Review*, 9 (3): 8–16.

Cole, Teju (2012), 'The White-Savior Industrial Complex', *The Atlantic*, March 21. Available online: http://www.theatlantic.com/international/archive/2012/03/the-white-savior-industrial-complex/254843/ (accessed 29 July 2014).

Cornwall, Andrea, and Susie Jolly (2009), 'Sexuality and the Development Industry', *Development*, 52 (1): 5–12.

CRR (2010), *In Harm's Way: The Impact of Kenya's Restrictive Abortion Law*. Available online: www.reproductiverights.org/sites/crr.civicactions.net/files/documents/InHarmsWay_2010.pdf (accessed 29 March 2017)

CRR (2014), 'Reproductive Injustice: Racial and Gender Discrimination in U.S. Health Care. A Shadow Report for the UN Committee on the Elimination of Racial Discrimination'. Available online: https://www.reproductiverights.org/press-room/un-committee-calls-on-united-states-to-immediately-address-racial-discrimination-in-health-care (accessed 2 April 2017).

Culler, Jonathan (2000), 'Story and Discourse in the Analysis of Narrative', in Martin McQuillan (ed.), *The Narrative Reader*, 104–8, London: Routledge.

Daiute, Colette (2011), 'Trouble: In, around, and between Narratives', *Narrative Inquiry*, 21 (2): 329–36.

Daly, Lois K., ed. (1994), *Feminist Theological Ethics: A Reader*, Louisville, KY: Westminster John Knox Press.

Das, Veena (2015), 'What Does Ordinary Ethics Look Like?' in Michael Lambek, Veena Das, Didier Fassin and Webb Keane (eds), *Four Lectures on Ethics: Anthropological Perspectives*, 53–125, Chicago: HAU Books.

Deeb-Sossa, Natalia (2007), 'Helping the "Neediest of the Needy": An Intersectional Analysis of Moral-Identity Construction at a Community Health Clinic', *Gender and Society*, 21 (5): 749–72.

Dhawan, Nikita (2013), 'The Empire Prays Back: Religion, Secularity, and Queer Critique', *boundary 2*, 40 (1): 191–222.

Dossa, Shiraz (2007), 'Slicing up "Development": Colonialism, Political Theory, Ethics', *Third World Quarterly*, 28 (5): 887–99.

Dube, Musa W. (2000), *Postcolonial Feminist Interpretation of the Bible*, St. Louis, MO: Chalice Press.

Dube, Musa W. (2002), 'Reading for Decolonization (John 4.1–42)', in Musa W. Dube and Jeffrey L. Staley (eds), *John and Postcolonialism: Travel, Space and Power*, 51–75, London: Sheffield Academic Press.

Dube, Musa W. (2007), 'Who Do You Say That I Am?' *Feminist Theology*, 15 (3): 346–67.

Dube, Musa W., and Jeffrey L. Staley (2002), 'Descending from and Ascending to Heaven: A Postcolonial Analysis of Travel, Space and Power in John', in

Musa W. Dube and John L. Staley (eds), *John and Postcolonialism: Travel, Space and Power*, 1–10, London: Sheffield Academic Press.

Duguid, Julian (1955), *The Blue Triangle*, London: Hodder and Stroughton.

Elkins, Caroline (2005), *Britain's Gulag: The Brutal End of Empire in Kenya*, London: Jonathan Cape.

Elmore-Meegan, Michael, Ronán M. Conroy and C. Bernard Agala (2004), 'Sex Workers in Kenya, Numbers of Clients and Associated Risks: An Exploratory Survey', *Reproductive Health Matters*, 12 (23): 50–7.

Farris, Sara (2017), *In the Name of Women's Rights: The Rise of Femonationalism*, Durham, NC: Duke University Press.

Fassin, Didier, ed. (2012), *A Companion to Moral Anthropology*, Malden, MA: Wiley-Blackwell.

FIDA-K and CRR (2007), *Failure to Deliver: Violations of Women's Human Rights in Kenyan Healthcare Facilities*. Available online: https://www.reproductiverights.org/sites/crr.civicactions.net/files/documents/pub_bo_failuretodeliver.pdf (accessed 29 March 2017)

Frank, Arthur (2010), *Letting Stories Breathe: A Socio-Narratology*, Chicago: University of Chicago Press.

Frazer, Elizabeth, and Nicola Lacey (1993), *The Politics of Community: A Feminist Critique of the Liberal-Communitarian Debate*, Hemel Hempstead: Harvester Wheasheaf.

Fretheim, Kjetil (2008), 'Whose Kingdom? Which Context? Ecumenical and Contextual Theology in the World Alliance of YMCAs', *International Review of Mission*, 97 (584–5): 116–28.

Furedi, Frank (1989), *The Mau Mau War in Perspective*, London: James Currey.

Ganusah, Rebecca (2014), 'The Church and Development: A Ghanaian Experience', in Cephas N. Omenyo and Eric B. Anum (eds), *Trajectories of Religion in Africa: Essays in Honour of John S. Pobee*, 203–18, New York: Editions Rodopi.

Garita, Alexandra (2014), 'Moving toward Sexual and Reproductive Justice: A Transnational and Multigenerational Feminist Remix', in Rawwida Baksh and Wendy Harcourt (eds), *The Oxford Handbook of Transnational Feminist Movements*, Oxford: Oxford University Press.

Garner, Karen (2007), 'World YWCA Leaders and the UN Decade for Women', *Journal of International Women's Studies*, 9 (1): 212–33.

Getman, Eliza, and Sarojini Nadar (2013), 'Natality and Motherism: Embodiment within Praxis of Spiritual Leadership', *Journal for the Study of Religion*, 26 (2): 59–73.

Getui, Mary N. (1998), 'Zelophehad's Daughters in Kenya', *Spectrum*, 26 (5): 52–9.

Getui, Mary N. (2003), 'Material Things in Contemporary African Society', in Jessie N. K. Mugambi and Anne Nasimiyu-Wasike (eds), *Moral and Ethical Issues in African Christianity*, 59–72, Nairobi: Acton.

Getui, Mary N., and Matthew M. Theuri, eds. (2002), *Quests for Abundant Life in Africa*, Nairobi: Acton.

Gez, Yonatan N. (2018), *Traditional Churches, Born Again Christianity, and Pentecostalism: Religious Mobility and Religious Repertoires in Urban Kenya*, Cham: Palgrave Macmillan.

Gifford, Paul (2009), *Christianity, Politics and Public Life in Kenya*, London: C. Hurst.

Gifford, Paul (2015), *Christianity, Development and Modernity in Africa*, London: C. Hurst.

Gitau, Wanjiru M. (2018), *Megachurch Christianity Reconsidered: Millennials and Social Change in African Perspective*, Downers Grove, IL: IVP Academic.

Gordon, David F. (1986), *Decolonization and the State in Kenya*, London: Westview.

Gordon, Natasha M. (1997), '"Tonguing the Body": Placing Female Circumcision within African Feminist Discourse', *Issue: A Journal of Opinion*, 25 (2): 24–7.

Grewal, Inderpal, and Caren Kaplan (2000), 'Postcolonial Studies and Transnational Feminist Practices', *Jouvert: A Journal of Postcolonial Studies*, 5 (1): n.p. Available online: https://legacy.chass.ncsu.edu/jouvert/v5i1/grewal.htm (accessed 13 January 2021).

Griffith, Saoyo T. (2014), 'Why Are Women in Kenya Still Dying from Unsafe Abortions?' *openDemocracy*, 20 January. Available online: https://www.opendemocracy.net/5050/saoyo-tabitha-griffith/why-are-women-in-kenya-still-dying-from-unsafe-abortions (accessed 20 August 2020).

Grosfoguel, Ramón (2016), 'What Is Racism?', *Journal of World-Systems Research*, 22 (1): 9–15.

Harcourt, Wendy (2009), *Body Politics in Development: Critical Debates in Gender and Development*, London: Zed.

Harley, Vera (1995), *Rickshaw to Jets: A History and Anecdotes of Kenya YWCA, 1912–1965*, London: Vera Harley/YWCA of England and Wales.

Haselbarth, Hans (2004 [1976]), *Christian Ethics in the African Context*, Nairobi: Uzima.

Hearn, Julie (2002), 'The "Invisible" NGO: US Evangelical Missions in Kenya', *Journal of Religion in Africa*, 32 (1): 32–60.

Higgs, Eleanor Tiplady (2016), 'Becoming "Multi-Racial": The Young Women's Christian Association in Kenya, 1955–1965', in Blanche Jackson Glimps and Theron N. Ford (eds), *Gender and Diversity Issues in Religious-Based Institutions and Organizations*, 24–50, Hershey, PA: IGI Global.

Higgs, Eleanor Tiplady (2019), 'From "Imperial Maternalism" to "Matricentrism": Mothering Ethics in Christian Women's Voluntarism in Kenya', *African Journal of Gender & Religion*, 25 (1): 20–44.

Hinga, Teresia M. (2017), *African, Christian, Feminist: The Enduring Search for What Matters*, Maryknoll: Orbis.

Hinyard, Leslie J., and Matthew W. Kreuter (2007), 'Using Narrative Communication as a Tool for Health Behavior Change: A Conceptual, Theoretical, and Empirical Overview', *Health Education & Behavior*, 34 (5): 777–92.

Hofer, Katharina (2003), 'The Role of Evangelical NGOs in International Development: A Comparative Case Study of Kenya and Uganda', *Africa Spectrum*, 38 (3): 375-98.

Horn, Jessica (2012), *Not as Simple as ABC: Christian Fundamentalisms and HIV and AIDS Responses in Africa*, Toronto: AWID.

House-Midamba, Bessie (1990), 'The United Nations Decade: Political Empowerment or Increased Marginalization for Kenyan Women?' *Africa Today*, 37 (1): 37-48.

Ingdal, Nora, Joyce Umbima and Anders Lamark Tysse (2008), 'Mid-Term Review of Project. Practice Reduction and Awareness on Female Genital Mutilation (FGM): YWCA Kenya', FOKUS/Nordic Consulting Group.

Izzo, Amanda L. (2018), *Liberal Christianity and Women's Global Activism: The YWCA of the USA and the Maryknoll Sisters*, New Brunswick: Rutgers University Press.

Jackson, Jeffrey T., Kirsten Dellinger, Kathryn McKee and Annette Trefzer (2016), 'Interdisciplinary Perspectives on the Global South and Global North', in Gregory Hook (ed.), *The Sociology of Development Handbook*, 129-52, Oakland: University of California Press.

James, Adeola (1990), *In Their Own Voices: African Women Writers Talk*, London: James Currey.

Jantzen, Grace (1998), *Becoming Divine: Towards a Feminist Philosophy of Religion*, Manchester: Manchester University Press.

Jindra, Ines W., Robert H. Woods, Diane M. Badzinski and Jenell Paris (2012), 'Gender, Religiosity, and the Telling of Christian Conversion Narratives', *Journal for the Sociological Integration of Religion and Society*, 2 (1): 1-23.

Johannsen, Dirk, Anja Kirsch and Jens Kreinath, eds. (2020), *Narrative Cultures and the Aesthetics of Religion*, Supplements to *Method & Theory in the Study of Religion*, 14, Leiden: Brill.

Kabeer, Naila (2015), 'Gender, Poverty, and Inequality: A Brief History of Feminist Contributions in the Field of International Development', *Gender and Development*, 23 (2): 189-205.

Kamaara, Eunice (1997), 'SAPs and Female Reproductive Health in Kenya', *Issue: A Journal of Opinion*, 25 (2): 16-19.

Kamaara, Eunice (1999), 'Reproductive and Sexual Health Problems of Adolescent Girls in Kenya: A Challenge to the Church', *Reproductive Health Matters*, 7 (14): 130-3.

Kamau, Nyokabi (2009), *AIDS, Sexuality and Gender: Experiences of Women in Kenyan Universities*, Eldoret: Zapf Chancery.

Kane, Rosalie A., and Arthur L. Caplan, eds. (1990), *Everyday Ethics: Resolving Dilemmas in Nursing Home Life*, New York: Springer.

Kangara, Lucy (2007 [2004]), *Youth, Church and Sexuality in Kenya. Post-Sexuality Leadership Development Fellowship*, Report Series No. 7, Lagos: Africa Regional

Sexuality Resource Centre. Available online: www.arsrc.org/downloads/sldf/ FinalReportLucyKangara2004.pdf (accessed 7 September 2020).

Kanogo, Tabitha (2005), *African Womanhood in Colonial Kenya 1900–50*, London: James Currey.

Kanyoro, Musimbi R. A. (1992), 'The Power to Name', in Musimbi R. A. Kanyoro and Wendy S. Robins (eds), *The Power We Celebrate: Women's Stories of Faith and Power*, 19–28, Geneva: WCC.

Kanyoro, Musimbi R. A. (1995), 'Cultural Hermeneutics: An African Contribution', in Ofelia Ortega (ed.), *Women's Visions: Theological Action, Reflection, Celebration*, 18–28, Geneva: WCC.

Kanyoro, Musimbi R. A. (1999), 'My Grandmother Would Approve: Engendering Gospel and Culture', *Feminist Theology*, 7 (20): 53–70.

Kanyoro, Musimbi R. A. (2001), 'Engendered Communal Theology: African Women's Contribution to Theology in the Twenty-First Century', *Feminist Theology*, 9 (27): 36–56.

Kanyoro, Musimbi R. A. (2006), 'Beads and Strands: Threading More Beads in the Story of the Circle', in Isabel A. Phiri and Sarojini Nadar (eds), *African Women, Religion, and Health: Essays in Honor of Mercy Amba Ewudziwa Oduyoye*, 19–42, Maryknoll: Orbis.

Kapinde, Stephen A. A. (2016), 'Prophetic Church Leadership in Kenya's Democratization Process between 1986 and 2010: A Case Study of the Most Rev. David Mukuva Gitari', MA thesis, Pwani University.

Kaoma, Kapya J. (2009), *Globalising the Culture Wars: U.S. Conservatives, African Churches, and Homophobia*, Somerville, MA: Political Research Associates.

Kaoma, Kapya J. (2012), *Colonizing African Values: How the U.S. Christian Right Is Transforming Sexual Politics in Africa*, Somerville, MA: Political Research Associates.

KCLF (Kenya Christian Leaders Forum) (2010), *Frequently Asked Questions on Contentious Issues in the Constitution Review Process*. Available online: https://web.archive.org/web/20130123085622/http://www.ncck.org/index.php/information/publications/158-brochure.html (accessed 1 February 2021).

Kemboi, Georgine J., Kennedy Onkware, and Omosa M. Ntabo (2011), 'Socio-Cultural Factors That Perpetuate the Spread of HIV among Women and Girls in Keiyo District, Kenya', *International Journal of Sociology and Anthropology*, 3 (5): 147–52.

KHRC and RHRA (2010), *Teenage Pregnancy and Unsafe Abortion: The Case of Korogocho Slums*. Available online: https://www.khrc.or.ke/mobile-publications/equality-and-anti-discrimination/69-teenage-pregnancy-and-abortion-case-study/file.html (accessed 13 January 2021)

Khader Serene (2019), *Decolonizing Universalism: A Transnational Feminist Ethic*, Abingdon: Oxford University Press.

King, Nicola (2000), *Memory, Narrative, Identity: Remembering the Self*, Edinburgh: Edinburgh University Press.

Klassen, Pamela E. (2013), 'Christianity as a Polemical Concept', in Janice Boddy and Michael Lambek (eds), *A Companion to the Anthropology of Religion*, 344–62, Chichester: Wiley Blackwell.

Kleinman, Sherryl (1996), *Opposing Ambitions: Gender and Identity in an Alternative Organization*, Chicago: University of Chicago Press.

Kothari, Uma (2006), 'An Agenda for Thinking about "Race" in Development', *Progress in Development Studies*, 6 (1): 9–23.

Kunhiyop, Samuel W. (2008), *African Christian Ethics*, Nairobi: WordAlive/Hippo.

Kwok, Pui-lan (2005), *Postcolonial Imagination and Feminist Theology*, London: SCM Press.

Lambek, Michael, ed. (2010), *Ordinary Ethics: Anthropology, Language, and Action*, Bronx: Fordham University Press.

Lewis, Desiree (2005), 'African Gender Research and Postcoloniality: Legacies and Challenges', in Oyèrónké Oyěwùmí (ed.), *African Gender Studies*, 381–96, New York: Palgrave Macmillan.

Lewis, Desiree (2008a), 'Rethinking Nationalism in Relation to Foucault's History of Sexuality and Adrienne Rich's "Compulsory Heterosexuality and Lesbian Existence"', *Sexualities*, 11 (1–2): 104–9.

Lewis, Desiree (2008b), 'Discursive Challenges for African Feminisms', *QUEST: An African Journal of Philosophy*, XX: 77–96.

Lewis, Desiree (2011), 'Representing African Sexualities', in Sylvia Tamale (ed.), *African Sexualities: A Reader*, 199–216, Dakar: Pambazuka Press.

Ligaga, Dina (2020), *Women, Visibility and Morality in Kenyan Popular Media*, Grahamstown: NISC/African Humanities Program.

Likimani, Muthoni (1985), *Passbook F.47927: Women and Mau Mau*, New York: Macmillan.

Likimani, Muthoni (2005), *Fighting without Ceasing*, Nairobi: Noni's Publicity.

Linde, Charlotte (2000), 'On the Acquisition of a Speaker by a Story: How History Becomes Memory and Identity', *Ethos*, 24 (4): 608–32.

Linde, Charlotte (2009), *Working the Past: Narrative and Institutional Memory*, Oxford: Oxford University Press.

Lorde, Audre (1984), 'Uses of the Erotic: The Erotic as Power', in *Sister Outsider*, 53–9, Freedom, CA: Crossing Press.

Lugones, María (2003), *Pilgrimages/Peregrinajes: Theorizing Coalition against Multiple Oppressions*, Lanham, MD: Rowman & Littlefield.

Lugones, María (2008), 'The Coloniality of Gender', *Worlds and Knowledges Otherwise*, 2 (2): 1–17.

Maathai, Wangari M. (2008), *Unbowed: One Woman's Story*, London: Arrow Books.

MacGaffey, Wyatt (2012), 'African Traditional Religion', *obo* in African Studies. doi: 10.1093/OBO/9780199846733-0064 (accessed 4 August 2020).

Machera, Mumbi (2003), 'Opening a Can of Worms: A Debate on Female Sexuality in the Lecture Theatre', in Signe Arnfred (ed.), *Re-Thinking Sexualities in Africa*, 157–70, Uppsala: Nordiska Africainstitutet.

MacIntyre, Alasdair (1974), *A Short History of Ethics: A History of Moral Philosophy from the Homeric Age to the Twentieth Century*, London: Routledge.

MacKenzie, Catriona, and Jacqui Poltera (2010), 'Narrative Integration, Fragmented Selves, and Autonomy', *Hypatia*, 25 (1): 31–54.

Maldonado-Torres, Nelson, Rafael Vizcaíno, Jasmine Wallace and Jeong Eun Annabel We (2018), 'Decolonising Philosophy', in Gurminder K. Bhambra, Dalia Gebrial and Kerem Nişancıoğlu (eds), *Decolonising the University*, 64–90, London: Pluto.

Maloba, W. O. (2017), *The Anatomy of Neo-Colonialism in Kenya: British Imperialism and Kenyatta, 1963–1978*, Cham: Palgrave Macmillan.

Mama, Amina (1995), 'Feminism or Femocracy? State Feminism and Democratisation in Nigeria', *Africa Development*, 20 (1): 37–58.

Mama, Amina (2011), 'What Does It Mean to Do Feminist Research in African Contexts?' *feminist review* (S1) [Conference proceedings 2011], e4–e20.

Mangena, Fainos (2009), 'The Search for an African Feminist Ethic: A Zimbabwean Perspective', *Journal of International Women's Studies*, 11 (2): 18–30.

Mantell, Joanne E., Jacqueline Correale, Jessica Adams-Skinner and Zena A. Stein (2011), 'Conflicts between Conservative Christian Institutions and Secular Groups in Sub-Saharan Africa: Ideological Discourses on Sexualities, Reproduction, and HIV/AIDS', *Global Public Health*, 6 (2): S192–S209.

Mapuranga, Tapiwa P. (2016), 'Churches and the Sexuality of Older Women', in Ezra Chitando and Njyambura Njoroge (eds), *Abundant Life: The Churches and Sexuality*, 59–74, Geneva: World Council of Churches.

Marlow, Heather M., Sylvia Wamugi, Erick Yegon, Tamara Fetters, Leah Wanaswa and Sinikiwe Msipa-Ndebele (2014), 'Women's Perceptions about Abortion in Their Communities: Perspectives from Western Kenya', *Reproductive Health Matters*, 22 (43): 149–58.

Mathangani, Mumbi (1995), 'The Triple Battle: Gender, Class, and Democracy in Kenya', *Harvard Law Review*, 39 (1): 287–335.

Mbithi, Philip M., and Rasmus Rasmusson (1977), *Self Reliance in Kenya: The Case of Harambee*, Uppsala: Scandinavian Institute of African Studies.

McGreal, Chris (2007), 'HIV-Infected Condoms Sent to Kill Africans, Claims Archbishop', *The Guardian*, 27 September. Available online: https://www.theguardian.com/world/2007/sep/27/aids.international (accessed 14 September 2020).

McGuire, Meredith B. (2008), *Lived Religion: Faith and Practice in Everyday Life*, Oxford: Oxford University Press.

McQuillan, Martin, ed. (2000), *The Narrative Reader*, London: Routledge.

Merab, Elizabeth (2018), 'Distributor Confirms Fake Condoms Are in the Market', *The Nation*, 12 February. Available online: https://nation.africa/kenya/news/distributor-confirms-fake-condoms-are-in-the-market-12348 (accessed 14 September 2020).

Mikell, Gwendolyn, ed. (1997), *African Feminism: The Politics of Survival in Sub-Saharan Africa*, Philadelphia: University of Pennsylvania Press.

Miller, Carol, and Shahrashoub Razavi (1995), 'From WID to GAD: Conceptual Shifts in the Women and Development Discourse', United Nations Research Institute for Social Development, Occasional Paper 1, New York: United Nations Development Programme. Available online: http://www.unrisd.org/80256B3C005BCCF9/ (httpPublications)/D9C3FCA78D3DB32E80256B67005B6AB5 (accessed 3 April 2017).

Miller, Richard E. (2005), *Writing at the End of the World*, Pittsburgh, PA: University of Pittsburgh Press.

Mitchell, Ellen M. H., Carolyn Tucker Halpern, Eva Muthuuri Kamathi and Shirley Owino (2006), 'Social Scripts and Stark Realities: Kenyan Adolescents' Abortion Discourse', *Culture, Health and Sexuality*, 8 (6): 515–28.

Mohanty, Chandra T. (1988), 'Under Western Eyes: Feminist Scholarship and Colonial Discourses', *Feminist Review*, 30: 61–88.

Mohanty, Chandra T. (1999), 'Women Workers and Capitalist Scripts: Ideologies of Domination, Common Interests, and the Politics of Solidarity', in Sharlene Hesse-Biber, Christina Gilmartin and Robin Lydenberg (eds), *Feminist Approaches in Theory and Methodology: An Interdisciplinary Reader*, 362–88, Oxford: Oxford University Press.

Mombo, Esther (2003), 'Doing Theology from the Perspective of the Circle of Concerned African Women Theologians', *Journal of Anglican Studies*, 1 (1): 91–103.

Momsen, Janet H. (2003), *Gender and Development*, Florence: Routledge.

Moore, Henrietta L. (2009), 'Epistemology and Ethics: Perspectives from Africa', *Social Analysis*, 53 (2): 207–18.

Muchomba, Felix M. (2014), 'Colonial Policies and the Rise of Transactional Sex in Kenya', *Journal of International Women's Studies*, 15 (2): 80–93.

Mudimbe, Valentin Y. (1997), *Tales of Faith: Religion as Political Performance in Central Africa*, London: Athlone Press.

Muhibbu-Din, Mahmudat O. (2011), 'The New Partnership for Africa's Development (NEPAD) Policy on Women Empowerment in Africa: A Critical Appraisal', *African Journal of Political Science and International Relations*, 5 (1): 1–9.

Muhonja, Besi Brillian (2018), *Womanhood and Girlhood in Twenty-First Century Middle Class Kenya: Disrupting Patri-Centered Frameworks*, Lanham, MD: Lexington.

Murunga, Godwin R., Duncan Okello and Anders Sjögren, eds. (2014), *Kenya: The Struggle for a New Constitutional Order*, London: Zed Books.

Mutongi, Kenda B. (2007), *Worries of the Heart: Widows, Family, and Community in Kenya*, Chicago: University of Chicago Press.

Mwaura, Philomena N. (2012), 'Concept of Basic Human Rights in African Independent Pentecostal Church of Africa and Jesus Is Alive Ministries', *Journal of World Christianity*, 5 (1): 9–42.

Mwikya, Kenne (2014), 'Unnatural and Un-African: Contesting Queer-Phobia by Africa's Political Leadership', *Feminist Africa*, 19: 98–105.

Narayan, Uma (1995), 'Colonialism and Its Others: Considerations on Rights and Care Discourses', *Hypatia*, 10 (2): 133–40.

Narayan, Uma (1997), *Dislocating Cultures: Identities, Traditions, and Third-World Feminism*, London: Routledge.

National AIDS Control Council (NACC) and National AIDS and STI Control Programme (NASCOP) (2012), *The Kenya AIDS Epidemic Update 2011*, Nairobi.

National Council of Churches of Kenya (NCCK) (2 August 2014). Our Programmes. '1(iii) Family Life Education'. Available online: https://web.archive.org/web/20141022071505/http://www.ncck.org/newsite2/index.php/our-work/k2-categories/our-programmes (accessed 1 February 2021).

National Council of Churches of Kenya (NCCK) and Kenya Christian Leaders Forum (KCLF) (2010), *Ten Reasons Why I Will Vote No at the Referendum* (leaflet).

Ndlovu-Gatsheni, Sabelo J. (2013), *Empire, Global Coloniality and African Subjectivity*, New York: Berghahn.

NEPHAK, BHESP, KESWA and GNP+ (2015), *Speaking Out: Personal Testimonies of Rights Violations Experienced by Sex Workers in Kenya*, Nairobi. Available online: http://www.nswp.org/resource/speaking-out-personal-testimonies-rights-violations-experienced-sex-workers-kenya (accessed 29 March 2017).

Newsinger, John (1981), 'Revolt and Repression in Kenya: The "Mau Mau" Rebellion, 1952–1960', *Science and Society*, 45 (2): 159–85.

Ngunjiri, Faith W. (2009), 'Servant-Leadership and Motherhood: Kenyan Women Finding Fulfillment in Serving Humanity', Working Paper #294, East Lansing: Michigan State University.

Ngunjiri, Faith W. (2010), *Women's Spiritual Leadership in Africa: Tempered Radicals and Critical Servant Leaders*, Albany, NY: SUNY Press.

Nichols, Joel A. (2009), 'Evangelicals and Human Rights: The Continuing Ambivalence of Evangelical Christians' Support for Human Rights', *Journal of Law and Religion*, 24 (2): 629–62.

Njambi, Wairimũ N. (2004), 'Dualisms and Female Bodies in Representations of African Female Circumcision: A Feminist Critique', *Feminist Theory*, 5(3): 281–303.

Njambi, Wairimũ N. (2007), '*Irua Ria Atumia* and Anti-Colonial Struggles among the Gĩkũyũ of Kenya: A Counter Narrative on "Female Genital Mutilation"' [*sic*], *Critical Sociology*, 33: 689–708.

Njambi, Wairimũ N. (2020), 'What Sexuality? Whose Knowledge? Mapping "Heterosexuality" and "Homosexuality" within Transnational Feminisms', *Gender and Women's Studies*, 2 (2): 1–16.

Njoroge, Nyambura J. (1996), 'Hannah, Why Do You Weep? I Samuel 1 and 2:1–21', in Grace Wamue and Mary Getui (eds), *Violence against Women: Reflections by Kenyan Women Theologians*, 21–6, Nairobi: Acton.

Njoroge, Nyambura (1997), 'The Missing Voice: African Women Doing Theology', *Journal of Theology for Southern Africa*, 99: 77–83.

Njoroge, Nyambura (2000), *Kiama Kia Ngo: An African Christian Feminist Ethic of Resistance and Transformation*, Accra: Legon Theological Studies.

Njue, Carolyne W., Hélène A. C. M. Voeten and Pieter Remes (2011), 'Porn Video Shows, Local Brew, and Transactional Sex: HIV Risk among Youth in Kisumu, Kenya', *BMC Public Health*, 11: 635.

Nussbaum, Felicity (1995), *Torrid Zones: Maternity, Sexuality, and Empire in Eighteenth-Century English Narratives*, Baltimore, MD: Johns Hopkins Press.

Nye, Mallory (2018), 'Race and Religion: Postcolonial Formations of Power and Whiteness', *Method and Theory in the Study of Religion*, 31 (3): 210–37.

Nzioka, Charles (2001), 'Perspectives of Adolescent Boys on the Risks of Unwanted Pregnancy and Sexually Transmitted Infections: Kenya', *Reproductive Health Matters*, 9 (17): 108–17.

Nzioka, Charles (2004), 'Unwanted Pregnancy and Sexually Transmitted Infection among Young Women in Rural Kenya', *Culture, Health and Sexuality*, 6 (1): 31–44.

Nzomo, Maria (1989), 'The Impact of the Women's Decade on Policies, Programs and Empowerment of Women in Kenya', *Issue: A Journal of Opinion*, 17 (2): 9–17.

Nzomo, Maria (1993), 'The Kenyan Women's Movement in a Changing Political Context', in Shanyisa A. Khasiani and Esther I. Njiro (eds), *The Women's Movement in Kenya*, 131–51, Nairobi: Association of African Women for Research and Development.

Oduol, Wilhemina, and Wanjiku M. Kabira (1995), 'The Mother of Warriors and Her Daughters: The Women's Movement in Kenya', in Amrita Basu (ed.), *The Challenge of Local Feminisms: Women's Movements in Global Perspective*, 187–208, Boulder, CO: Westview.

Oduyoye, Mercy A. (2000), *Hearing and Knowing: Theological Reflections on Christianity in Africa*, Nairobi: Acton.

Oduyoye, Mercy A. (2001), *Introducing African Women's Theology*, Sheffield: Sheffield Academic Press.

Okech, Awino (2009), 'Aid from a Feminist Perspective', in Hakima Abbas and Yves Niyiragira (eds), *Aid to Africa: Redeemer or Coloniser?*, 26–41, Oxford: Pambazuka Press.

Okech, Awino (2016), *Unlocking the Doors: Feminist Insights for Inclusion in Governance, Peace and Security. Primer 3*, Accra: African Women's Development Fund (AWDF).

Okech, Awino (2019), *Widow Inheritance and Contested Citizenship in Kenya*, London: Routledge.

Okeke, Philomina E., and Godwin Oru (2006), 'Women, NEPAD and Nation Building: Revisiting a Dying Debate', *African Sociological Review*, 10 (2): 72–93.

Oloo, Habil, and Monica Wanjiru, with Katy Newell-Jones (2011), *Female Genital Mutilation Practices in Kenya: The Role of Alternative Rites of Passage*, London: Feed the Minds.

Oluoko-Odingo, Alice A. (2009), 'Determinants of Poverty: Lessons from Kenya', *GeoJournal*, 74 (4): 311–31.

Omosa, Mary (1995), 'Persistent Cultural Practices: A Review of the Status of Women in Kenya', in AAWORD, *From Strategies to Action, a Research Perspective*, 61–85, Nairobi: Association of African Women for Research and Development.

Open Society (2012), *Criminalizing Condoms: How Policing Practices Put Sex Workers and HIV Services at Risk in Kenya, Namibia, Russia, South Africa, the United States, and Zimbabwe*. Available online: https://www.opensocietyfoundations.org/reports/criminalizing-condoms (accessed 29 March 2017).

Osur, Joachim (2011), *The Great Controversy: A Story of Abortion, the Church, and Constitution-Making in Kenya*, Nairobi.

Ouko-Otieno, John (2009), 'Feminist Bioethics in the Global Scene: The Case of Kenya as a Developing Nation', *International Journal of Feminist Approaches to Bioethics*, 2 (1): 59–70.

Outka, Gene (2005), 'Christian Ethics?' in William Schweiker (ed.), *The Blackwell Companion to Religious Ethics*, 197–203, Oxford: Wiley-Blackwell.

Owiti, Louisa A. (1992), 'Muguna B Water Project Provides Water for a Variety of Purposes in Rwanyanga Community, Meru District, Kenya', in Waafas Ofosu-Amaah and Wendy Philleo (eds), *Proceedings of the Global Assembly of Women and the Environment: 'Partners in Life' November 4–8, 1991, Volume II*, Washington, DC: UNEP.

Oxfam (2012), *Public Health at Risk: US Trade Policy Endangers Access to Affordable Anti-Retroviral Medicines*, Available online: https://web.archive.org/web/20120815184129/http://www.oxfam.org/sites/www.oxfam.org/files/international-aids-conference-oxfam-media-brief-july2012.pdf (accessed 1 February 2021).

Oyěwùmí, Oyèrónkẹ (1997), *The Invention of Women: Making an African Sense of Western Gender Discourses*, Minneapolis: University of Minnesota Press.

Oyěwùmí, Oyèrónkẹ (2016), *What Gender Is Motherhood? Changing Yorùbá Ideals of Power, Procreation, and Identity in the Age of Modernity*, Basingstoke: Palgrave Macmillan.

Pailey, Robtel (2019), 'De-Centring the "White Gaze" of Development', *Development and Change*, 51 (3), 729–45.

Parsitau, Damaris S. (2009), ' "Keep Holy Distance and Abstain till He Comes": Interrogating a Pentecostal Church's Engagements with HIV/AIDS and the Youth in Kenya', *Africa Today*, 56 (1): 44–64.

Parsitau, Damaris S. (2012), 'From Prophetic Voices to Lack of Voice: Christian Churches in Kenya and the Dynamics of Voice and Voicelessness in a Multi-Religious Space', *Studia Historiae Ecclesiasticae*, 38 (Supplement): 243–68.

Pasture, Patrick, Jan Art and Thomas Buerman, eds. (2012), *Beyond the Feminization Thesis: Gender and Christianity in Modern Europe*, Leuven: Leuven University Press.

Pedwell, Carolyn (2007), 'Theorizing "African" Female Genital Cutting and "Western" Body Modifications: A Critique of the Continuum and Analogue Approaches', *Feminist Review*, 86: 45–66.

Pigg, Stacey L. (2005), 'Globalizing the Facts of Life', in Vincanne Adams and Stacey L. Pigg (eds), *Sex in Development: Science, Sexuality, and Morality in Global Perspective*, 39–66, Durham, NC: Duke University Press.

Pigg, Stacey L., and Vincanne Adams (2005), 'Introduction: The Moral Object of Sex', in Vincanne Adams and Stacey L. Pigg (eds), *Sex in Development: Science, Sexuality, and Morality in Global Perspective*, 1–38, Durham, NC: Duke University Press.

Pope Pius XI (31 December 1930), *Casti Connubii*. Available on: https://www.papalencyclicals.net/pius11/p11casti.htm (accessed 13 January 2021).

Presley, Cora A. (1988), 'The Mau Mau Rebellion, Kikuyu Women, and Social Change', *Canadian Journal of African Studies*, 22 (3): 502–27.

Price, Kimala (2010), 'What Is Reproductive Justice?: How Women of Color Activists Are Redefining the Pro-Choice Paradigm', *Meridians*, 10 (2): 42–65.

Quijano, Aníbal (2007), 'Coloniality and Modernity/Rationality', *Cultural Studies*, 21 (2–3): 168–78.

Qureshi, Sadiah (2004), 'Displaying Sara Baartman, the "Hottentot Venus"', *History of Science*, 42 (2): 233–57.

Ramugondo, Elelwani (2018), 'Healing Work: Intersections for Decoloniality', *World Federation of Occupational Therapists Bulletin*, 74 (2): 83–91.

Rao, Rahul (2014), 'Re-membering Mwanga: Same-Sex Intimacy, Memory and Belonging in Postcolonial Uganda', *Journal of Eastern African Studies*, 9 (1): 1–19.

Rivera, Mayra (2007), *The Touch of Transcendence: A Postcolonial Theology of God*, Louisville, KY: Westminster John Knox Press.

Robbins, Joel (2016), 'What Is the Matter with Transcendence? On the Place of Religion in the New Anthropology of Ethics', *Journal of the Royal Anthropological Institute*, NS (22): 767–808.

Robinson, Fiona (2015), 'Care Ethics, Political Theory, and the Future of Feminism', in Daniel Engster and Maurice Hamilton (eds), *Care Ethics and Political Theory*, 293–312, Oxford: Oxford University Press.

Rodney, Walter (2018), *How Europe Underdeveloped Africa*, London: Verso.

Roy, Arundhati (2014), 'The NGO-ization of Resistance', *Massalijn*. Available online: http://massalijn.nl/new/the-ngo-ization-of-resistance (accessed 21 September 2020).

Rubenstein, Mary-Jane (2004), 'An Anglican Crisis of Comparison: Intersections of Race, Gender, and Religious Authority, with Particular Reference to the Church of Nigeria', *Journal of the American Academy of Religion*, 72 (2): 341–65.

Sabar-Friedman, Galia (1996), 'The Power of the Familiar: Everyday Practices in the Anglican Church of Kenya (CPK)', *Journal of Church and State*, 32 (2): 377–95.

Sabar, Galia (2002), *Church, State and Society in Kenya: From Mediation to Opposition 1963–1993*, New York: Frank Cass.

Said, Edward W. (1978), *Orientalism*, New York: Random House.

Salemink, Oscar (2015), 'The Purification, Sacralisation, and Instrumentalisation of Development,' in Philip Fountain, Robin Bush and R. Michael Feener (eds), *Religion and the Politics of Development*, 35–60, Basingstoke: Palgrave Macmillan.

Saunders, Kriemild, ed. (2002), *Feminist Post-Development Thought: Rethinking Modernity, Post-Colonialism and Representation*, London: Zed.

Scott, Joan C. (2009), 'Sexularism', Ursula Hirschmann Annual Lecture on Gender and Europe, European University Institute, Florence. Available online: http://cadmus.eui.eu/bitstream/handle/1814/11553/RSCAS_DL_2009_01.pdf?sequence=1 (accessed 1 March 2017).

Seims, Sara (2011), 'Maximizing the Effectiveness of Sexual and Reproductive Health Funding Provided by Seven European Governments', *International Perspectives on Sexual and Reproductive Health*, 37 (3): 150–4.

Selinger, Leah (2004), 'The Forgotten Factor: The Uneasy Relationship between Religion and Development', *Social Compass*, 51 (4): 523–43.

Sewpaul, Vishanthie (2005), 'Feminism and Globalisation: The Promise of Beijing and Neoliberal Capitalism in Africa', *Agenda: Empowering Women for Gender Equity*, 64: 104–13.

Seymour-Jones, Carole (1994), *Journey of Faith: The History of the World YWCA*, London: Allison and Busby.

Shadle, Brett (2015), *The Souls of White Folk: White Settlers in Kenya, 1900s–1920s*, Manchester: Manchester University Press.

Shannon, Kate, Steffanie A. Strathdee, Shira M. Goldenberg, Putu Duff, Peninah Mwangi, Maia Rusakova, Sushena Reza-Paul, Joseph Lau, Kathleen Deering, Michael R. Pickles and Marie-Claude Boily (2015), 'Global Epidemiology of HIV among Female Sex Workers: Influence of Structural Determinants', *Lancet*, 385: 55–71.

Shaw, Carolyn M. (1995), *Colonial Inscriptions: Race, Sex, and Class in Kenya*, Minneapolis: University of Minnesota Press.

Sheffield, James R., and Victor P. Diejomaoh (1972), *Non-Formal Education in African Development: Report of a Survey Conducted by the African-American Institute, with financial support from the United States Agency for International Development*, New York: African-American Institute. Available online: https://files.eric.ed.gov/fulltext/ED100767.pdf (accessed 21 September 2020).

Shell-Duncan, Bettina (2008), 'From Health to Human Rights: Female Genital Cutting and the Politics of Intervention', *American Anthropologist*, NS 110 (2), 225–36.

Shorter, Aylward, and Edwin Onyancha (1997), *Secularism in Africa. A Case Study: Nairobi City*, Nairobi: Paulines.

Singhal, Arvind, and Everett M. Rogers (2003), *Combating AIDS: Communication Strategies in Action*, New Delhi: Sage.

Sistersong (2015), *What Is Reproductive Justice?* Available online: http://sistersong.net/index.php?option=com_contentandview=articleandid=141andItemid=8 (accessed 4 April 2017).

Sivelä, Jonas (2012), 'Infected Condoms and Pin-Pricked Oranges: An Ethnographic Study of AIDS Legends in Two Townships in Cape Town', *Cultural Analysis*, 11: 45–66.

Sjørup, Lene (1997), 'Negotiating Ethics: The Holy See and the Fourth World Conference on Women, Beijing, 1995', *Feminist Theology*, 5 (14): 73–105.

Somers, Margaret R. (1994), 'The Narrative Constitution of Identity: A Relational and Network Approach', *Theory and Society*, 23 (5): 605–49.

Spivak, Gayatri C. (2010), 'Can the Subaltern Speak? Revised Edition', in Rosalind Morris (ed.), *Can the Subaltern Speak? Reflections on the History of an Idea*, 21–78, New York: Columbia University Press.

Spronk, Rachel (2005), 'Female Sexuality in Nairobi: Flawed or Favoured?', *Culture, Health and Sexuality*, 7 (3): 267–77.

Stamp, Patricia (1986), 'Kikuyu Women's Self-Help Groups: Toward an Understanding of the Relation Between Sex-Gender System and Mode of Production in Africa', in Claire Robertson and Iris Berger (eds), *Women and Class in Africa*, 27–46, New York: Africana.

Stanley, Brian (1990), *The Bible and the Flag: Protestant Mission and British Imperialism in the 19th and 20th Centuries*, Leicester: Apollos.

Steady, Filomena Chioma (2005), 'An Investigative Framework for Gender Research in Africa in the New Millennium', in Oyèrónkẹ Oyěwùmí (ed.), *African Gender Studies*, 313–31, New York: Palgrave Macmillan.

Stiglitz, Joseph (2002), *Globalisation and Its Discontents*, New York: W.W. Norton.

Stoler, Ann (1989), 'Rethinking Colonial Categories: European Communities and the Boundaries of Rule', *Comparative Studies in Society and History*, 31 (1): 134–61.

Stoler, Ann (1992), 'Sexual Affronts and Racial Frontiers: European Identities and the Cultural Politics of Exclusion in Colonial Southeast Asia', *Comparative Studies in Society and History*, 34 (3): 514–51.

Stroebel, Johannes, and Artur Van Benthem (2012), 'The Power of the Church: The Role of Roman Catholic Teaching in the Transmission of HIV', *SSRN Electronic Journal*, 1–32. Available online: https://ssrn.com/abstract=2018071 (accessed 1 March 2017).

Switzer, Heather (2010), 'Disruptive Discourses: Kenyan Maasai Schoolgirls Make Themselves', *Girlhood Studies*, 3 (1): 137–55.

Switzer, Heather (2013), '(Post)Feminist Development Fables: The Girl Effect and the Production of Sexual Subjects', *Feminist Theory*, 14: 345–60.

Syed, Jawad, and Faiza Ali (2011), 'The White Woman's Burden: From Colonial Civilisation to Third World Development', *Third World Quarterly*, 32 (2): 349–65.

Tamale, Sylvia (2011), 'Researching and Theorising Sexualities in Africa', in Sylvia Tamale (ed.), *African Sexualities: A Reader*, 11–36, Dakar: Pambazuka Press.

Taylor, Charles (1994), 'The Politics of Recognition', in Amy Gutmann (ed.), *Multiculturalism*, 24–48, Princeton, NJ: Princeton University Press.

Taylor, Charles (2006), *Sources of the Self: The Making of the Modern Identity*, Cambridge: Cambridge University Press.

Thomas, Lynn (1998), 'Imperial Concerns and "Women's Affairs": State Efforts to Regulate Clitoridectomy and Eradicate Abortion in Meru, Kenya, c.1910–1950', *Journal of African History*, 39 (1): 121–45.

Thomas, Lynn (2003), *Politics of the Womb: Women, Reproduction, and the State in Kenya*. Berkeley: University of California Press.

Tonkin, Elizabeth (1992), *Narrating Our Pasts: The Social Construction of Oral History*, Cambridge: Cambridge University Press.

Tronto, Joan C. (1993), *Moral Boundaries: A Political Argument for an Ethic of Care*, New York: Routledge.

Udvardy, Monica L. (1998), 'Theorizing Past and Present Women's Organizations in Kenya', *World Development*, 26 (9): 1749–61.

UN (United Nations) (1996), *Report of the Fourth World Conference on Women*, Beijing, 4–15 September 1995. Available online: www.un.org/womenwatch/daw/beijing/pdf/Beijing%20full%20report%20E.pdf (accessed 21 September 2020).

UNICEF (2008), *The State of the World's Children*. Available online: http://www.unicef.org/publications/files/The_State_of_the_Worlds_Children_2008.pdf (accessed 22 November 2015).

Von Bülow, Dorthe (1992), 'Bigger Than Men? Gender Relations and Their Changing Meaning in Kipsigis Society, Kenya', *Africa*, 62 (4): 523–46.

Van Klinken, Adriaan (2014), 'Homosexuality, Politics and Pentecostal Nationalism in Zambia', *Studies in World Christianity*, 20 (3): 259–81.

Van Klinken, Adriaan (2015), 'Queer Love in a "Christian Nation": Zambian Gay Men Negotiating Sexual and Religious Identities', *Journal of the American Academy of Religion*, 83 (4): 947–64.

Van Klinken, Adriaan (2019), *Kenyan, Christian, Queer: Religion, LGBT Activism, and Arts of Resistance in Africa*, Penn: Penn State University Press.

Van Klinken, Adriaan, and Masiiwa R. Gunda (2012), 'Taking Up the Cudgels against Gay Rights? Trends and Trajectories in African Christian Theologies on Homosexuality', *Journal of Homosexuality*, 59 (1): 114–38.

Van Tol, Deanne (2015), 'The Women of Kenya Speak: Imperial Activism and Settler Society, c.1930', *Journal of British Studies*, 54 (2): 433–56.

Van Tonder, C. L., and B. C. Lessing (2003), 'From Identity to Organisation Identity: The Evolution of a Concept', *SA Journal of Industrial Psychology*, 29 (2): 20–8.

Vial, Theodore (2016), *Modern Religion, Modern Race*, Abingdon: Oxford University Press.

Vuola, Elina (2002), *Limits of Liberation: Feminist Theology and the Ethics of Poverty and Reproduction*, London: Sheffield Academic Press.

Wainaina, Binyavanga (2005), 'How to Write about Africa', *Granta*, 92: 92–5.

Walker, Margaret Urban (2007), *Moral Understandings: A Feminist Study in Ethics*, 2nd edn, Abingdon: Oxford University Press.

Wane, Njoki (2013), '[Re]Claiming my Indigenous Knowledge: Challenges, Resistance, and Opportunities', *Decolonization: Indigeneity, Education and Society*, 2 (1): 93–107.

Wangari, Esther (2002), 'Reproductive Technologies: A Third World Feminist Perspective', in Kriemild Saunders (ed.), *Feminist Post-Development Thought: Rethinking Modernity, Post-Colonialism and Representation*, 298–312, London: Zed.

Ware, Vron (1992), *Beyond the Pale: White Women, Racism, and History*, London: Verso.

Warhol, Robyn (2012), 'A Feminist Approach to Narrative', in David Herman, James Phelan, Peter J. Rabinowitz, Brian Richardson and Robyn Warhol (eds), *Narrative Theory: Core Concepts and Critical Debates*, 9–13, Columbus: Ohio State University Press.

Webster, Wendy (1998), *Imagining Home: Gender, Race and National Identity, 1945–64*, London: UCL Press.

Wertsch, James V. (2008), 'The Narrative Organization of Collective Memory', *Ethos*, 36 (1): 120–35.

White, Luise (1990), *The Comforts of Home: Prostitution in Colonial Nairobi*, Chicago: University of Chicago Press.

Wignall, Ross (2014), *Our Brother's Keeper: Moralities of Transformation at YMCA Centres in UK and Gambia*, unpublished PhD thesis, University of Sussex, UK.

Wilson, Kalpana (2012), *Race, Racism, and Development: Interrogating History, Discourse and Practice*, London: Zed Books.

Wilson, Kalpana (2015), 'Towards a Radical Re-appropriation: Gender, Development and Neoliberal Feminism', *Development and Change*, 46 (4): 803–32.

Win, Everjoice J. (2004), 'Not Very Poor, Powerless or Pregnant: The African Woman Forgotten by Development', *IDS Bulletin*, 35 (4): 61–4.

Wipper, Aubrey (1995), 'Women's Voluntary Associations', in Margaret J. Hay and Sharon Stichter (eds), *African Women South of the Sahara*, 2nd edn, 164–86, Harlow: Longman Scientific and Technical.

Woollacott, Angela (1998), 'From Moral to Professional Authority: Secularism, Social Work, and Middle-Class Women's Self-Construction in World War I Britain', *Journal of Women's History*, 10 (2): 85–111.

World YMCA (2013), 'Paris Basis – 1855'. Available online: https://www.ymca.int/about-us/ymca-history/paris-basis-1855/ (accessed 13 January 2021).

World YWCA (2002), 'HIV/AIDS [to] Be Made a Major Movement-Wide Priority over the Next Four Years'. Available online: http://www.oikoumene.org/en/resources/

documents/other-ecumenical-bodies/church-statements-on-hivaids/world-ywca (accessed 15 March 2017).

World YWCA (2007), *World YWCA Statements of Policy Adopted at Legislative Meetings 1894–2007*, Geneva: World Young Women's Christian Association.

World YWCA (2011), *Annual Report April 2011–December 2011*, Geneva: World Young Women's Christian Association.

World YWCA (2012), *Annual Report 2012*, Geneva: World Young Women's Christian Association.

World YWCA (2015), *World YWCA Constitution*, Geneva: World Young Women's Christian Association.

World YWCA (2019), 'DOC BM INFO 1 – List Member Associations Status of Affiliation', Geneva: World Young Women's Christian Association (distributed at World YWCA Council, Johannesburg, November 2019).

World YWCA (2020), *World YWCA Glossary*, Geneva: World Young Women's Christian Association. https://www.worldywca.org/wp-content/uploads/2020/12/1. World-YWCA-Movement-Glossary-and-Definitions-1-3.pdf (accessed 1 February 2021).

Wynter, Sylvia (1996), 'Is "Development" a Purely Empirical Concept or Also Teleological?: A Perspective from "We the Underdeveloped"', in Aguibou Y. Yansané (ed.), *Prospects for Recovery and Sustainable Development in Africa*, London: Greenwood Press.

Yount, Kathryn M., and Bisrat K. Abraham (2007), 'Female Genital Cutting and HIV/AIDS among Kenyan Women', *Studies in Family Planning*, 38 (2): 73–88.

Yuval Davis, Nira (1998), 'Gender and Nation', in Rick Wilford and Robert L. Miller (eds), *Women, Ethnicity and Nationalism*, 21–35, London: Routledge.

YWCA of Kenya (2008), *YWCA of Kenya Annual Council Report 2008*, Nairobi: Kenya YWCA.

YWCA of Kenya (2009), *YWCA of Kenya Annual Council Report 2009*, Nairobi: Kenya YWCA.

YWCA of Kenya (2010), *YWCA of Kenya Annual Council Report 2010*, Nairobi: Kenya YWCA.

YWCA of Kenya (2011), *YWCA of Kenya Annual Council Report 2011*, Nairobi: Kenya YWCA.

YWCA of Kenya (n.d.), *Young Women's Christian Association of Kenya*, Nairobi: Kenya YWCA.

Zabus, Chantal, ed. (2013), *Out in Africa: Same-Sex Desire in Sub-Saharan Literatures and Cultures*, Woodbridge: James Currey.

Zigon, Jarrett (2014), 'An Ethics of Dwelling and a Politics of World-Building: A Critical Response to Ordinary Ethics', *Journal of the Royal Anthropological Institute*, NS (20): 746–64.

Zimbizi, George, Gertrude Kopiyo and Jeremiah Owiti (2011), *Mid-Term Evaluation of the Gender and Governance Programme III in Kenya (2008–2011): Final Report*, Nairobi: UN Women Regional Office for East and Southern Africa.

Zizzo, Natalie, Emily Bell and Eric Racine (2016), 'What Is Everyday Ethics? A Review and a Proposal for an Integrative Concept', *Journal of Clinical Ethics*, 27 (2): 117–28.

Index

Abok, Mwajuma Alice 83–4, 156–9
abortion 16, 40, 64–5, 100–5, 119–20, 127, 130–1, 136–41, 147–50, 164–5, 183–5, 205 n.2 (*see also* Kenyan constitution, controversial faith issues)
abstinence 112, 121, 133–5
abundance 180–7, 198
Africa
   British colonization 16, 36–7, 51–60, 181
   orientalism 77
   representations 36, 74–7, 178, 204–5 n.1
African instituted churches (AICs) 56, 177, 205 n.3
African values 16, 41–3, 62–5, 73, 97–8, 99–125
   Ubuntu 26
African women
   representations 10, 52, 54, 56–61, 93, 97
   YWCA 24–5, 48, 65–71, 80–90, 201
AIDS (*see also* HIV) 34, 87, 90–5, 111–18, 135, 169, 172, 185, 205 n.4, 206 n.8
Atkins, Kim 21, 32, 39
autobiography 3, 25, 27, 153, 202

Beijing (Fourth World Conference on Women, 1995) 80, 91
Bible 14, 22, 56, 167, 180, 188
   ethics 50, 103, 172, 184, 197
   imperialism 181, 194
   Jn 10.10 180–4
   New Testament 180–4, 187
   Old Testament 22, 147, 194
   stories 22, 23, 180-4, 194, 202
   study 52, 81, 148, 159–60, 167, 170
biography 17–18, 23, 26–7, 39, 43, 92, 108, 202
bisexual 16, 142, 146, 207 n.3 (*see also* controversial faith issues, LBTQI women, LGBTQ, sexuality)

boys
   circumcision, 106, 187
   contemporary 114, 206 n.7
   servants 55, 60, 67
Britain 14, 47, 49–52, 56–9, 70, 169
   British Empire 14–16, 25–7, 47–72, 74

Cairo (International Conference on Population and Development, 1994) 40, 80, 91
Cairo Consensus, 91–2, 96
capitalism 5, 37, 39, 53, 59, 74–5, 78
care 114–15, 138, 179, 182, 185–6, 206 n.8
Catholicism 49–50, 79, 132–3, 137, 139, 162–5, 170, 187, 202, 204 n.1
Cavarero, Adriana 21, 27, 32
Christian emphasis 17–18, 28, 148, 151–2, 166–74, 180, 195, 198
   committee 148, 160, 185, 208 n.4
Christian ethics 14–19, 35, 65, 72, 139, 149, 156, 161, 173–7, 182–90, 190–9, 201–2 (*see also* ethics)
   adiaphora 187–8
   African Christian Ethics 139
Christian identity 3–4, 10–18, 35, 148–50, 166–72 (*see also* Christian emphasis)
   boundary work 29, 130–1, 139–43, 150
   'C' in the 'Y', the 164–70
   Paris Basis 51–5
   staunch 29, 163–6, 196
   unity 17, 49–51, 145, 163–6, 171, 176, 187, 189, 200
   use 83, 112, 123, 127, 152, 158, 180, 188–9
   whiteness 53–7
church 3, 24, 25, 41, 49, 52, 55–6, 62–3, 67–8, 83, 87
   Anglican 55, 67, 69, 139, 145, 205 n.1
   ethics 35, 102–5
   harambee 78–9
   Nairobi 5 95–7

Seventh Day Adventist (SDA) 161–2, 204 n.1
Circle of Concerned African Women Theologians, the 175–6, 182–7, 191, 194–7
civilization 53–5, 65, 73, 77, 80, 128, 181
clergy 15–16, 69, 104, 115, 123, 144, 176, 188, 190, 198, 205 n.1
coloniality 15–16, 33, 48, 127, 177, 200
   gender 31, 42, 54–6, 72
   rejection 42
colonization 12, 15–16, 38, 48, 51–60, 67–8, 71–6, 92–5, 128, 147, 154, 177, 181–2
common sense 34–5, 177–8, 198
condoms 131–6, 147–50, 162–3, 206 n.6, 206 n.7
   contraception 113–14
   controversial 16, 100, 123, 132–5
   Christian stance 116, 127, 132–3, 137, 163
   female 133
   prophylaxis 93–4, 111–17, 134–5, 185, 187
constitution
   Kenyan 87, 97, 101–5, 136, 183, 189, 205 n.1
   World YWCA 49–50, 169
contraception 73, 94, 129, 133, 145, 183–4 (*see also* condoms)
controversial faith issues 9, 16–17, 34, 65, 89, 100, 123–4, 127–50, 151–2, 158, 192, 198–200 (*see also* abortion, condoms, LGBTQ)
   Christian ethics 188–9
   definition 129–32
   YWCA identity 161–74

development industry 4, 9, 15, 35–40, 99–100, 128, 178, 195, 200
   Bretton Woods 75
   gender 86–95, 145, 150
   postcolonial critique 74–9, 90–8
   structural adjustment programmes (SAPs) 38, 77–8
discourse 23, 33–7, 39–40, 79, 202
Dube, Musa 10, 147, 181, 186, 192, 194–5

ecumenism 17, 35, 49–50, 95–100, 149–52, 155, 161–6, 193, 200
Eldoret 171
ethics (*see also* African values, Christian ethics, life, theology)
   care 36–7, 115, 182
   commitments 15, 22, 29, 32–3, 40, 99–101, 123, 152, 184, 193, 196, 202
   definition 35, 187, 190–2, 203 n.1
   everyday 16–19, 24, 35, 124, 147, 187–90
   identity 13, 15, 32–3, 63, 103–4, 151–2
   maternal 112, 116, 182–5
   ordinary 18, 35, 189–93
   sexual 104, 112, 117, 127, 132, 135, 149, 174, 178, 185

faith-based organizations (FBO) 127, 169, 178
family life education 83, 96–7, 108 (*see also* sex education)
family planning 96, 162, 165 (*see also* sex education)
family values 16, 41, 96–7, 205 n.2
Federation of Women Lawyers, Kenya (FIDA-K) 87, 94, 102
female genital practices 56, 62–3, 72, 106
   female circumcision crisis 61–5, 71–2, 102, 111, 177
   female genital mutilation (FGM) 7, 15, 21, 84–6, 90, 99–100, 130–2, 172, 205 n.3
   YWCA 105–11, 117, 129–32
feminism 9–10, 38–9, 82, 151
   African 31, 42, 76–7, 92–5, 129, 203 n.3
   Christianity 4, 15, 128, 206 n.1
   development industry 90–5, 99, 117–22
   femonationalism 38
   theology 3, 10, 175–7, 182–6, 192–7
   YWCA 30–2, 47, 100, 179, 195
field research 3–13, 20–1, 105–7, 115–16, 130–1, 142–3, 158–66, 203 n.1
Foucault, Michel 23, 191
fulfilled lives 18, 116, 175, 179–82, 185

gay rights 141–2, 146, 205 n.2 (*see also* LGBTQ)
gender
   cisgender 40, 142, 145

coloniality 31, 42, 54-6, 72
gender and development (GAD) 76, 84, 88
gender studies 11, 24, 31, 129
gender work 76, 86, 96, 99-100, 123, 149, 160
transgender 16, 142
Gifford, Paul 78, 95
girls
　abortion, 136-8, 185
　genital practices, 21, 61-5, 106-11
　modern 41
　narratives 34, 37-8, 52, 67-9, 155, 203 n.3
　sexuality 111-22, 127, 178, 206 n.7
grammar 25-6, 67, 152-3, 155, 158, 182

Harley, Vera 7, 47-8, 65-71, 90, 148, 153-5, 162, 170, 196, 207 n.2
health 37-40, 61-2, 71-3
　care 39, 79, 82, 90, 94-5
　development industry 91-2
　maternal 37, 40, 73, 77, 90-2, 94, 99, 119, 128, 138 186, 204 n.1
　public 57-61, 77-9, 90-3
　YWCA programmes (see SRHR)
heteronormativity 16, 24, 40, 54, 58, 97, 119, 132-3, 143-5, 147, 151, 185-6, 201
Hinga, Teresia 176, 186, 206 n.1
history
　institutional 23-9, 151-4, 159
　Kenya 57-65, 81-90, 100-5
　YWCA 7, 13-15, 47-57, 65-71, 80-90, 99-102, 104-24, 152-61, 166-72
HIV 34, 73, 86, 97-8, 99-100
　development industry 90-5
　positive 34, 111-16, 121, 185
　YWCA 111-17 (see also AIDS, condoms, SRHR)
homophobia 77, 144, 146, 198

identity 61-4, 77, 91, 122-4, 127, 129, 147, 184
　Christian 53-4, 83, 103-4, 112, 139, 143, 149, 176, 188-90
　moral 39, 56-8, 99, 108, 140, 178
　narrative 9-11, 13-18, 20-43, 48, 71, 148, 159, 164-6, 158, 173, 175, 196

organizational 7, 21, 25-32, 117, 127, 131, 152-9, 173, 195-7
World YWCA 48-51
YWCA 52, 55, 65-71, 99-100, 109, 123, 140-1, 147-50, 151-74, 179-82
imperialism 27, 42, 52-8, 103-5
　Christianity 55-6, 123, 127, 146, 177, 182-4
　development industry 37-8, 73, 76, 94-5, 98, 127-9, 146
　imperial maternalism (see maternalism)
　sexuality 42, 52, 58, 143
institutions
　ethics 16, 35, 132, 175, 188-9, 193, 195-8, 201-2
　identity 7, 12-18, 21, 23-32, 43, 100, 117, 127, 131, 133, 149, 152-9, 173, 179, 195-7
　structure 14, 51-3, 86, 105, 185, 192, 200 (see also organizations)
international development (see development industry)

Kanogo, Tabitha 51-2, 57-63
Kant, Immanuel 191
Kanyoro, Musimbi 157, 176, 182, 194, 208 n.4
Kaoma, Kapya 97, 104, 139, 177, 205 n.2
Kenyatta, Jomo 78, 81-3
Khader, Serene 38, 88
Kisii 8, 84, 106-11, 118
Kisumu 8, 118
Kwok, Pui-lan 22, 35, 52, 141, 147, 189, 192 (see also feminist theology)

League of Kenyan Women Voters (LKWV) 29, 87
Lewis, Desiree 37, 42, 73, 76, 77, 93, 97
LGBTQ 16, 42, 101, 141-7, 150, 183, 186, 201 (see also controversial faith issues, LBTQI, sexuality)
　LBTQ women 122, 131-3, 141-7, 149, 163, 183, 186
　lesbian 16, 141-7 (see also LBTQI women)
life
　abundant (see fulfilled lives)
　ethics 18, 35-6, 43, 75, 175, 182-7
　fulfilled 18, 116, 175, 179-82, 185

pro-life 102–3
stories 27–8, 32, 116
Ligaga, Dina 33–4, 41–2, 97, 120 (*see also* moral narrative)
Likimani, Muthoni 56, 60, 68–70
Linde, Charlotte 17, 22, 25–33, 153, 159 (*see also* narrative identity)

Maathai, Wangari 56, 81
Maendeleo ya Wanawake (MYW) 66, 68, 70, 83, 109
Maguna B 84–6
maternalism 10, 36, 74, 80, 111, 115, 182–5
  imperial 14–15, 47–72, 170, 182, 200
medicalization 92, 98, 109, 123
memory 13, 17, 25, 27–8, 48, 160, 168, 173
men 60, 66–7, 69, 93
  colonizers 14, 59–60
misogyny 14, 23, 77, 112, 188, 197–8
missionary Christianity 14, 36, 51, 55–6, 61–72, 73, 88, 177, 179, 184, 204 n.1
missionary feminism 38–9
modernity 38, 41–2, 49, 53–4, 73–5, 88, 91–2, 95–6, 98, 108, 128, 171, 178–9
Mohanty, Chandra Talpade 31, 76, 91, 93, 203 n.3
Moi, Daniel Arap 83, 86, 89
Mombasa 8, 65, 67, 70, 71, 81, 83, 84, 113, 132, 155
Mombo, Esther 194
moral narrative 28, 33–5, 43, 58, 195–8
  cautionary tale 33, 122
  development industry 35–40
  gender 40–2, 97, 102, 122, 138, 178
  identity 21, 108, 149
  sexuality 40–2, 114–16, 134, 150, 187
mothers 10, 21, 35–8, 56–7, 63–4, 68, 81, 93, 100, 129, 138, 178, 183–6
  motherhood 36, 41, 53–7, 92, 120, 149, 183–6
  mothering 15, 36, 41, 183–6
  teenage mothers 34, 136–8, 178
Mugo, Margaret 70–1, 83, 155–6, 171, 204 n.5, 207 n.1

Nairobi 4–6, 40, 71, 80–4, 92–3, 97–8
  colonial 48, 51–3, 70, 112, 160
  YWCA branch 8, 12, 108, 113, 117

narrative
  ethics 32–5, 190–7
  identity 3–4, 10, 13–18, 20–43, 63, 188, 195
  public 21, 25–6, 28, 202
  ontological 21, 25–6, 28, 202
  urban legends 34, 116
  YWCA 17, 151–73, 195–7 (*see also* history: YWCA)
National Council of Churches of Kenya (NCCK) 83, 87, 96–7, 101–4, 123, 134, 138–9, 150, 189, 201, 205 n.4
National Council of Women of Kenya (NCWK) 81–2
nationalism 58, 65–6, 78–9, 94, 97, 100–5, 194, 197
NGO-ization 15, 80, 82, 89, 127
Njambi, Wairimu 56–7, 62–4, 72, 106, 111, 147, 204 n.2
Njoroge, Nyambura 132, 146, 176, 182–4, 194

Oduyoye, Mercy Amba 182, 194–5 (*see also* Circle of Concerned African Women Theologians, feminist theology)
Okech, Awino 37, 41–2, 89, 98, 104, 129, 177–9
ontological narrative 21, 25–6, 28, 202
origins story 17, 25–6, 28, 31, 151, 157–61, 166–8, 202
Oyewumi, Oyeronke 31, 91, 177, 184

Pailey, Robtel 39, 73
parenting 40, 53, 62–3, 90, 93–4, 97, 106–8, 111, 122, 185–6
Paris Basis 49–50, 179
piousness 29, 35–6, 57, 163–6, 200
pleasure 4, 16, 27, 61, 92, 118, 122, 128, 132, 141, 166
postcolonial theory 3, 9, 11, 31, 38–9, 90–5, 124, 141, 147, 154, 181, 191, 195
poverty 38, 75–8, 80–2, 84, 91, 94, 99, 120–2, 142, 177, 183, 200
power 12, 26, 32, 36, 43, 201–2, 203 n.3, 204 n.3
  colonial 48, 54–5, 58, 65–6
  narrative 12–13, 22–5, 34, 39
  in research 10–11

pregnancy 102, 107, 134, 139 (*see also* abortion, controversial faith issues, motherhood)
   foetus 103–4, 139
   teenage 120
   unwanted 102, 134–8
progress 23, 39, 65, 73–4, 85, 88, 92, 98, 123
pronatalism 18, 41, 58, 102, 113, 116, 129, 151, 182–6
public narrative 19, 24–6, 29, 34, 195, 202
purity 114, 117, 120, 133–5, 185
   impurity 14, 116

queer 129, 141–4, 147 (*see also* LGBTQ, sexuality)

racism 31, 37–40, 48, 66, 68, 77, 88, 153, 204 n.1
   race 54, 57, 66, 69, 76, 89, 171, 181, 207 n.2
reproductive justice 40, 98, 122, 138, 186, 198, 204 n.6
repronormativity 16, 56, 112, 116, 138, 145, 183–6
Rickshaws to Jets 7, 47–8, 148, 154–6, 207 n.3
rural 60, 62–3, 67, 79, 80–6, 93, 97–9, 110, 114–15, 200

saviourism 38–9, 178, 182, 204 n.5
   Cole, Teju 38–9
secular 30, 38, 130, 164, 169, 188, 201
   development industry 95, 123–4, 128
   secularism 30, 42, 105, 140, 146, 184, 189
   secularization 30, 42, 49, 95, 140, 166, 168–9
   secularized 95, 160
   values 97, 99, 123–4
   Western 38, 128, 187
segregation
   gender 38, 59, 109
   race 59–60, 65, 68
sex education 83, 86, 90, 96–7, 108, 129, 131–2, 185
sex work 34, 40–2, 56–61, 90, 93, 112–14, 119–20, 124, 131–3, 146–7
sexual health (*see* SRHR)

sexuality 15, 40–2, 73 (*see also* controversial faith issues, LGBTQ)
   African 65, 90–3, 98
   boys 114, 206 n.7
   Christianity 105, 112, 122–4, 182–7
   development industry 90–5
   girls 34, 41, 102, 114, 117, 134, 143–7, 206 n.7
   heterosexuality 40–1, 57, 114, 122, 132, 142, 147, 206 n.1
   identity 143–7
   men 93
   women 56–7, 98
   youth 17, 40–2, 90, 96, 113, 118–19
sexual and reproductive health and rights (SRHR) 91–3, 95–6, 99–100, 117–22 (*see also* controversial faith issues)
Siaya 8, 87, 118
sin 14, 104, 116, 136, 140, 176
Somers, Margaret 21–6, 32, 152, 173
Spronk, Rachel 92, 112, 118
story 13, 23, 27, 33, 43, 151–2, 204 n.4 (*see also* narrative)
   'Be yourself face the darkness wisely' 121–2
   good shepherd 180–1
   Hannah 194
   Nyaboke 20–1
   origins 159–61
   story-data 13
   storytelling 16, 18, 23–7, 32, 43, 191, 194
   'Subira smiles at last' 121
   'When the deal is too good, think twice' 120–1

Tamale, Sylvia 98, 129
Tana River 8, 87, 113
theology 3, 191–2 (*see also* abundance, the Circle of Concerned African Women Theologians, fulfilled lives)
   abortion 102–4, 139
   anthropology 47, 50, 133
   contextual 177, 194
   ethics 14–15, 18, 127, 187, 192–3, 197–8
   narrative 22, 24, 194–5
   ordinary 18, 175–6, 189–93
   racism 156
YWCA 144, 161, 172, 181–2

Thomas, Lynn 57, 62–4, 129
tradition
    African traditional religion (ATR) 128, 184, 194
    Christian 14, 19, 35, 187–8, 192, 196
    culture 41, 75, 128
    vs modernity 91, 98, 128
    practices 179
    values 99, 123
transactional sex (*see* sex work)

UKAID 75
United Nations (UN) 4–5, 37, 40, 80, 82, 86, 91, 101, 201
urbanization 41–2, 50, 58, 74, 80–1, 93, 96–8, 128
USAID 75, 91, 205 n.4

violence
    against women 117
    colonial 55, 60
    post-election 100–1, 185
    sexualized 59, 91, 112, 119

Wainaina, Binyavanga 77
water 82, 84–7
wealth 64, 75, 94, 181
welfare 73–98
whiteness 15, 36, 52, 53–7, 95, 128, 154, 156, 170, 187, 199, 204 n.5
Wilson, Kalpana 37–8, 60, 73–5, 88, 90, 129, 142
womanhood (*see also* mothers)
    African 34, 52
    Christian 52–4, 177, 196
    proper 34–6, 122, 178, 196
    white 5, 52, 56–7, 170, 207 n.2
women (*see also* young women)
    'bad' 34, 50, 196
    Christian 14, 18–19, 23, 30, 182, 196–7, 202
    and development (WAD) 89
    in development (WID) 82, 84, 87–8
    older 20, 53, 115, 185–6
    rural 63, 67, 79–82, 86, 93, 99, 110, 114–15
    urban 41, 81, 92–3, 99
    white 31, 38, 53–5, 60, 69–71
World YWCA 14–7, 201
    Christianity 169–70, 179–80
    constitution 50–1, 179–80
    development industry 80–1, 88–9, 114
    early history 49–50
    feminism 30–1, 137, 143
    Kenya 52, 62, 67, 85–6, 117–18, 124, 137, 143, 157
    World's YWCA 49–50

Young Men's Christian Association (YMCA) 18, 47, 148, 168, 205 n.5
    World Alliance of YMCAs 48–9
young women 13–14, 40–2, 47–52, 68, 98, 115–19, 132–41, 169–70
Young Women's Christian Association (YWCA) movement 8, 14–15, 23, 36, 47–51, 123, 160, 169–73, 201
    Great Britain 49–52, 207 n.4
    Uganda 84

www.ingramcontent.com/pod-product-compliance
Lightning Source LLC
Chambersburg PA
CBHW062142300426
44115CB00012BA/2009